# Team Organization

5

# WILEY SERIES IN
# Industrial and Organizational Psychology

*Series Editors:*

## CARY L. COOPER
*University of Manchester Institute of Science and Technology, UK*

## NEAL SCHMITT
*Michigan State University, USA*

Image Theory: Decision Making in Personal and Organizational Contexts

**Lee Roy Beach, University of Arizona, USA**

Team Organization

An Enduring Competitive Advantage

**Dean Tjosvold, Simon Fraser University, Canada**

# Team Organization

## An Enduring Competitive Advantage

**DEAN TJOSVOLD**
*Faculty of Business Administration*
*Simon Fraser University*
*Burnaby, British Columbia*
*Canada*

**JOHN WILEY & SONS**
Chichester · New York · Brisbane · Toronto · Singapore

*Other Wiley Editorial Offices*

John Wiley & Sons, Inc., 605 Third Avenue,
New York, NY 10158-0012, USA

Jacaranda Wiley Ltd, G.P.O. Box 859, Brisbane,
Queensland 4001, Australia

John Wiley & Sons (Canada) Ltd, 22 Worcester Road,
Rexdale, Ontario M9W 1L1, Canada

John Wiley & Sons (SEA) Pte Ltd, 37 Jalan Pemimpin #05-04,
Block B, Union Industrial Building, Singapore 2057

***Library of Congress Cataloging-in-Publication Data:***

Tjosvold, Dean.
    Team organization: an enduring competitive advantage /
Dean Tjosvold.
    p.   cm.—(Wiley series in industrial and organizational
psychology)
    Includes bibliographical references and index.
    ISBN 0-471-92301-X
    1. Work groups. 2. Organizational effectiveness. I. Title.
II. Series.
HD66.T55 1990
658.4'02—dc20                                    90–12600
                                                      CIP

***British Library Cataloguing in Publication Data:***

Tjosvold, Dean.
    Team organization.
    1. Organizations. Teams. Management
    I. Title
    658.402

ISBN 0-471-92301-X (ppc)
ISBN 0-471-93483-6 (pbk)

Typeset by the Alden Press, London and Northampton
Printed and bound in Great Britain by
Biddles Ltd, Guildford and King's Lynn

To My Home Team
Dale, Margaret, Tak Kwan, Dale Jr,
Mary, Jenny, Jason, Wesley, Lena
and Colleen

Team Organization

An ~~introducing~~ enduring
Competitive advantage

Dean Tjosvold

# Contents

# Series Foreword

The purpose of this **Industrial and Organizational Psychology Series** is to provide a range of high quality books covering 'leading edge' and significant topics in both industrial and organizational psychology. This series will help develop both theory and research in topics of interest to industrial and organizational psychologists in industry, in academia and in private and public organizations. We hope to explore such themes as job analysis, employee recruitment, psychology in the unions, motivation, employee satisfaction, counselling at work, job design and a range of subjects of topical interest to the international community of industrial and organizational psychology. We hope this series will be used by applied practising psychologists, as well as by graduate students in psychology departments and business schools throughout the world.

This book explores group processes in organizations and how those processes can be used to promote overall organization effectiveness. It joins Lee Roy Beach's book titled *Image Theory: Decision Making in Personal and Organizational Contexts* as the second volume in our series. We hope these books and many others in this new series will contribute to the vastly expanding field of industrial and organizational psychology.

Cary L. Cooper
Neal Schmitt

# Preface

*benefits*

*Team Organization* shows how working as a team up and down and across the organization creates value and serves customers. Most competitive advantages are increasingly fragile in the intensely competitive, global marketplace. A money-making product is imitated; a lucrative market attracts aggressive competitors. Teamwork is an ultimate competitive advantage for it fuels the continuous improvement necessary to adapt and prosper in a turbulent world.

This book integrates research findings into a framework that clarifies confusions: working as a team does not mean stifling sameness, but spirited individuality and controversy. Unity cannot be assumed, but is forged through debate and discussion. Strong interpersonal relationships are not harmonious, but continually renewed through conflict managing. Successful teams *envision* a common direction, recognize that their goals are *united*, feel *empowered* and skillful, *explore* alternative positions before deciding, and *reflect* on their progress.

You and your associates can use *Team Organization* to develop a common conviction and priority to work as a team. You will find a model of productive joint work, the ingredients to structure teams, and suggestions how to shape teamwork's principles to fit your circumstances.

Teamwork is not easy. It requires courage to break out of suspicious, cautious ways of working. In the mistrustful, impersonal climates of many organizations, people must give before they are assured of getting, they must reach out before they know others will reciprocate. Departments must relinquish feelings of self-righteousness and superiority to recognize their interdependence. Fair division of work and distribution of rewards must be negotiated, opposing positions integrated, and frustrations addressed.

But teamwork is possible. Most of us have belonged to fun, involving, and productive teams. We wanted each other to succeed, felt bonded, and got an extraordinary job done. The challenge is not to do something that we have not done before, but to form teams under the pressure to produce quickly and efficiently with people we do not know well, who are trained in another speciality, and have a different cultural background. Many teams, spread out around the world, must coordinate by fax and computer. Hundreds of employees in different business units are asked to be synergistic. Humans have worked together for tens of thousands of years, but have little experience in the conditions of contemporary organizations.

## THE BOOK'S PURPOSE

Our challenge is to appreciate how teamwork contributes to organizations, understand the conditions that make interaction between people and groups highly effective, and develop the procedures and plans that put this effectiveness to work. How can groups be challenged and managed so that they become invaluable allies as organizations cope with threats and exploit opportunities?

The book does not try to critique group studies or review them comprehensively, but *uses group research to develop a comprehensive framework to managing and leading in an organization*. It develops a straightforward, powerful model that simultaneously identifies the nature of productive teams and how to create them. Organizational leaders work with employees to *envision* an engaging, common direction, feel *united* in their objective and interests, be *empowered* and skillful to work together, *explore* alternative solutions to problems, and *reflect* and continuously learn from their experiences. This teamwork helps teams and their organizations nimbly respond to their environments with innovation and strengthened commitment.

## TELLING THE STORY OF TEAMS

Discussing relationships and teamwork can seem abstract and elusive. This book's framework is a general one that can be applied in many industries and settings. But working with other people is a full, concrete reality.[1]

I have used an extended case with characters and dialogue to tie the ideas down to situations and to show how the ideas might be applied. The company is fictitious, but the scenes are based on actual people and situations that I have encountered as a researcher, educator, consultant, business owner and employee. The people at Savory Foods confronted real obstacles that required competent, persistent action to overcome. However, your group may be more distracted with short-term issues, more mistrustful, and less willing to experiment than Savory. Your company may have to be more patient and courageous to overcome barriers and work as a team.

## THE BOOK'S STRUCTURE

The book has four sections. Part I, Applying Group Research to the Workplace, outlines the book's model and its research support. Chapter 1 argues that organizations are increasingly relying on teams and defines groups and organizations. Chapter 2 describes the components of the team organization model. Chapter 3 provides the theory and research for the model and shows how its components are mutually reinforcing. Chapter 4 examines popular alternative frameworks and suggests that the team organization model has considerable power to apply in many settings, but does not provide specific strategies.

Part II, Teamwork for Effective Organizations, summarizes the research on team potentials and pitfalls. Chapter 5 argues that teams are vital for continuous improvement and innovation. In Chapter 6, research is reviewed on how teams gain commitment and loyalty by fulfilling basic human needs to achieve and be respected. However, a great deal of research has documented that teams are often frustrating and unproductive. Chapter 7 argues that leadership is needed to develop successful teams.

Part III, Creating Teamwork, describes the major ingredients of successful teams and shows how they can be developed. Chapter 8 examines envisioning, Chapter 9, uniting, Chapter 10, empowering, Chapter 11, exploring, and Chapter 12, reflecting.

The last section, Toward an Integrated Company, focuses on how the team organization model can be applied to the organization as a whole. Chapter 13 looks at integrating employees and managers, and Chapter 14 investigates how to bind divisions together to form a synergistic company. Chapter 15 addresses the major steps necessary to become a team organization.

## CONCLUDING COMMENTS

*Benefits*

Teamwork stimulates ongoing innovation and gains employee commitment. Teams are good for the company and its people; they integrate the individual and the organization. But making teamwork a reality requires knowledge, sensitivity, and persistence. Teamwork is such a critical competitive advantage because potential competitors, though they may have deep pockets to buy the latest computer and production technology, cannot buy and put teamwork in place. Though there is no guarantee of long-term success today, productive teamwork provides an edge by being a sustainable competitive advantage.

I want you and your associates to use this book to obtain the tools to sharpen your teamwork. I have tried to make the team organization ideas accessible and usable, yet still suggest their richness and research base. I trust you will discuss the ideas with your colleagues and together implement them. Remember, understanding and creating teamwork is something that you do together, not alone.

# REFERENCE

1. Tjosvold, D. (1989). *Managing Conflict: The Key to Making your Organization Work*. Minneapolis, MN: Team Media.

# Acknowledgements

It may seem odd that a book on teamwork was authored by one person. But this book, like most achievements, is a 'we' thing, and I am very indebted to a great many people for their ideas and encouragement. This book reflects the deep influence of my mentor, David W. Johnson at the University of Minnesota, and his mentor, Morton Deutsch at Columbia University. I used research by many capable persons on group processes and understanding the role of groups in organizations. I am grateful to all the authors and publishers who have granted me permission to use quotations from their work in this volume. Cary Cooper and Neal Schmitt graciously asked me to participate in their series, and offered constructive feedback. Mark Wexler and Lu Fernandes made a number of useful suggestions. Choy Wong and others on the research team have contributed greatly to the studies that directly tested and extended the framework of this book.

I thank Mike Conroy, Bruce Fraser, Bob Heywood, Mike Jones, Bob Lewis, Len McNeely, Denis Martel, Allan Moore, Paul Weener, and the many other managers and employees whom I have worked with over the years. These experiences have been instrumental in developing my ideas. My colleagues at Simon Fraser University in organizational behavior, accounting, marketing, management information sciences, and finance have broadened my perspective. Mary Tjosvold and Margaret Tjosvold demonstrated many ways to work together as a team. Jenny Tjosvold helped with the research and the writing, and, along with our sons and daughters, creates a warm, rich family 'team.'

# Introduction

The greatest improvement in the productive powers of labour, and the greater part of the skill, dexterity, and judgment with which it is anywhere directed or applied, seem to have been the effect of the division of labour.

Adam Smith, *Wealth of Nations*

We are going to win and the industrial West is going to lose out: there's nothing much you can do about it, because the reasons for failure are within yourself . . . for you the essence of management is getting the ideas out of the heads of the bosses into the hand of labour . . . for us, the core of management is precisely the act of mobilizing and pulling together the intellectual resources of all employees . . . only by drawing on the combined brainpower of all its employees can a firm face up to the turbulence and constraints of today's environment.

Konosuke Matsushita, Executive Director, Matushita Electric

Confronted with intense competition, shareholder and employee demands, and global possibilities, managers are reinventing their profession and transforming their companies. They involve employees through participative management and quality circles; circumvent the traditional hierarchy, push decision making deep down into the organizations, and make their organizations flatter; form partnerships with suppliers to reduce inventory costs and serve customers effectively; strike up alliances with foreign companies to penetrate new markets and with competitors to combine research and development efforts; and restructure to reduce costs and put business units closer to their customers. Mechanical, bureaucratic, impersonal ways of working are giving way to lean, entrepreneurial ones. Teamwork is needed to make these new ways of managing and organizing effective.

While we now recognize that changing how we are organized is needed to realize competitive advantages, less appreciated is that the organization is itself the most enduring of competitive advantages. An effective team organization builds upon itself and continues to bear fruit. John Robinson, Chief Executive Officer (CEO) of American Express, concluded, 'Quality is the only patent protection we've got.' And a well-run organization improves quality, keeps customers, checks costs—and makes potential competitors look elsewhere for opportunities.

# TEAMWORK AS COMPETITIVE ADVANTAGE IN MANUFACTURING

The competitive factory of today uses computers, robots, and flexible machines to lower costs, improve quality, and offer greater product variation. The competitive factory of tomorrow will bundle services with products that meet a range of customer needs.[1] Even today production workers are marketing by talking to customers about their needs. They are consulting with customers on how to maintain and use products effectively. The factory has become a showroom for customers to appreciate how the company's products can solve problems. *Teamwork developed the competitive factory of today; it is even more critical for the service factory of the future.*

In mass production, the production core was separated from upstream activities of new product development and design, and from downstream activities of sales and service. For decades manufacturing managers tried to maximize their efficiency, and complained that the demands of new product engineers and sales interfered.

As many Japanese manufacturers showed, breaking down barriers between the upstream activities of new product and processes and the shop-floor fostered innovation and improved manufacturing performance. Getting product designers, manufacturing engineers, and shop-floor managers and employees talking and working together was critical for manufacturing excellence. Understanding the aspirations and ideas of new product people and manufacturing engineers, factory managers and workers became invaluable allies as they provided feedback on the manufacturability of new designs, constructed prototypes quickly, and introduced engineering changes.

In the service factory of tomorrow, shop-floor managers and workers will also be linked with downstream activities in support of the sales force, service technicians, and consumers. They will give their companies competitive advantages by serving customers before and after the product has been built as well as manufacturing high-quality, specialized, cost-effective products.

Manufacturers are already experimenting with the service factory. For example, Tektronix, a manufacturer of electronic equipment, has set up direct communication between customers and shop-floor employees. The company inserts a card within every oscilloscope that lists the names of the workers who built it along with a toll-free number. Customers call with questions about the use of their oscil-loscopes, complaints about its performance, and requests for additional products. The workers meet daily with managers to discuss the phone calls and necessary follow-up. Workers also call customers and ask how well their products are performing.

At Hewlett-Packard's Fort Collins Systems Division, which makes computers and technical workstations, the factory's quality department supports marketing. The marketing staff is in position to know the information customers want. The quality department collects and presents information on test results and conditions in easy-to-understand ways, including video-tapes, that inform and impress customers. The quality department also works directly with sales people through training and guided tours to better prepare them to serve customers.

Allen-Bradley, a manufacturer of industrial automation controls, uses its Milwaukee computer-integrated manufacturing operation to demonstrate its products. Within 24 hours of the order, the factory can produce 1025 different electronic contactors and relays in lot sizes down to one and with zero defects. Customers can see first-hand how various levels of controls work together and how Allen-Bradley's software products and systems architecture can help them.

Teamwork is key to making the full-scale service factory a reality. Factory people must work with marketing and service if they are going to understand customer expectations, become skilled in making presentations and consulting with them, and opening up their factories as showrooms. Marketing and service people gain essential product information and capabilities by talking to people who build and know the product the best.

Technology helps. Computerized ordering systems, expert systems to manage complex sales, computerized logs for after-sale support, computerized catalogs for replacement parts, and 24-hour answering machines to take customers' complaints all speed up communication and break down barriers between production and upstream and downstream activities. However, *understanding the value of teamwork and knowing how to work together drive the move to the service factory*.

Manufacturing operations continue to require fewer people. However, those that remain must do much more than any robot can. They have proven themselves indispensable members of the teams that design and develop new products. They will increasingly become partners with marketing, sales, and after-sales service as their companies strive to meet comprehensive customer needs. The days of functional groups doing their own thing with a few managers trying to coerce some coordination are gone. It is ongoing, face-to-face (and computer-to-computer) spirited teamwork that propels innovation and competitive advantage in manufacturing.

## THE PROMISE OF TEAMS

Managers are using a wide variety of teams for highly practical reasons: they get things done. Not ordinary things, for most of these can be accomplished by individuals working alone. *Teams get extraordinary things done.* Companies face incredible challenges to serve and respond to customers, adapt to new technology, instill employee commitment to a shared vision, and compete in the crowded international marketplace. Managers do not just want to 'manage' in the sense of bureaucratic handling of the status quo, but they want to lead their employees on a journey. They strive to tap the ideas and energy of all employees. Synergy, synchrony, and integration are their guides to innovate.

*Teams are practical ways to foster communication and integrated effort.* Professionals and employees can combine their specialized knowledge to develop unified solutions that work from various perspectives. *Teams are politically useful in that they are concrete ways to involve stakeholders.* Although it is impractical to have large departments gather to debate issues, their representatives can hammer out a consensus.

### CONTINUOUS IMPROVEMENT

Teams have the potential to solve two essential issues every organization confronts. The first is to keep *the organization responsive and open to its environment.* No organization exists in a vacuum, but must serve its customers, investors, and other stakeholders or face the possibility of reduced support and resources. Today's organizations must be alert to changes and adapt to remain viable. Organizations from universities to preschools, from high tech to low tech must *innovate.* Teams are practical ways to create the wherewithal to manage change.

### COMMITMENT

The second issue is to *integrate employees into the organization.* No company can survive unless employees commit their energies and ideas to use its resources to satisfy stakeholders. Ordering and paying are not by themselves sufficient to motivate people to meet today's challenges. Organizations must foster *high commitment*. Teams can be rich, intrinsically meaningful experiences that touch and enrich the lives of people.

The use of teams is a gradual transformation, but its impact dramatic. *Groups are becoming the basic building blocks of organizations and are vital in rejuvenating them.* This movement has far-reaching implications for leadership, training, compensation, and organizational design.

# ROADBLOCKS TO TEAMWORK ⬅

Many managers find the rewards of teamwork distant and its road bumpy and winding; they are ambivalent and skeptical rather than passionate. Their reservations are not overcome by top management rhetoric and sloganning. They put their energies into areas where they expect more certain returns.

## AMBIVALENCE AND UNCERTAINTIES

Teamwork requires passion and commitment. Cohesive, lively teamwork will not develop unless people feel an urgency to move towards it. But the movement to the team organization, like other important challenges to the status quo, evokes misgivings and confusions that resist change. Can a leader be strong and effective yet work as a team with employees? Aren't heads of the business units supposed to be aggressive and competitive? Won't asking them to cooperate water down their effectiveness?

To many, groups and teamwork are weak and ineffectual—signs that managers and their companies have become soft and wishy-washy. Teams involve never-ending meetings and are cop-outs and delaying tactics so that managers do not have to take risks and exercise authority. Groups squelch ideas and sink to the lowest level because they can be no better than the most incompetent individual member. They exclude the hard-charging and independent.

Popular ideas about how to structure and lead groups compound the confusion. It is often assumed that cohesion, similarity, and harmony are critical for a team to cooperate and work together. Yet this 'human relations' approach is unrealistic because employees will inevitably have opposing ideas and interests. Cohesion is thought undesirable because it induces conformity and stifles creativity. Many people suspect that gains in social solidarity come at the expense of creativity and innovation, and the price is too high.

There are, especially in North America, mixed values about groups. Teamwork and cooperation are often thought of as motherhood statements,

**Table 1** Comparison of models

| Human relations model | Team organization model |
| --- | --- |
| Modest goals | Inspiring vision |
| Assume unity | Forge unity |
| Assume skilled | Stimulate development |
| Compromise | Explore opposing views |
| Smooth over | Manage conflict |
| Steady work | Innovation |
| Job acceptance | Commitment |

the value of which no reasonable person would dispute. The very rationale for an organization is to capture teamwork and coordinate the work of many to accomplish tasks no one person can do efficiently or at all. Yet companies and managers are expected to be independent-minded and competitive. Competition makes capitalism more efficient than socialism; competition makes one firm superior to others in the marketplace. From this standpoint, cooperative teamwork sounds wishy-washy and wrong.

These questions and uncertainties make teamwork sound abstract, vague, and mysterious. Managers and employees need a focused understanding of teamwork and its consequences before they can be expected to commit themselves fully. A comparison of models is shown in Table 1.

## CAN WE DO IT?

A pervasive reason that teamwork is underdeveloped is that managers do not have a clear map to achieve it. Developing teamwork seems like a comprehensive, elusive notion that offers few clues where to begin and few signposts along the way.

Teamwork challenges traditional ways of working. Are managers prepared and equipped to inspire, persuade, and negotiate? Teamwork is a powerful idea with broad implications for links between individual managers and employees as well as between union and management, and between executives as well as their departments and divisions. But how can such a multifaceted jelly-fish be wrestled with, tracked down, and tackled? What are the first, middle, and last steps?

There are doubts that teamwork can be developed with different people. Perhaps teamwork is possible with 'gold'-collar high-tech workers, but not with white-collar middle managers. Perhaps it works with outgoing types, but not with introverted techies. Production people might like it, but sales people will shake their heads in disbelief. Working in teams is possible in protected public services, but is it compatible with a bottom-line company? Teamwork may be a vital weapon in Japan's success or in excellent companies in North

America and Europe, but can it happen in an average small company in the American Midwest or English Midlands?

## LOST CREDIBILITY

In the 1980s, many managers pressed for a new partnership between management and labor; for greater trust and cooperation and a new partnership. Expressing sincere intentions, while a vital first step, is insufficient. Talking about teamwork and managing its symbols, without follow-through, backfires.

US employees, surveys suggest, actually became less trusting in the 1980s.[2] Employees want to believe: respect from managers, recognition of their contributions, and honest communication were more important to them than job security. However, middle managers, professionals, and workers all indicated they were getting less respect, less recognition, and less honesty.

Espousing teamwork values, however sincere, must be supported with credible, consistent action. Many employees believe their bosses 'talk the talk, but don't walk the walk.' Top management waxes on about people as the most important resource, but then without warning terminates people. One day they are into sloganning about quality, the next day they push for reduced costs. Employees doubt increasingly the ability of top management to deliver. Less than a third of the employees surveyed believed that management even provided clear goals.

# GROUP RESEARCH'S MESSAGE

Although many people have ambiguous attitudes toward groups in organizations, *research knowledge presents a consistent, useful message about groups in organizations.* While knowledge is far from complete, social psychologists, sociologists, and other social scientists have joined management researchers to develop an extensive knowledge base about interpersonal relations, interdependence, and groups. Surely groups and related phenomena are among the most widely researched areas in the social sciences. There is a need to integrate this research to draw implications for the role and management of teams in organizations.[3]

The message of group research, however, is not a simple one. Certainly teams are not a cure-all for organizational ills or a sure-fire route to a competitive company. *Researchers have documented the potential value of group work, but they have also identified pitfalls and problems that threaten groups.* Forming teams is not by itself an effective strategy.

Sometimes groups are assumed to replace the authority hierarchy and managers in particular. Nothing could be further from the truth. *Teams require skillful leadership and a great deal of management.* Using teams demands that managers understand what groups can and cannot do, and be sensitive to their pitfalls. They must have a solid sense of what makes a group effective, and have the skills to create the conditions that foster group success. They should know how to select people for a team, help them create a common vision, hold individuals responsible, and help the groups discuss their differences and solve problems. The human resource systems of compensation, training, and development need to reinforce teamwork.

*Research does not imply that every task and issue should be assigned to a team.* For many simple tasks, having individuals working alone is efficient and avoids costly coordination.[4] Individuals find the task challenging and rewarding, and need not rely on others. Traditional hierarchical organizations that assign employees independent roles and have managers coordinate may be able to operate satisfactorily in a stable environment.

Competitively trying to outdo others is another alternative to cooperative teamwork. At times, competition is inevitable as people compete over a new promotion. Competition can be useful: departments are energized as they vie to see which one can raise more funds for a charity. However, neither independent work nor competition have proven effective for dealing with complex problems or managing change.[5]

I argue that for most organizations, especially those that must adapt to change and are striving for excellence, *cooperative teamwork should be the dominant, but not the only, way of working.* People will still at times work independently. Often a team will divide up its task and hold individuals accountable for completing their part. Competition over who has the best skits at the company party can be fun and exciting, and a break from cooperative teamwork. However, the vast majority of teams and organizations are much more successful when they recognize that their independent and competitive work occurs within a more general cooperative context.

## BECOMING A TEAM ORGANIZATION

Teamwork is *not* an off-the-shelf product; it is more like a computer information system than a personal computer. Teamwork has general principles and logic as well as defined components, but these have to be melded and formulated to fit the people and their circumstances. As a computer system requires coordinated work between designers and users, so too does teamwork.

What is needed is for managers and employees to develop a common commitment and understanding of teamwork and to work together to create a unified direction and make teamwork a part of their daily work. They need to keep enriching and strengthening teamwork, or risk falling back to traditional habits.

## SHARED CONVICTION

Wanting to is an important first step. But it is not enough that the CEO of the company or the manager of the department thinks teamwork is a good idea. Everyone should believe it is vital to sustain the success of their company and their own prosperity and security. It is through teamwork that the company delivers high-quality products that customers value; it is through teamwork that the company adapts and innovates; it is through teamwork that the company selects, trains, and retains competent, energetic employees.

People have an urgency to develop the team organization. They care about their company and their relationships, and are passionate about becoming a team. But it is a passion based on realistic appraisal of the potential of working as a team.

## COMMON KNOWLEDGE BASE

Teamwork is so basic that people often assume they know what it means. But there is a great deal of confusion about the nature of effective work relationships. In fact, teamwork challenges outmoded ways of thinking about organizations. Power as the ability to get people to do what they would not choose to do is being replaced by empowering others to believe and act. Making decisions as determining who is right and who is wrong is giving way to incorporating different points of view into creating solutions that work for all. Rather than a fight over scarce resources, conflict is becoming an opportunity to strengthen common ground.

People will be uncertain about how they are to communicate, deal with their differences, and manage their conflicts unless they have clear norms and expectations. To the extent they have publicly acknowledged the kind of teamwork they aspire to, people will operate on the same wavelength. Otherwise, they risk misunderstandings, embarrassments, and uncertainties that make them doubt their co-workers' sincerity and ability to work as a team.

## MUTUAL WORK

The ideas of vision, unity, empowerment, exploration, and managing conflict must be translated into the actual operations and day-to-day work of the organization. But there are no set procedures that are universally applicable. Some teams need to meet daily; others quarterly. Some teams will communicate face to face, others by fax. Some teams will all work on the same problem, others will assign people independent tasks.

Team members themselves decide how tasks should be structured, work distributed, and rewards given to strengthen their unity. They create the settings and venues and computer networks they need to stay in touch, and identify the training they need to work together. The manager urges, orchestrates, and approves, but members are highly involved for they are in the best position to determine the most effective and efficient way to work together. They must be convinced, moreover, that they are all committed to working as a team.

Teamwork is everyone's responsibility. One person cannot cooperate or manage a conflict. Teamwork is needed to become a team organization; the method reinforces the message.

## CONTINUOUS DEVELOPMENT

There are forces pushing team members to become more effective. They are united behind their common challenge, feel motivated to support their friends, and want the rewards of success. But there are forces pushing against the team. Team members have inevitable frustrations and undiscussed suspicions that other activities and priorities are more important. Teamwork is either growing or declining; there is no maintaining the status quo. Without attention and work, teams will gradually wither. Like improving service or reducing costs, *teamwork is an ongoing journey, not a destination.*

In addition to strengthening departments and groups internally, teamwork should also spread throughout the organization. The efforts of one area to work as a team need to be supported by others. While groups can become cooperative and cohesive when they are in competition with others, this approach is seldom effective in organizations. The marketing group will want to work with a production group that is open to their suggestions for how they can improve customer service; otherwise they will question why they should bother to work as a team for the organization.

Developing teamwork, I have argued, is much like improving product quality, customer service, and other comparative advantages. It will not happen unless people are convinced, understand what it is, implement it, and strive for continuous improvement. But teamwork does not compete with other changes; it supports them. The drive to quality and customer service unites individuals and groups, gives them a benchmark for how they can integrate their efforts and ideas, and provides a rationale for why they should resolve their differences. Teamwork is necessary to achieve competitive advantages; the company's business mission gives teamwork a vital meaning. A united company succeeds.

# REFERENCES

1. Chase, R. B. and Garvin, D. A. (1989). The service factory. *Harvard Business Review*, July–August, 61–69.
2. Farnham, A. (1989). The trust gap. *Fortune*, December 4, 56–78.
3. Cummings, L. L. (1986). Reexamining our thoughts concerning groups in organizations. In P. S. Goodman (ed.), *Designing Effective Work Groups*. San Francisco: Jossey-Bass, 350–361.
4. Johnson, D. W. and Johnson, R. T. (1989). *Cooperation and Competition: Theory and Research*. Edina, MN: Interaction Book Company.
5. Johnson, D. W. and Johnson, R. T. (1989). *Cooperation and Competition: Theory and Research*. Edina, MN: Interaction Book Company.

# Part I:   Applying Group Research to the Workplace

We are not going to overtake the Japanese in this decade in those industries in which we have fallen behind. There is no way in which that can happen. We will do very well to overtake them in the next decade, and to do so, we will have to change our ways rather dramatically.

Joseph M. Juran, 1987

Our organization is based on mutual respect: The contributions of each person are essential to our success. We have learned that creating a business (or a product) depends on people who care about each other and about the customers we serve. This caring for one another translates into integrity in our operating style. We live up to our commitments: . . . We share the fun, excitement, and triumph of group and individual success. We have pride in our accomplishments. We do it together, and we're the best in the business.

Maria Straatmann, Computer Technology and Imaging

Managers and employees usually want to work as a team, and teamwork has become a rallying cry for many organizations. But there is a great deal of confusion about what teamwork is and suspicion whether it can be created. Chapter 1 discusses the movement toward becoming a team organization. Chapter 2 introduces the team organization model and the major levers available to managers and employees to develop it. A great deal of theorizing and empirical work, summarized in Chapter 3, supports this model. Chapter 4 reviews major alternative approaches to organizational groups that have been tested and developed; considering these approaches highlights the uses and limitations of the team organization model.

# 1 Moving to the Team Organization

'I want to help our managers develop teamwork at Savory Foods,' Marian Moberg said to Jerry Leppa. Marian had worked at Savory Foods for eight years, and was now manager of Employee Services. She welcomed the challenge her boss, Walt Newhouse, the vice president of Human Resources, gave the department to work directly with managers to strengthen their abilities and the company's organization.

'Sounds noble—sounds like something you would want to do,' Jerry replied. Jerry had been with the company for 12 years, and was now in charge of the industrial relations section. He was by nature skeptical, and he couldn't help thinking that Walt was just trying to butter up the CEO, Allan Lindberg.

'I'm excited that Allan and Walt want us to take this proactive role in developing the company.' Marian recognized but did not take Jerry's suspicions too seriously. She knew she could count on him. 'That's a lot better than just worrying about sick leave, and all that administration stuff.'

'Let's charge ahead to the great unknown, only to be left out on the range when the winds turn,' Jerry said. 'Remember my first rule of working here: face reality, not wish things are different from what they are.'

'But we need challenging aspirations and to create a new reality, as Allan said.'

'Talk, talk, talk—sometimes it just burns me up when the high flyers get on their podiums and talk about teamwork and meeting the challenges of tomorrow. I think these guys all go to the same public relations firm for their speeches.'

'But it's not just words,' Marian said earnestly. 'The world of food is changing, and we have to change with it or fade into the background. Our competitors are not standing still; they are buying this and that company— getting ready to compete worldwide.'

'That's scare talk,' Jerry replied. 'We're still selling lots of noodles, canned soups, frozen vegetables—we've got lots of products.'

'But like Allan said, lifestyles are changing. People will pay premium prices for microwave foods they can fix in five minutes that taste good and are nutritious. The question is whether we'll be supplying them or will someone else.'

'Not everyone likes microwave food.'

'You're supposed to be the one who likes to face reality, but you seem to have forgotten those numbers that were passed around. You don't have to be the CEO or a financial wizard to get the message of our lackluster bottom line. Sales growth is slowing, prices are being squeezed, and we're not cashing in on new types of convenience foods. It seems clear that unless we get our act together, we face downsizing and layoffs.'

'It just rubs me the wrong way when I hear the CEO or any of those bosses talk about pulling together, being a team, and we're all in this together. Whenever I hear these things, I always wonder what this guy is trying to pull over me.'

'Teamwork sounds great to me.'

'These guys just want everyone to shut up and do it their way.'

'But Allan said he wanted participation, a thousand ideas to flourish, and bottom-up management. He's asking us to speak out and take initiative, isn't he?' Marian hoped that she had interpreted Allan correctly.

'Words, words. You can be too naive, you know.'

'But the CEO is doing something. He's trying to get the top team together —he admitted that the VPs had not set a good example of teamwork, and that would have to change.'

'Do Allan and Walt walk the walk, or do they just talk the talk? They wax on about excellence, teamwork, and a caring company, but they are still shouting about efficiency, productivity, and profits. They talk about long-term development, but demand short-term bottom-line results.'

'But you need all of that, the short term and long term, productivity and people.'

'And what are *you* going to do about that?'

'My idea is that I ask a number of managers to meet regularly and become a study group. We will read common articles and have some hard hitting discussions about what makes an effective group that innovates and supports our employees.'

'But if you're going to do this, Marian, you should do it right. You've got to get them to do more than talk. If our employees just hear more and more people talk about corporate culture, innovation, and teamwork without action, we might be sowing the seeds of a revolution by raising expectations and not delivering. Besides, our managers will say that studying groups is a good thing to do, but then find all sorts of excuses why they just can't make it to the next meeting.'

'But they could also think together about what they can do to develop their departments into productive, supportive teams. It's got to mean something to them.'

'Why not let them work side by side to do it? I've often thought that our managers are too isolated.' Jerry wanted to help Marian.

'Too isolated? Now it is your turn to be out of touch. They're always complaining about how they go from one meeting to another and never have any time alone.' Marian liked to prick Jerry's at times overbearing manner.

'What I'm talking about is that they have no one to talk to about their concerns and frustrations, and to draw up plans. They can't really talk to their employees, say, about what to do about one of them.'

'They do complain that they have no one to bounce an idea off, except if they're lucky enough to have another manager as a close friend.'

'Or unlucky.'

'I need a name. I could call it the "Team Leaders Corps—TLC."'

'You could—if you had no sense of modesty, to say nothing of good taste,' Jerry laughed.

'So we discuss ideas, and we help each other put them into practice. We become a real team so that we can become better leaders.'

'Sounds like a possibility—who knows, maybe even a winner, stranger things have happened.'

Marian knew several managers were struggling to develop strong teams. Listening to Allan and Walt talk about the need for teamwork gave her the idea that these managers should get together. It hit her that in their own ways they were each trying to overcome many of the same barriers. She would be more efficient and less pressured because they could learn the ideas together. And as Jerry suggested, they could act as consultants to each other. They could also learn as they themselves developed as a team.

It was not really part of her character to take the lead to organize the management development team. She would have to call and make appointments, sometimes with managers whom she did not know well and who might tell her 'No.' She would have to persuade them that her idea was good and practical, go through rounds of negotiating to find a suitable time, and may have to readjust her own calendar. And she still had all her own regular work to do. But she was encouraged, even inspired, by the Allan and Walt talk about the importance of leadership and teamwork for Savory. She was determined to be a leader and give her idea a good shot.

Two weeks of persistence paid off, and four managers agreed to participate in the team. Marian was concerned that the managers came from different sections of the company. She worried that they might not find a common language and ground, but liked the challenge of applying ideas in different settings. If successful, the group might help bridge the divisions that separated people at Savory.

After introductions, Marian began, 'What I thought we might do today is to share our thoughts and hopes about what each one of you wants to learn from this group, specifically how you want to become more effective leaders and develop teamwork with your people. That would help us get focused on the challenges we have before us, and what we have in common. I hope this discussion will also help us to get to know each other as people and as managers better.'

Art Slavik from Marketing offered to begin. He had begun as a sales representative 15 years ago, and had worked himself up to management. He made the transition, and indeed surprised himself at how seriously he identified with being a manager. 'Despite all the talk about how marketing people are favored in this company, not everything is rosy.'

'Jet lag from flights to Hawaii,' quipped Scott Westman from Research & Development.

'Indigestion from fancy restaurants, perhaps,' said Miles Lennon from Production.

'I can see we have a supportive group here,' Marian said.

'We're trying to be understanding, but in our own peculiar Savory way,' said Kyle La Mont, the controller.

Marian was nervous about such teasing for it touched on destructive prejudices people at Savory had about other areas. And she did not want the meeting to degenerate into one-liners. She hoped though that such joking was an indirect, enjoyable way to get these issues out on the table.

Art explained that if the company was going to enter global niche markets, as the CEO wanted, its marketing staff would have to learn to do things much differently. They would have to work with and through foreign distributors and the joint venture partners that the company was trying to develop. He had been concerned for some time about the marketing culture of 'every man for himself' and the requirement that sales people should be aggressive and individualistic. The marketing people considered any direction or rule as an infringement of their freedom to operate and be successful. They brushed aside teamwork as irrelevant. But now they would surely have to pull together to learn the new languages and skills of working with foreign customers and joint ventures. 'They believe they are ready for the new challenges. I don't. And I might as well be talking Greek when I tell them we need teamwork.'

'My people are skeptical about teamwork, but for different reasons,' Miles said. 'They're at each other's throats.' He explained that one reason he was hired two years ago was that, as a black man, top management thought he would be able to deal quickly with the racial and other conflicts in the production plant. It hadn't worked out that way. Sometimes he feared he was contributing to the backbiting. Black employees accused him of betrayal; white supervisors accused him of appeasement. Even the female and male employees were hostile toward each other.

'Make no mistake, it is not just because I am committed to good race relations on the job that I'm concerned,' Miles continued. 'We waste a lot of time talking, brooding, and attacking that could be better spent doing the job. What's more, we can't seem to look further down the road and think about how we can attain excellence in production. There are exciting things happening in food production. I'm afraid the rest of the world is passing us by. I warn them that the company will move its production facilities abroad if we don't get our act together.'

'My problems are not so dramatic—they're puzzling,' Scott from R&D said. He was young, but respected for his creative ideas. Accustomed to quick success, he was beginning to worry that he might not become a successful manager. His VP wanted to use new product teams as they had in his former company. Rather than have the Research people develop a product, then have Marketing evaluate it, then Industrial Engineering design production, and finally hand it over to Production, representatives from all these groups were to form a team for each new significant product possibility. But Scott couldn't get people to believe. When they showed up for meetings, they were ill-prepared to work together. They'd nod their heads, walk away, and not much happened. 'Talk about foreign languages. They all speak and think differently, and there's little real communication. I try to set up relaxed times for them to talk, but they seem afraid to take the initiative and really open up. I can't remember being so frustrated, and having so little idea about what I can do.'

'Our situation in Accounting is somewhat similar,' Kyle, the controller, offered. He had only been on the job for six months, and had spent that time just trying to figure out what was going on. But he was not linked to the old habits or problems, and spoke candidly about the accounting group. 'We are a dispirited, disjointed group. The CEO and our VP keep telling us that we need to serve "our customers" better and provide the new profit and cost centers with the timely information they need to run their business. That kind of talk doesn't go over too well. If we ask for more computers to help us get information to "our customers," we're told that there's no money in the budget. But other groups seem to get money for doing much less basic things. We're isolated from the other areas at Savory and from each other. Getting us to work better by working together seems to me to be one of the keys we need to move forward.'

Marian summarized: 'I think what we've said today reinforces what Allan has been telling us. Savory has pressing challenges ahead, and teamwork will help us meet them. We—our team here—have important work ahead.'

'Let's have some fun, too,' Miles said to general agreement.

 ## CONFRONTING CHALLENGES

Managers at Savory had good reasons to develop teams. Art wanted the sales people to become more sensitive and savvy to deal with foreign customers as Savory entered global markets. Miles believed teamwork would improve the quality of work life, and help Production use new techniques and methods on the shop floor. Scott wanted to reduce the time from interesting idea to marketable product. Kyle hoped to create a team that could give the cost and profit centers the timely, useful information needed to make good business decisions.

Groups are developing and marketing products, solving production problems, and creating corporate strategy. Managers want an open, organic organization that discards formalism and fosters the ongoing communication and exchange needed for hustle and swift action.[1] They are experimenting with participation, high-commitment organizations, quality circles, semi-autonomous work teams, new product rugby, labor–management cooperation, and the Scanlon plan and gainsharing programs. These innovations, though they have different philosophies, language, and focus, all involve the explicit use of teams to accomplish vital organizational missions.

Team marketing has become logical and effective, especially for large, national accounts; sales representatives receive commissions based on the account's sales volume.[2] Teamwork is spilling out across organizational and national boundaries. Many manufacturers form teams with suppliers to boost quality, reduce costs, and assure continuous improvement. International joint ventures are becoming ubiquitous. Even traditional competitors such as American and Japanese auto-makers are engaged in a wide variety of cooperative strategies. Increasingly, people with different organizational and national loyalties from diverse cultural backgrounds are working together.

## WHAT ARE ORGANIZATIONAL GROUPS?

Groups are prominent in organizations, even traditionally managed ones. Executives form the top management team, customer representatives the sales force, and assembly-line operators the work group. Managers from all plants in the Midwest division meet regularly to discuss production problems and new ideas about leadership. Employees put great stock in their membership in organizational groups; typically they introduce themselves by identifying their department.

Groups are vital outside the workplace: we live, play, worship, and relax in groups. Our interest here is in groups associated with organizations. Typically, the people and purpose of the group are based in one company: a task force is struck to recommend a new software program for accounting. However, groups that span organizations are also vital as managers pool resources across companies. Marketing people from a radio station and an airline might form a team to develop a contest to win trips abroad both to strengthen the loyalty of the station's listeners and to advertise the airline's new routes.

### ORGANIZATIONS

Organizations are extremely flexible and useful social inventions. There are organizations for every conceivable purpose—and a few inconceivable ones! They are designed to accomplish goals—put people on the moon, produce and market hamburgers, elect politicians, and protect grizzly bears—through *the combined, integrated effort of many persons.* Usually these goals cannot be reached by one person acting independently. Official goals define in abstract terms what the organization wishes to accomplish. These formal goals are found in charters, annual reports, and public statements. Operational goals are more specific guides for how the official goals are to be achieved.

Organizations are open systems: they depend upon the environment for support and resources, and offer market products and services to the environment in exchange for resources. *Organizations use structured relationships in which people are assigned responsibilities and have interrelated roles to coordinate the effort of many people to transform inputs into products and services that can be marketed.* The management system oversees and integrates the technology and people so that the coordination is efficient and obstacles are overcome.

## GROUPS

Groups are even more pervasive than organizations. Although we all have extensive experience with groups, and have little trouble identifying groups in our lives, defining groups so as to encompass all their variety is difficult. Groups have many characteristics, and there is no consensus which one is distinguishing. Social scientists have typically emphasized one aspect of groups in their definitions.

Some researchers have argued that the central characteristics of groups involves *face-to-face interaction and mutual influence.* Homans[3] proposed that groups are small enough for people to communicate in a face-to-face manner over a period of time. Shaw[4] defined groups as two or more persons interacting with each other over a period of time so that each person influences others and is influenced by them.

Relatedly, social scientists have emphasized *interdependence and structured relationships.* Lewin[5] proposed that interdependence was central to the understanding of groups. Fiedler[6] characterized groups as individuals who share a common fate in that an event which affects one affects the others. Sheriff and Sheriff[7] argued that group members have reciprocal roles and norms that regulate their behavior.

*Perceived membership* has also been considered critical. Bales[8] argued that group members develop a distinct impression of each other. Shea and Guzzo[9] emphasized that people see themselves as a group and are seen by others as a group.

*Common goals and tasks* also characterize groups.[10] Group members need to believe that they are united and can act in unison. They are thought to have a common purpose and their interaction helps them accomplish their objectives and meet their needs.[11]

Groups are best defined by combining interaction, structured relationships, and goals and membership into a single definition.[12] *Groups are two or more persons who interact and influence each other directly, who are mutually dependent and have interlocking roles and common norms, and who see themselves as a unity in pursuit of common goals that satisfy their individual aspirations and needs.*

A basic characteristic of groups, especially organizational ones, is that they are open systems. They, like organizations, depend upon their environment and must negotiate this dependence. Groups get their members, mission, and resources from the organization and the rest of the environment, and are expected to return benefit.

Groups do not meet all these criteria all the time. Members may resist influence; they may have incompatible role expectations and assume different norms. Group members may not agree what its goals are or have goals that are very meaningful for individuals. The definition incorporates ideals to strive for as well as descriptions of reality.

Our definition helps to indicate what is not a group. Singapore, Digital Equipment Corporation, Lutherans, and new high school graduates are not groups. These people may see themselves as belonging together, have some common values and norms, and even be mutually dependent, but they do not have face-to-face interaction in which they communicate and try to influence each other directly.

Organizations are distinct from groups in that they can be much larger, and may involve thousands of people most of whom never see or speak to each other. Organizations tend to be more complex and incorporate many groups with diverse interests and aspirations. Typically they have a more formalized mission, division of labor, and authority hierarchies.

Yet groups and organizations are highly similar. They are both designed to coordinate effort to accomplish goals. They are mechanisms for pooling the resources, energy, and ideas of people to accomplish tasks that an individual cannot accomplish efficiently. Groups and organizations both involve interaction, interdependence, influence, reciprocal roles, common goals, and perceived membership.

*Groups, as microcosms of organizations, are highly compatible ways for organizations to structure work.* Groups foster integrated work that helps an organization coordinate people to accomplish its ends. Their size makes them more easily managed than organizations. Yet the central role of groups for organizations has not been obvious. Since Frederick Taylor, the founder of modern management theory, managers have tended to think of individuals, not groups, as the basic building block of their organizations.

## EFFECTIVENESS

Effective organizational groups, as open systems, must serve the interests of the organizations from which they draw their charter and resources. Similarly, effective organizations, as open systems, must serve their customers and other stakeholders or they will eventually suffer the loss of support and resources.

Groups and organizations must also serve their members to develop motivation and commitment. If persons believe that the group and organizational goals, experience, and rewards are trivial and meaningless, they may go through the motions but will not provide the effort and persistence necessary to get something extraordinary done.

Groups and organizations must normally serve both the short term and the long term. A marketing group is expected to develop an effective plan to sell microwave hot chocolate sundaes for the coming summer season, and, if possible, create more effective plans for future seasons. A marketing plan that sells sundaes this year but alienates customers for next season is not a good plan. It becomes imperative then that organizational groups strengthen themselves so that they can work together productively in the future.

This reasoning suggests that effective groups and organizations must satisfy several criteria:[13]

(1) Groups and organizations appreciate how they can add value for their 'customers' and other stakeholders, recognize changes in their environment, and adapt so that they can continue to provide value for them, and receive their support in turn. They are effective in that they are doing the right thing.

(2) Groups and organizations complete their tasks and accomplish their goals in ways that are acceptable to stakeholders within the time, resources, and other constraints deemed appropriate. They are efficient: they are doing things right.

(3) Members find their work motivating and rewarding so that they exert effort, use their abilities, and persist to do their jobs well.

(4) People develop their individual skills and effective work relationships to tackle future tasks with confidence.

(5) Members become committed and identify with their group and organization so that they take the long-term view and have the energy to pursue future assignments.

These criteria are in an overall sense compatible and reinforcing. They are not, though, always equally important, and in the short run there are tradeoffs: a solution is rammed through to meet a deadline, although it increases suspicion and undermines future collaboration. Because of the strong emphasis on the short term, the focus in many organizations is getting the present task completed efficiently, at the expense of the other criteria of group and organizational effectiveness and long-term excellence. The next chapter outlines major characteristics that make groups and their organizations effective.

## REFERENCES

1. Peters, T. (1987). *Thriving on Chaos: Handbook for a Management Revolution*. New York: Knopf.
2. Cespedes, F. V., Doyle, S. X. and Freedman, R. J. (1989). Teamwork for today's selling. *Harvard Business Review*, March–April, 44–53.
3. Homans, G. (1950). *The Human Group*. New York: Harcourt, Brace.

4. Shaw, M. (1976). *Group Dynamics*. New York: McGraw-Hill.
5. Lewin, K. (1951). *Field Theory in Social Science*. New York: Harper.
6. Fiedler, F. (1967). *A Theory of Leadership Effectiveness*. New York: McGraw-Hill.
7. Sheriff, M. and Sheriff, C. (1956). *An Outline of Social Psychology*. New York: Harper & Row.
8. Bales, R. F. (1950). *Interaction Process Analysis*. Reading, MA: Addison-Wesley.
9. Shea, G. P. and Guzzo, R. A. (1987). Groups as human resources. *Research in Personnel and Human Resources Management*, **5**, 323–356.
10. Shea, G. P. and Guzzo, R. A. (1987). Groups as human resources. *Research in Personnel and Human Resources Management*, **5**, 323–356.
11. Bales, R. F. (1950). *Interaction Process Analysis*. Reading, MA: Addison-Wesley. Cattel, R. (1951). New concepts for measuring leadership, in terms of group syntality. *Human Relations*, **4**, 161–184. Smith, M. (1945). Social situation, social behavior, and social group. *Psychological Review*, **52**, 224–229.
12. Johnson, D. W. and Johnson, F. P. (1987). *Joining Together: Group Theory and Group Skills*. Englewood Cliffs, NJ: Prentice-Hall. Shea, G. P. and Guzzo, R. A. (1987). Groups as human resources. *Research in Personnel and Human Resources Management*, **5**, 323–356.
13. Hackman, J. R. (1983). *A Normative Model of Work Team Effectiveness*. Technical Report No. 2, Research Program on Group Effectiveness, Yale School of Organization and Management.

# 2 The Team Organization Model

'At our first meeting, Art said that talking about teamwork with his sales people was like speaking in Greek,' Marian opened up the second session of the Team Leaders Corps. 'It got me thinking that we need a common language and framework to think about groups.'

'There seems to be an endless way to analyze them,' Kyle said. 'I took a course some time ago, and we studied various models of effective organizational teams. Interesting, but difficult to decide which one to use.'

'There's been a lot of interest and work on autonomous groups in production,' Miles said. 'Give the group some breathing room, and watch them work hard. Sounds great.'

'I'm wondering if we can really have one approach, given that we manage in such different areas,' Scott said. 'I think our new product teams have been rather autonomous, but to me that's part of the problem rather than the solution.'

'But if we're going to help each other, as I believe we want to, we need a common set of guides for how we should proceed,' Miles said.

'That's right,' said Art. 'But let's make sure that we get some tools that we can work with—that suggest how we can develop our teams. Now I grant you that studying groups can be intellectually challenging and all, and I'm not against that by any means. I'm sure that you could study groups and the different approaches for years, and keep learning. But we are practical people using company time, and we all want some payoff in how we manage.'

'It's not that we are uninterested in truth,' Kyle remarked. 'We are interested. But we want to be able to do something with it.'

'I don't think there's anything wrong with that, or that wanting guidelines for action is anti-intellectual,' Marian said. 'We used to say in graduate school, "If you want to understand something, try changing it," ' Marian had learned not to get defensive about managers' wanting procedures. After earning her Ph.D., four years in teaching college, and a brief stint consulting for Savory,

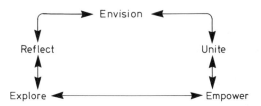

**Figure 2.1** Team organization model

she had taken the plunge into full-time management. She at first missed teaching and felt awkward dealing with action-oriented people, but now had no regrets. She saw herself at the exciting crossroads between theory and action.

'Group researchers,' she continued, 'have long been interested in application. Kurt Lewin, the founder of contemporary group dynamics and my hero, used to say, "There's nothing so useful as a good theory." He wanted to bridge theory and action. He rejected both mindless action and heartless social science.'

'Well, this is helping fill in a missing piece from last week,' Art said. 'We all talked about our hopes and goals but, Marian, you were a little quiet.'

Marian saw that others shared Art's interest. She talked about her hopes to work closely with managers to help them develop on-the-job skills that really made a difference. She hoped that the group could demonstrate the value of synergy and teamwork, and perhaps bring the different divisions and areas at Savory together more. 'I also want to be part of a team, to develop my own abilities to be a team leader. And you are my guinea-pigs!'

They laughed. 'Just don't put on a white lab coat and dissect us,' Miles said. 'I still have vivid memories of my tenth grade biology class.'

Marian felt more relaxed, and more a part of the team. 'We're a laboratory in a sense. We want to practice using strategies to develop ourselves as a team.'

'I like that,' Scott said. 'We should be able to practice what we preach.'

'What our workers don't need is a lot more talk,' Miles said.

'Don't we need talk *followed* by action?' Kyle asked.

'That's a better way of putting it,' Miles said. 'Talk is useful as long as we follow through. If we don't, we'll lose credibility and then we might as well throw in the towel.'

'Here's the model, the common language that I'd like us to consider as a guide for team development,' Marian said, passing out the team organizational model. (See Figure 2.1.) She explained that the model has five components:

Envision, Unite, Empower, Explore, and Reflect. These parts are not only mutually compatible, but very reinforcing. Effective groups just don't do one of them well, but all five.

'I guess the "envision" part is what we've been doing so far,' Scott said. 'We've been talking about what we want to accomplish, how we would like things to be different.'

'We all, including Marian, have also been establishing a vision for this group as well as for our own work groups,' Art said.

'We've already begun the "unite" part of the model,' Miles said. 'I can see where we are better off together, that we all want to learn about teamwork, and we can help each other become more effective managers.'

Marian explained that a critical aspect of uniting is that their common vision as well as their individual goals gives them a strong sense of cooperative interdependence, that is, as one is successful the others are successful. People feel that they 'are in this together.'

'In a way, we are also on the third part of empowering,' Kyle mused. 'I feel more confident about developing teamwork just by the sense of common effort. But I'm not there yet; I need to learn a lot more.'

'The "we can do it" feeling, the conviction that the group will be successful, is at the heart of empowering,' Marian said. People in the group believe they have the abilities and resources to overcome obstacles and accomplish their visions. The skills and opportunities to work together are vital to this sense of power, for people who can't work together can't integrate their efforts productively.

'"Explore" is also an important step to team success,' Marian continued. Inevitably, any group confronts obstacles, difficulties, and problems as they try to accomplish their tasks and realize their vision. Not all situations can be anticipated, and some issues will be particularly difficult. Groups are often tempted to grab the first solution without a thorough examination of the issues or creation of alternative solutions. Groups must be able to explore problems and possible solutions to arrive at ones that are effective and efficient.

Groups are not machines to set up and let run smoothly. Teams must continually examine and strengthen their abilities to envision, unite, empower, and explore. As the environment of the group and the needs of individuals change, the vision needs to be updated. Frictions and conflicts may gnaw away at the sense of unity. People may become worn down and out, or use sloppy problem-solving methods and be wedded to old ways. The status quo is seldom possible to maintain; teams either grow or decline. Continuous learning and improvement should be on the team's agenda.

'So it is not simple,' Kyle said. 'Too bad—I like simple solutions. You know, have a meeting or two and then move on to the next problem. We're going to have to think long-term, that teamwork is an ongoing process.'

'That will be a switch,' Miles said. 'We go in for crisis management and getting through the day at Savory. There's a theory in production management that the things that we can accomplish quickly are the ones that we do. But there's got to be a better way than trouble shooting all the time.'

'Your model also means that we have to work hard on the people side of the business,' Scott said. 'Sometimes I think that we're so preoccupied with the tasks that developing a group takes a backseat.'

'I agree with you guys, but at the same time the model seems basic to me,' Art said. 'I do these things already, but I know that I could do them much better and more consistently.'

'I'm hoping that the model can guide our efforts to develop teams, and also to let our people know what we're trying to do—where we're coming from and where we're heading,' Marian said.

'Isn't the model a part of our visions for our departments and Savory as well as this group?' Kyle asked.

'A critical part,' Art said.

## WHAT IS A TEAM ORGANIZATION?

Employees at Stagnate Inc. want to get through the day without being harmed. Their motto is 'live and let live,' and they take satisfaction in doing their own independent job and protecting their 'turf.' Cool to each other except for a few people who get together to gossip and complain, they're uptight and worry that they may be misunderstood or say the wrong thing. They protect themselves by keeping their ideas and feelings in check. Hoping not to offend others and get themselves in trouble, they try to figure out what the powerful want to hear before they speak. To advance in the company, they imitate the ideas and manners of the powerful and think of people who differ from the powerful in background, gender, or values as 'losers.'

They like to smooth over and get by any problem or difficulty. However, when confronted, people rigidly argue that their ideas and positions are right and should prevail. Disagreements are taken as personal attacks that make them look weak and incompetent; they derogate and sabotage those who oppose them. They bear grudges and don't forget slights and opposition. People at Stagnate believe fate and external forces determine the company's destiny. Complex problems hang around, until a crisis forces the boss to act. People feel unappreciated, fear being blamed, and put their hopes and energies into their lives outside the company.

It does not have to be this way. Dynamic Inc. has developed a *team organization*. Employees are excited about the company's vision and want to serve its customers. They are in ongoing dialogues about how they can get their jobs done and make continuous improvements. They easily ask for assistance and feel free to speak their minds. They respect and appreciate each other as persons and as contributors; they also directly challenge each other's ideas and positions. They want everyone to feel powerful, valuable, and included, not just those in the top positions. They forgive slights, misunderstandings, and opposition.

They realize their various perspectives and training are needed if the company is going to flourish. Confronted with complex problems, they form teams of diverse people who open-mindedly listen to various views to hammer out recommendations that make sense from a number of perspectives. They relish the give and take of discussing issues; they work to make their solutions high-quality ones that deserve their internal commitment. They take pride and celebrate their individual and company achievements.

How did Dynamic Inc. get this way? The managers and employees confronted several challenges. They met the *managerial challenge to structure and facilitate teams*. The managers created an environment in which employees feel committed and work effectively. They monitor their groups to identify and knock down barriers that get in the way of employees' working together. They structure controversy so that people dig into issues and create new, workable solutions.

Dynamic Inc. has also met the *leadership challenge to invigorate the organization*. The teams feel valued and know that top management will consider their ideas and recommendations seriously. They are able to negotiate so that they can have appropriate resources and time to complete their tasks. The reward, training, and promotion systems support teamwork within and between groups.

Managers and employees also met the *personal challenge to strengthen their attitudes and skills to work productively with each other*. They learned to communicate openly, support others, and manage their conflicts.

In the team organization, managers and employees are *committed to their vision*. People understand how their own efforts fit into the objectives of their department and the goals of their company. They believe that *this vision unites them*. They and their bosses and co-workers have cooperative goals so that they can be successful together. They feel *powerful and confident* they have the technical skills and interpersonal abilities to combine their resources to accomplish tasks and move toward goal attainment. They *explore problems* by exchanging information and discussing opposing views openly to dig into issues and create solutions. They *reflect on their experiences* to celebrate progress and learn from conflicts and mistakes.

Teamwork is part of the company's approach to getting things done. *The organization as a whole envisions, unites, empowers, explores, and reflects.* Groups believe that they share a common vision with other teams and individuals, they have cooperative goals, complement each other, discuss problems, and strengthen their work relationships.

# ENVISION: WHAT DIRECTION?

If a man does not know to which port he is sailing, no wind is favorable.
Seneca

A clear, engaging direction is a central first step to developing a team organization.[1] All members are fully aware of the team's business objectives and its organization framework: they know what they are expected to accomplish and how they will work together to achieve it. They understand the importance of this vision for themselves and others, and are committed to pursuing it. This vision motivates and directs.

Visions must be created; they do not just appear. Effective leaders look beyond the everyday distractions of work to ponder the future of how things might be. Leaders are pioneers who challenge the status quo, and are willing to risk failure to search for a better way.[2] Though not necessarily originators of innovations, they recognize good ideas and work to get them implemented. They challenge, experiment, and innovate.

Yet leaders cannot create the vision alone. They listen to employee concerns and ideas to help them create the group's vision. They enlist employees to help them mold the vision. They realize they cannot command commitment, they must inspire it. Leaders are 'keepers of the dream,' as Steve Jobs (the founder of Apple Computers) said, but they must inspire others to share this dream.

## ENVISIONING

Ways leaders can create a shared vision include:

(1) *Assess the business mission* Customers, industry, experts, and competitors help team members examine the present business strategy to assess its viability and risks.

(2) *Reflect on the organization framework* Team members discuss the nature

of productive teamwork and compare their work relationships to the team organization model.

(3) *Confront relationship issues* Dealing directly with grievances and conflicts sets the stage for forging a common vision. It demonstrates management's credibility that they want a team organization.

(4) *Search for opportunities to initiate change, innovate, and grow* Rather than wait for a crisis to hit, the team finds something that is 'broken' it can fix. They break out of the routine and the usual, and consider their work an adventure to enjoy. Employees talk about their concerns about the business strategy, and what bugs and annoys them about their jobs and work environment. They let each other know what they would like to change in the strategy and management of their team.

(5) *Take risks and learn from mistakes* People gather new ideas and try little experiments.

(6) *Present a short vision statement* A leader or task force evokes images and metaphors in describing the business mission and organization framework for the company.

(7) *Dialogue and include* Team members discuss the vision and its potential significance for them and the company. They integrate their ideas so that the business strategy and organization framework make sense to them.

(8) *Update* The team revises its vision in light of changes in and outside the group. It again hears customers' ideas and complaints, and the predictions of industry experts, and reviews the competition.

(9) *Appreciate accomplishments* The team celebrates its capacity to change and rewards progress on its vision.


## UNITE: ARE WE TOGETHER?

Together we stand, divided we fall.
                              Watchword of the American Revolution

An effective vision convinces team members they are united in a common effort. Sensing they are moving in the same direction, they communicate openly and understand each other. They realize they need the information, knowledge, ideas, support, and energy of others to get their jobs done and to contribute successfully to the company.

Cooperative unity cannot be taken for granted. Even a vision does not guarantee it. Employees might believe that they should compete against each other to show the boss they are the most committed to the vision. They may want to prove to themselves that they are better than others. Cooperative work at times seems impractical and costly. Employees would rather work on their own individual task rather than take the time from a busy day to coordinate.

The costs of scheduling another meeting and rearranging vacation time are often very immediate whereas the benefits of working together to develop a new program are more distant.

Nor can unity be decreed. It is not enough for managers to talk about how employees should cooperate, or blame them for not doing so. People must come to their own conclusion that what is good for one is good for all; success for one is success for all. Moreover, cooperative dependence needs to be a shared conclusion. One person cannot cooperate alone. Everybody sees the positively related goals and is willing to work with others to accomplish them.

## UNITING

People use various cues and information to conclude that they have cooperative goals. The levers managers can use include:

(1) *Explore the team's vision* All members know the purpose and value of the vision. They understand that no one can fulfill the vision alone; they must work together.

(2) *Assign a task and ask for one product* The team as a whole is to develop a new product or solve a problem. The manager wants team members to integrate their ideas and develop one solution. All team members sign off on the team's output indicating that they have contributed to and support it.

(3) *Keep track of group productivity* All workers average their individual output to form a group average for each week. Individual workers are responsible for keeping their output up, and for helping others improve theirs.

(4) *Promote group learning* All group members are expected to improve their skills in managing, selling, or operating machinery, and to help each other learn. The manager will chose at random one team member to demonstrate learning, and the team is rated on that basis.

(5) *Praise the team as a whole for its success* The manager recognizes all members of the team and their accomplishments are written up in the company newsletter.

(6) *Reward individuals based on group performance* Each team member receives a monetary bonus based on the team's success.

(7) *Hold an unproductive group accountable* Managers confront failed teams and have them suffer some consequence, rather than single out people to blame.

(8) *Make the task challenging* Team members will be highly motivated to accomplish achievable, but difficult tasks, and will recognize they need everyone's ability and support to do so.

(9) *Pledge to cooperate* Team members begin meetings by all openly declaring that they will cooperate and work together. Trust can be established when

team members believe all of them have decided to promote common goals, and reciprocate cooperation.

(10) *Limit the resources to the group* Team members realize that as individuals they cannot each try to accomplish the task, but must pool their resources.

(11) *Assign complementary roles* An employee is asked to record ideas, another to encourage full participation, another to be a devil's advocate to challenge common views, and a fourth to observe and provide feedback to help the group reflect on its workings.

(12) *Encourage team identity* Teams devise and publicize their own name and symbol. Members focus on their common characteristics and backgrounds.

(13) *Promote personal relationships* Team members discuss their feelings and values they consider important. 'Small talk' about family and oneself develops personal, trusting relationships. Social gatherings such as Friday afternoon 'beer busts' and Christmas parties encourage such interaction.

(14) *Write a philosophy* Team members develop their own value statement. The values emphasize that they belong together, care about each other, and should be helpful 'citizens.' Employees recall stories and examples that illustrate the vision, values, norms, and unity of the team.


## EMPOWER: CAN WE DO IT?

I never got very far until I stopped imagining I had to do everything myself.
Frank W. Woolworth

Feeling united in a common effort contributes to confidence that the team can realize its vision. But that is insufficient. Team members do not exert themselves fully unless they believe that they have the technical resources, the organizational mandate, and the skills to combine their ideas and efforts successfully. Empowering, like envisioning and uniting, cannot be done to people; they themselves must believe that they can do it.[3]

Teams are not islands. They need the *organization's mandate, permission,* and *support* to be highly effective. The company provides the new product team with the time, money, and other resources to do its job. Team members also must believe that management will give the approval to produce and market their product if it meets requirements. Without such expectations, team members feel 'what's the point of trying.'

Believing that team members have the necessary *technical skills and resources* to reach the group goal is central to a sense of power and confidence. When the new product team members believe that together people have the research, development, industrial engineering, production, and marketing expertise to be successful, they are prepared to join forces in a common effort.

*Interpersonal and social skills* are also vital. Cooperative goals themselves do not result in productive work; people must actually work together effectively. Working together requires sensitivity, empathy, and confrontation. People should be aware of the feelings and needs of others, and respond to them. They must exchange information and at times challenge each other's position and thinking. If a new product team believes that meetings will be unproductive and unhappy because of indifference or acrimony, they won't have much enthusiasm. Relatedly, they need the opportunities of team meetings and gatherings to exchange ideas and assist each other.

*Individual responsibility and team accountability* empower a group. Employees do not want others to be 'free riders' who take them for 'suckers' who end up doing all the work. People avoid situations in which they suspect that they will be unjustly exploited. Team members want to divide the labor fairly and effectively. They feel a sense of personal accountability to complete their tasks so that other team members can complete theirs. They do their own jobs and whatever else it takes so that the team as a whole is successful.

## EMPOWERING

(1) *Relate the team's vision to the organization's* Employees discuss how their team's goals further the business strategy and teamwork of the organization. Executives indicate how they see the team's role in the company and discuss with employees their common direction.

(2) *Allocate resources* The company backs up its talk with a budget and assigning people to the team to complete its mission.

(3) *Include skilled, relevant people* People who are specialists in technical areas, in facilitating groups, and linking with management will all help the team accomplish its goals. Team members discuss their previous accomplishments, experiences, and credentials, and in other ways realistically disclose their personal strengths.

(4) *Develop abilities* Team members take courses, read books and journals, and discuss ideas to keep current in their specialties. Readings, workshops, and reflection on experiences develop skills in dealing with conflicts and other group issues.

(5) *Structure opportunities to work together* Regular meetings, having offices close together, electronic mail, and computer systems help team members exchange information and keep each other posted.

(6) *Commit publicly* The team members indicate they are personally motivated to get the group's job done well. Their public announcement convinces themselves and others that the team will apply its collective abilities to get the job done.

(7) *Hold individuals accountable* All team members report on their activities
to the group and show their personal responsibility. Individuals who complete
their assignments are recognized. The team confronts individuals who fail to
fulfill their obligations, and may decide to encourage and give assistance, or
reprimand and punish the individual.

(8) *Structure team human resource systems* The organization rewards group
effort, uses teamwork as a criterion for promotion, provides training in group
skills, and makes consultation on teamwork available.

## EXPLORE: HOW TO MAKE DECISIONS?

> Since the general or prevailing opinion on any subject is rarely or never the
> whole truth, it is only by the collision of adverse opinion that the remainder of
> the truth has any chance of being supplied.
>
> John Stuart Mill

> The best way ever devised for seeking the truth in any given situation is
> advocacy: presenting the pros and cons from different, informed points of view
> and digging down deep into the facts.
>
> Harold S. Geneen, former CEO, ITT

Working together and feeling empowered do not mean smooth sailing and
inevitable success. Teams hit bumps and bruises along the way. Every group
needs the ability to identify and dig into issues, and overcome barriers to move
toward its vision.

Issues and decisions come in such a great variety that there is no one
particular way that they should be approached. The first rule is that the team
must be *flexible and use the approach appropriate for the situation.* A leader or
coordinator can dispense with minor issues efficiently. Some decisions are not
worth the effort to explore in great depth, and previous solutions can be
reasonably applied. At times, some decisions must be made quickly with little
or no consultation.

However, what is critical is how the team approaches important, ongoing
issues, for these are the decisions that give the group its character and impact
on people's involvement and team success. For these issues, the team should
dig into possibilities, create alternatives, and choose a high-quality solution
that solves the problems and strengthens the group. The second rule of
decision making is that teams need to *promote constructive controversy to
explore issues and alternatives.*

Controversy involves differences of opinion that temporarily prevent, delay,
or interfere with reaching a decision. Controversy, when constructively
handled, very much contributes to successful teamwork. Through controversy, people become open to new and opposing information. Confronta-

tion with an opposing view creates doubts that one's own position is adequate. People become interested in the arguments of opponents and ask questions to explore the view. They take the information seriously, develop a more complex and accurate view of the problem, and incorporate the opposing positions into their own thinking and decisions. Controversy creates new solutions by integrating previously assumed unrelated or opposing information and ideas. People appreciate the issues more completely, and are committed to implementing solutions because they understand their rationale and purpose.

The controversy must reaffirm the team's unity and empowerment to be successful. Controversy discussed in a win–lose, competitive, 'I'm right, you're wrong' way or that questions people's abilities and motives tears teams apart and creates closed-mindedness and one-sided, ineffective solutions.

## EXPLORING

Teams explore issues thoroughly by protecting and stimulating diverse views. They search opposing ideas and integrate them to create workable solutions. Strategies to encourage exploring are:

(1) *Include diverse people* Independent people who differ in background, expertise, opinions, outlook, and organization position are likely to disagree.

(2) *Establish openness norms* Everyone is encouraged to express their opinions, doubts, uncertainties, and hunches. Ideas are not dismissed because they first appear too unusual, impractical, or undeveloped.

(3) *Protect rights* The right to dissent and free speech reduces fears of retribution for speaking out.

(4) *Assign opposing views* Coalitions are formed and given opposing positions to present and defend. One person is assigned to take a critical evaluation role by attacking the group's current preference.

(5) *Probe* Team members stop defending their own views long enough to ask each other for more information and arguments. They put themselves in each other's shows by listening carefully and reflecting back the other's position and arguments.

(6) *Use the golden rule of controversy* Discuss issues with others as you want them to discuss with you. If you want people to listen to you, then listen to them.

(7) *Consult relevant sources* Articles, books, consultants, and experts can provide experiences and ideas that can help the group decide which course of action is superior.

(8) *Emphasize common ground* Throughout the discussion, they remind each other that they are working for a solution that benefits all. Team

members recognize that they want to resolve the controversy so they can make a decision and accomplish common goals.

(9) *Show personal regard* They criticize ideas rather than attack an individual's motivation and personality. Insults or implications that challenge another's integrity, intelligence, and motives are avoided.

(10) *Combine ideas* Team members avoid 'either my way or your way' thinking and try to use many ideas to create new, useful solutions. They may be able to create a totally new solution.

## REFLECT: HOW CAN WE IMPROVE?

Habits can't be thrown out the upstairs window. They have to be coaxed down the stairs one step at a time.

Mark Twain

Groups have a choice between becoming more committed to their visions, more united, more empowered, and more able to explore issues or undermining their purpose and confidence. Teams need to be able to assess their present state of functioning, celebrate and build upon their accomplishments, learn from mistakes, and deal with frustrations. Effective groups monitor and regulate themselves so that they can continue to work together without a great deal of intervention by managers. They build themselves up into an independent team that will be productive in the future as well as the present.

The status quo has the illusion of permanence. Kurt Lewin argued that the present state of affairs is created by the equilibrium of forces that are presently in balance. But these forces will inevitably change and push groups to a new plateau. There are, for example, forces that help them feel united, but also ones that push them apart. Their present sense of unity results from the balance of these forces. But if a fight convinces people they cannot work together, they feel less confident and united. Groups are *either growing or declining*. Maintaining the status quo is seldom a real alternative.

An essential first step is to create valid, useful information about the group's present functioning.[4] Organization development specialists have created a rich array of methods to collect data. Team members complete a survey questionnaire and later receive a summary of the results. Process consultation focuses on observing group functioning and then discussing these findings with the group to help them become more aware and effective. Interviewing identifies the perspectives and experiences of group members. Group members as well as outside consultants use these methods to assess the present dynamics of the team.

The data should be useful; they should focus on areas that the group can influence. The team organization model identifies envisioning, uniting, empowering, and exploring as areas to assess and develop.

Avoiding and smoothing over frustrations and conflicts are seldom effective. Indeed, dealing openly and directly with conflicts is critical for groups to maintain and strengthen themselves. Through conflict, people become aware of frustrations and where their vision, unity, empowering, and exploring are deficient. Conflict creates the incentives and energy to deal with problems. Well-managed conflict is the medium to update and develop teams.

The team assesses its strengths and successes as well as its frustrations and limitations. Celebrating 'small wins' encourages the team to build upon its abilities to accomplish its long-term vision. The team recognizes that it must go through the envision, unite, empower, explore, and reflect cycle continually. An effective team does not appear quickly or easily; team members must think in terms of continuous improvement and ongoing development, not a one stop, quick fix.

## REFLECTING

The ways teams can analyze their interaction, deal with frustrations, and celebrate their successes include:

(1) *Collect data* Questionnaires are relatively inexpensive ways for team members to indicate how they view the group's vision, unity, empowerment, exploring, and reflection. In interviews, people explain the specific behaviors and incidents that lie behind their perceptions and generalizations about the group. A team member, an employee from another group, or a consultant can observe the actual interactions within the group.

(2) *Structure times to discuss findings* Team members avoid surprises that catch people off guard, but have regular, scheduled times to discuss their relationships.

(3) *Put self in others' shoes* Team members ask about and try to know each other's perspective so they can appreciate the problem fully and be in position to develop solutions that work for all. They stop defending their own views long enough to listen carefully to others, and demonstrate their understanding of the others' positions and arguments.

(4) *Define issues specifically* Teams can resolve concrete conflicts more easily than general principles and grand ideas. People fight over issues, not personalities. People talk about their feelings and reactions to the team and its members and describe what led them to draw their conclusions.

(5) *Use exploring and controversy skills* Team members invite various possibilities, avoid assuming that it has to be one person's way or another's, and combine ideas.

(6) *Recognize the gains for resolving conflicts, and the costs for not* It takes a team to get itself into a fight, and it takes the team to get out of it. When everyone realizes the costs and the benefits, discussion is apt to be fruitful.

(7) *Be firm, yet flexible* Team members should be firm in their resolution to develop useful solutions, but flexible about what they might be.

(8) *Strive for ongoing improvement* Teams need time to develop, and interpersonal problems are not easily solved. The goal is to make progress through repeated discussions rather than to solve all issues and become a completely successful team instantly.

## CONCLUDING COMMENTS

The team organization model identifies major hurdles a collection of individuals must overcome to be a high-performance team. Teams require much. Employees must be committed to the team's vision and task, feel united in their purposes, feel empowered that they can do it, be able to explore opposing views, and reflect on their experiences to strengthen their vision, unity, empowerment, and exploring. But these teams give much. As discussed in Chapters 5 and 6, they drive organizational innovation and continuous improvement, and provide a rich, human experience that binds people together and to their organization. The next chapter reviews theory and research behind the team organization model.

## REFERENCES

1. Hackman, J. R. and Walton, R. E. (1986). Leading groups in organizations. In P. S. Goodman (ed.), *Designing Effective Work Groups*. San Francisco: Jossey-Bass, 72–119.
2. Kouzes, J. M. and Posner, B. Z. (1987). *The Leadership Challenge*. San Francisco: Jossey-Bass.
3. Congor, J. A. (1989). Leadership: the art of empowering others. *Academy of Management Review*, **3**, 17–24.
4. Argyris, C. (1970). *Intervention Theory and Method: A Behavioral Science View*. Reading, MA: Addison-Wesley.

# 3 Theory and Research: Team Organization Model

'We agree we need a framework we can use,' Scott began the third meeting of the Team Leaders Corps. 'Our discussion last time and the readings you passed out helped me understand your team organization model, Marian. I can see how we can use the model, but I'm uneasy about it—I have some doubts.'

Art saw that Marian looked concerned and said, 'I'm sure he doesn't want to rain on your parade, Marian.'

Several years before Marian had bristled when Art made similar comments; she thought he was too paternalistic. But afterwards he had assured her that he was trying to be supportive. She now accepted his comments as well-intentioned, and a smile slipped onto her face as she said, 'We're supposed to be able to explore issues and examine different points of view!'

'Quick on your feet, Marian, especially for someone from Human Resources,' joked Miles to general laughter. 'Seriously, we're not going to get very far if we can't apply our model to ourselves.'

'That's right,' Marian deadpanned. 'So tell me what are you *now* complaining about, Scott?'

'I suggest that we look into the idea of an outside consultant to give us a broader perspective,' Scott returned the deadpan. More laughter.

'I'll rush in to protect you, Scott,' Kyle said. 'Seriously, I too have some questions.'

'One trouble I have with the model,' Scott continued, 'is we want unity yet we are also to explore different points of view. I'm not saying it can't happen, but how realistic is that?'

'The theory makes a critical distinction that people in effective teams believe their goals are compatible and reinforcing, but that they can have opposing views about how to reach these goals,' Marian said. 'Agreement on ends does not mean agreement on means. They may disagree about how to proceed and about the correct approach to overcoming obstacles, though they are all totally committed to their common goal.'

'That may take a while to sink in,' Scott said. 'Let's see, my new product team may all want the most profitable product, but disagree what product that might be.'

'Even after they settle on the product, they may disagree about how to market it, how to produce it, what colors it should be—the possibilities are endless,' Marian said.

'No wonder these teams can be hard to pull off,' Scott remarked.

'If it were easy, we wouldn't need this group,' Marian said. 'But it is not just managing these teams that's hard. 'Creating a successful new product in the competitive marketplace is very challenging and difficult. The team, anyone, is going to have to ask a lot of hard questions.'

'OK, having these common goals and different opinions isn't contradictory, but that does not mean that people actually make such a distinction.'

'That's a research issue, and there are a number of studies that indicate that people do clearly distinguish the two,' Marian said. 'In fact, studies show that people express their opposing views more openly and more productively with cooperative goals. Competitive, win–lose conflict leads to avoidance or escalation.'

'Interesting. Do you have material I can read?'

'Sure, I'll send some things in the internal mail,' Marian said. She looked around, and added, 'Perhaps everyone wants some reading? OK, you'll all get copies.'

'I've got a problem with the model,' Kyle said. 'It extolls the virtues of a shared vision, but also emphasizes power. I thought shared vision was an alternative to the old ways of using power to force people to do things.'

'You mean the good old days,' Art said.

'The model is aligned with contemporary thinking that power is not itself a dirty word,' Marian said. 'We're used to thinking that power is a game of who has more than the other and who can get the other to do their bidding.'

Miles said, 'Power is getting other people to do things.'

'But the model suggests a different way of considering power, namely, that power represents the resources and abilities to get things done,' Marian said. 'We can both have power, and if we can combine our power, we'll be dynamite —pardon the pun. Power then need not be a club to make people do things through fear, but it enables us to get things done.'

'I've heard people say power is not necessarily a zero-sum game. Just because I have more does not mean you have less,' Art offered.

'That fits in with what I'm saying,' Marian said. 'If team members recognize and appreciate each other's abilities to do the job, they all have power. That in turn should increase their confidence that they can be successful, which in turn is motivating. Nothing discourages people more than a sense of powerlessness, that they do not have what it takes to reach their goals.'

'But can people really think about power in this way?' Scott asked. 'It sounds idealistic.'

'There's a number of studies showing, for instance,' Marian said, 'that when people believe they have cooperative goals they are willing to appreciate and use each other's resources and information. They are open to being influenced, and forget about tough, coercive ways to influence. Competitive people try to demand and force others which only alienates people further.'

'I think we should have some reading on this too,' Kyle said.

'I'll be glad to—I do have resources that will help us accomplish our common vision,' Marian said.

'Still quick on your feet, Marian,' Miles commented.

Marian smiled and said, 'Good discussion. We've learned more about the team organization model.'

'I feel better,' Scott said. 'I want our vision for our teams to be sensible.'

'Our vision should be rational as well as inspiring,' Marian concurred.

She continued after a pause. 'We don't have a lot of time left. I'd like us today, and on a regular basis, to reflect on our own group to see how we are doing as a team, as the model suggests. I think that this can strengthen ourselves as a team, but also can help us learn more about teams that we can apply in our own work groups.'

'I think we were mostly exploring today,' Art said. 'We had some problems understanding the part of our vision which involves using the team organization model; we did a good job exploring these questions.'

'I hope I didn't dominate the conversation or close off debate,' Marian said.

'You were responding to our questions and doubts; that was good,' Scott said.

'You were demonstrating your abilities to help us learn about teams,' Kyle said. 'Isn't that part of the empowering and giving us the confidence that together we can learn?'

'We were in the unity stage as well,' Art added. 'Certainly we were working together, we weren't trying to outdo each other—except, of course, who could get the most laughs.'

'That's part of the empowering—or is that just showing off?' Miles said laughing.

'So we can say that we were in an exploring mode, but we were also certainly working on our vision and perhaps even clarifying it some,' Marian said. 'We were also developing our abilities, and are now reflecting on how we have done.'

'We're going around the cycle, but hopefully not around in circles,' Scott said.

'Looping through the vision, unity, empowering, and exploring stages is a way to get started and build up momentum,' Miles said.

'So let's celebrate our success over lunch,' Kyle suggested. 'Isn't that part of the model too? Marian, I know you've got an expense account, and I can vouch that this is a legitimate business expense.'

'Sure, I'll be glad to take you out for lunch, if it's not too hard on your male egos,' Marian said.

'It is, but let's do it anyway,' Art said.

'One more thing,' Marian continued. 'Our people will probably be like us. They will need time to think about the team model and to ask questions about it. Showing the model and one-way explanation won't be enough. We need to understand the basic theory and research behind the model. Then we can discuss it confidently and help our people learn and use it.'

'I can see that it is important for us managers to understand the model because we have to use it to manage our teams. But do our people have to?' Scott asked.

'I think so,' Art said. 'Isn't the model really part of our vision for our teams? I want my people to know what kind of team they are striving to be so that they can all work to make the team effective.'

'Having them learn the model is a way of sharing a part of your vision for the team,' Marian added.

'It's part of empowering too, because the model can help them develop the confidence that they can make their teams work,' Kyle said. 'We want everyone in the group to help make the team successful.'

'Understanding the model will also help your group members reflect and learn from their experience,' Marian said.

'Interesting,' Scott said.

# TEAM POTENTIAL AND PITFALLS   ←

In reviewing research, social scientists have concluded that teams have considerable potential to combine the ideas and actions of many to solve complex problems.[1] Team members can combine their strengths and efforts to complete tasks that individuals working alone could not efficiently do. Through discussion, they challenge and correct each other's errors and biases in reasoning, present a variety of information that no one person has or can adequately remember, and combine perspectives into new solutions not previously considered.

Recent meta-analyses have statistically summarized the results of hundreds of studies. Findings, when considered together, show cooperative groups were more productive than individuals working competitively or independently.[2] Specifically, the average cooperator performed at about three-fifths of a standard deviation above the average person working competitively or independently. Results of the research are so strong that it would take thousands of studies showing no difference to reach the conclusion that cooperative groups were not more productive than individuals.

Laughlin,[3] for example, has conducted a series of studies documenting how groups can pool their information to solve a variety of intellectual tasks. The evidence suggests that *truth wins*; once the correct solution is in the group, it stays in the group. People are willing to be persuaded to accept another's solutions when it can be demonstrated to be correct.[4] Larger groups are more effective because with more people there is a greater chance the correct information is in the group. Even highly competent group members are able to combine their ideas and information to solve problems more successfully together than alone.

However, the demonstrated potential of groups must be considered in light of studies documenting that interaction can interfere.[5] Prestigious, but less informed, people may dominate the discussion and decision.[6] Group members may cope with stress and tension by demanding conformity and isolating those who offer contradictory, challenging information and ideas.[7] Some people will loaf and will let others be 'suckered' into working harder.[8]

It is not surprising, therefore, that some researchers have concluded that interaction makes rational, comprehensive problem solving unlikely. Through such dynamics as 'groupthink,' team members reinforce their biases and simplifications.[9] Alternatively, conflict can make the decision making political and an exercise in bargaining and trading.[10] Coalitions form to promote their special interests with little concern for a decision good for the whole.

Teams have potential, but are not invariably effective. Team members may work together in ways that impede or facilitate productivity. *The critical issue for managers and researchers is to identify interaction that facilitates team productivity and the conditions that promote this interaction.* The team organization model uses the theory of cooperation and competition and related research to analyze interaction in a team. Four hundred studies conducted over the past four decades have developed this approach to understanding interaction and identifying its antecedents and consequences.[11]

*Pitfall*

# THEORY OF COOPERATION AND COMPETITION

In the 1940s, Morton Deutsch argued that studying how people believe their goals are related is a useful way to understand the dynamics and outcomes of interaction. Interaction can take on very different characteristics. Employee beliefs about how they depend upon each other drastically affect their expectations, communication, exchange, problem solving, and productivity. Deutsch identified three alternatives: cooperation, competition, and independence. What is critical is how people believe their goals are predominantly linked because these perceptions affect their expectations and actions.

## THE ALTERNATIVES

*team benefit*

In cooperation, employees believe their goals are positively linked so that as one moves toward goal attainment, others also move toward reaching their goal. They understand one's goal attainment helps others reach their goals; as one succeeds, others succeed. People in cooperation appreciate that they want each other to pursue their goals effectively, for the other's effectiveness helps all of them reach their goals.

Individual achievement depends upon the achievement of others. *Cooperation is not based on altruism, but on the recognition that, with positively related goals, self-interests require collaboration.* Cooperative new product team members want each other to develop useful ideas and work hard to create a new product that makes everyone feel successful. *Cooperative work integrates self-interests to achieve mutual goals.*

Alternatively, employees may believe their goals are competitive in that one's goal attainment precludes or at least makes less likely the goal attainment of others. If one succeeds, others must fail. If one 'wins,' others 'lose.' People in competition conclude that they are better off when others act ineffectively;

when others are productive, they are less likely to be successful themselves. Competitive team members want to prove they are the most capable and their ideas superior; they are frustrated when others develop useful ideas and work hard. *Competitive work pits self-interests against each other in a fight to win.*

Independence occurs when people believe their goals are unrelated. The goal attainment of one neither helps nor hinders the goal attainment of others. Success by one means neither failure nor success for others. People in independence conclude that it means little to them if others act effectively or ineffectively. Independent team members care little whether others develop useful ideas or work hard. *Independent work creates disinterest and indifference.*

## INTERACTION

Whether people believe their goals were predominantly cooperative, competitive, or independent, Deutsch theorized, profoundly affects people's orientation toward each other. In cooperation, people want others to act effectively and expect others to want them to be effective because it is in each person's self-interest to do so. They trust their risks and efforts will be supported and reciprocated.

Studies document that people in cooperation share information, take each other's perspective, communicate and influence effectively, exchange resources, assist and support each other, discuss opposing ideas openly, use high-quality reasoning, and manage conflicts constructively.[12] These interaction patterns in turn result in task completion, problem solving, reduced stress, attraction, strengthened work relationships, and confidence in future collaboration.

Competition and independence, compared to cooperation, typically restrict information and resource exchange, distort communication, and escalate or avoid conflict; these patterns in turn frustrate productivity (except on some simple tasks), intensify stress, and lower morale. Research has not so clearly distinguished between competition and independence, although generally independence has a similar though not as negative an impact on interaction dynamics and outcomes as competition.

Deutsch's theory distinguishes cooperative interaction as critical for team success. Cooperative goals will have a greater impact if team members are highly committed to them. When they believe their goals are related to their personal interests, promote their values, and are supported by significant others, they exert more effort to pursue team goals and strengthen their cooperation.

Putting people into teams will not by itself be successful, for team members may compete or work independently. Cooperation research documents that getting team members to believe their goals are positively related is a powerful strategy to induce productive interaction.

# POSITIVE POWER

Traditionally, power has been thought to be a largely disruptive force; it may corrupt persons with it and enfeeble those without it. From this perspective, power is best 'equalized' to minimize its effects.[13] A contemporary view emphasizes the inevitable and potentially constructive role of power in organizations.[14] Power may energize and promote productivity[15] and the desire to wield power may aid managerial effectiveness.[16]

The theory of cooperation and competition has proved useful to understand the positive and negative faces of power. The dynamics and outcomes of power depend significantly on whether organizational members believe their goals are cooperative or competitive.

Experiments and field studies have found, using a variety of operations and samples, that cooperative compared to competitive goals induce higher expectations of assistance, greater support, more persuasion and less coercion, and more trusting and friendly attitudes in power relationships.[17] For example, powerful supervisors in cooperation supported and assisted their subordinates and used their resources to aid them; high-power supervisors in competition and independence had the capacity but were not motivated to assist their subordinates.[18]

Traditionally, power is defined as overcoming resistance and getting others to do what they would not otherwise do.[19] However, such a definition places power in a win–lose mode. People are assumed to be competitive, unwilling to assist each other, and caught in a struggle to see who can dominate.

Power is based on the control over valued resources that means one can affect the goals of others. A team member has power when others believe that person has information, assistance, emotional support, problem-solving ability, organizational clout, or other strength that can help them accomplish their goals. Cooperative goals promote the exchange and use of these resources to accomplish organizational tasks. Positive power is based on employee recognition of each other's resources and beliefs that goals are cooperative.

Positive power enhances teamwork. *Employees who recognize their team members have the skills and resources to achieve common goals, and have the cooperative interest to share them, are confident.* Without this empowerment, team members feel demoralized and doubtful their effort will pay off. They may decide to pursue other goals.

# CONSTRUCTIVE CONTROVERSY

Controversy, the discussion of opposing positions, has been found to be an important complement to cooperative goals. Cooperation does not avoid or suppress conflict, but encourages mutual discussion and productive manage-ment. Employees who discuss their opposing ideas openly can integrate their perspectives to solve problems and pursue their cooperative goals success-fully.

*Controversy, when discussed in a cooperative context, stimulates elaboration of views, the search for new information and ideas, and the integration of apparently opposing positions.* These dynamics result in understanding the problem, more adequate solutions, and commitment to implement them.[20]

## CONTROVERSY DYNAMICS

A number of experimental studies indicate that controversy can contribute to problem solving. Maier[21] and his colleagues found that groups composed of persons with different views and outlooks and groups whose leader en-couraged expression of minority opinions made high-quality decisions. Diver-sity of possible solutions was found to improve the quality of group decisions.[22] Hall's[23] studies suggest that consensus decision making is useful 'because it stimulates open controversy. Researchers have found that structur-ing controversy aids policy making.[24]

Recent experiments document the dynamics in controversy and, specific-ally, show how controversy can help manage the biases of individuals and promote decision making.[25]

Decision makers in controversy have been found to be open to new and opposing information. Confronted with an opposing opinion, they felt uncer-tain about the adequacy of their own positions, indicated interest in the opponent's arguments, and asked questions to explore the opposing views. They demonstrated they knew the opposing arguments and understood the reasoning others used to examine the problem and develop the opposing perspective.

In addition to openness to new information and ideas, decision makers in controversy have taken the information seriously, developed a more complex and accurate view of the problem, and incorporated the opposing position into their own thinking and decisions. The conflictful interaction has also resulted in the creation of new solutions not originally proposed. They have used information and ideas from others to develop a more complete awareness and appreciation of the complexity of the problem and arrived at a solution that responded to the complete information.

Controversy creates high-quality, innovative solutions and agreements. The mix and clash of the discussion creates new positions not previously considered. These positions combine the arguments and perspectives of several people in elegant ways. People are satisfied and feel they have benefited from the discussion. They enjoy the excitement, feel aroused by the challenges of the conflict, and develop positive attitudes toward the experience. They are committed to the new agreements and positions because they understand how they are related to their own interests and positions, and why the adopted position is superior to their original one. Controversy is critical for successful participation in which people 'own' and feel committed to decisions.[26]

## MINORITY INFLUENCE

Attention has traditionally focused on how the majority make independent team members conform through normative influence.[27] The normative influence of the majority pressures people to conform to expectations.[28] It can be powerful because people depend upon others to compare and evaluate their feelings and beliefs. Disagreement can imply that one's beliefs are ill-founded and that one is rejected as a competent person. Yet this influence is not always successful. Individuals who believe that at least one other team member shares their misgivings about the group's consensus, or are highly confident in their views, resist majority pressure.[29]

Normative influence and pressures to conform are only half the story. Team members also use informational influence.[30] People are willing to be influenced because they want evidence about the nature of reality and what positions are correct and useful. They want to know what is true and they look to persuasive arguments, especially on intellectual tasks that have superior answers.[31] Minorities can influence majorities through persuasive logic and documentation.

Influence is two-way; the minority influence the majority as well as being influenced by them. Indeed, while majority influence may induce public compliance, minority influence often results in private acceptance.[32] Groups with exposure to persistent, credible minority views employ divergent thinking that leads to detection of novel, correct solutions and to acceptance of new positions.[33] Minority views stimulate controversy and innovation.

## ORGANIZATIONAL STUDIES

The demands of the marketplace and workplace require organizations to innovate and adapt. They are experimenting with new procedures and management styles, and developing new products and services to respond to technological advances, competition, and consumer preferences. Controversy is essential for successful innovation.

Faculty members and employees of a large Canadian post-secondary educational institution were interviewed on specific times they were able to solve problems in new, creative ways.[34] When they discussed their opposing views openly and forthrightly and considered all views, they were able to develop innovative solutions. When they discussed issues from only one point of view and were unable to incorporate different views, then they failed to make progress and developed solutions low on quality and creativity.

Managers have long complained that employees are unmotivated and resist new technological innovations and, as a consequence, the investments do not pay off in expected productivity increases. Less recognized are the intellectual demands in that employees must identify problems and discuss solutions to use the technology. Employees of a retail chain were found to use new scanning technology more efficiently when they exchanged information and hammered out ideas about how to solve the many problems the technology created.[35]

Managers are restructuring and transforming organizations. They are cutting management levels, splitting up businesses, forming links across business units, and using task teams and parallel structures to create synergy. However, restructuring seldom results in the expected improved quality of products, productivity, and quality of work life for employees, and returns for shareholders. A large telecommunications high-technology firm had undergone waves of restructuring, without noticeable improvement. Interviews revealed that changing structures was insufficient.[36] Employees had to make use of any new order, and to do this they had to coordinate and discuss their conflicts. When they were able to manage their difficulties and reassure and support each other, they were able to make use of the new structures.

Controversy has proved important to accomplish a wide range of organizational objectives. Pilots, first officers, and flight attendants who discussed their views openly and skillfully were found to maintain the margin of safety of their airplane. They worked efficiently and together to deal with a wide range of threats to airplane safety in order to restore safety, use safe procedures, and gain confidence in each other.[37]

Constructive controversy helps serve customers. Engineers from different departments and with varied training needed to discuss their views openly and coordinate their work in order to win and complete projects for clients.[38] Customer representatives, repairmen, and technical staff used constructive controversy to deal with customer complaints. Sales people who use controversy were found to be more successful in developing a successful marketing relationship.[39] Constructive controversy is also useful for performance appraisal[40] and managers' making effective use of accounting services.[41]

## REFLECTION AND DEVELOPMENT

Researchers have proposed various models of the stages of group development.[42] While documenting that groups go through phases has proved difficult, teams need experience and practice to develop into a productive unit. The involvement of team members so that they see themselves as having a common task, rewards, and feedback and the ability to identify interpersonal difficulties and manage conflicts, contributes significantly to cooperative teamwork.

## FORMING A TEAM

Setting group goals, receiving feedback, and getting incentives have all been found to strengthen team motivation and productivity. Pritchard and his colleagues[43] worked with army groups to help them identify their goals, how their productivity could be measured, and the incentives that the team would find attractive. Through systematic involvement in many discussions and meetings to develop the system, team members created reasonable goals, were aware of what they needed to do to accomplish them, and knew how they would be rewarded. They came to see themselves as a unit.

For the first five months, the researchers provided feedback for each group in terms of the percentage of their maximum output at the end of each month, and they held meetings to review the feedback. In the next phase of the experiment, team members established aspiration levels, that is, how much of the goals they wanted to achieve in the next month. In the final phase, they added the incentive of time off work for maintaining a high level of performance and additional incentives for exceeding that level.

The results indicate that the program was highly successful in motivating team members. The group involvement and feedback were particularly useful; adding the goal setting and incentives were not critical. This and other studies underscore the value of team members' participation to develop and strengthen their ties. They have to understand their goals are cooperative, see that they have resources to reach their goals, and plan to use constructive controversy to solve problems.

## CONFLICT MANAGEMENT  & belinda's

Surveys indicate that managers spend over 20% of their time dealing with conflicts.[44] They also work hard to avoid conflict.[45] People in organizations deal with the conflict in many ways. They discuss jointly, convince, show up, throw, cry, avoid, listen, sabotage, gossip, drink, get even, leave, use authority, transfer, complain to higher-ups, and form an alliance.[46] They have been found to conflict over goals, unclear task assignments, unfair evaluations, insults and criticism, unrealistic workloads, unfair distribution of rewards, refusal to interact, and a lack of feedback, challenges, and efficiency.

Managing these conflicts can be highly useful. Frustrations are identified and dealt with so that people can work effectively. Through conflict, people keep in touch with their own emotions and learn more about themselves. They also learn how others react and think, and improve their sensitivity. Conflict tests relationships and, if properly discussed, strengthens them.[47]

Cooperation and competition have proved useful to analyze the inevitable frustrations, disappointments, and other conflicts that occur in teams. Conflicts involve incompatible activities where one person is interfering, obstructing, or making another's actions less effective.[48] However, conflicts are by no means invariably competitive. People with compatible, cooperative goals not only can conflict, they often do. They conflict over how they can efficiently divide their work, whether they have been given the proper respect and recognition, who should be held responsible for failure, and a fair way to distribute the rewards of their joint success.

Cooperative goals encourage initiating discussions of conflict and making them productive. With cooperative goals, people deal openly with their frustrations and grievances, listen and understand others' feelings and complaints, work for solutions that are mutually advantageous and reach agreements they are willing to implement.[49]

Reflecting on experiences and dealing directly with conflicts are important to develop long-term team cooperation.[50] Avoiding conflict can be useful at times and help get tasks completed in the short run. However, for a team to enhance its capabilities, identify and reduce frustrations, and strengthen trust and emotional bonds, ongoing processing and reflecting on the team is critical.

## CONCLUDING COMMENTS

Strong commitment to cooperative goals, recognition of the team's abilities and strengths, the capacity to discuss opposing positions on problems encountered, and ongoing development and reflection on successes and conflicts transform a collection of people into a productive force. Cooperative goals and the capacity to work together and discuss opposing views, recent studies document, have helped engineers win and complete contracts for clients, utility departments answer customer complaints, crew members cope with threats to the safety of the airplane, and sales representatives serve their customers. Cooperative teamwork has proven, extensive value to organizations.

# REFERENCES

1. Hill, G. W. (1982). Group versus individual performance: are N + 1 heads better than one? *Psychological Bulletin*, **91**, 517–539. Kelley, H. H. and Thibaut, J. W. (1968). Group problem solving. In G. Lindzey and E. Aronson, *Handbook of Social Psychology*. Reading, MA: Addison-Wesley, vol. 3, 1–105. Johnson, D. W., Maruyama, G., Johnson, R. T., Nelson, D. and Skon, S. (1981). Effects of cooperative, competitive, and individualistic goal structures on achievement: a meta-analysis. *Psychological Bulletin, 89*, 47–62.
2. Johnson, D. W., Maruyama, G., Johnson, R. T., Nelson, D. and Skon, S. (1981). Effects of cooperative, competitive, and individualistic goal structures on achievement: a meta-analysis. *Psychological Bulletin, 89*, 47–62.
3. Laughlin, P. R. (1988). Collective induction: group performance, social combination processes, and mutual majority and minority influence. *Journal of Social and Personality Psychology, 54*, 254–267.
4. Laughlin, P. R. and Earley, P. C. (1982). Social combination models, persuasive arguments theory, social comparison theory, and choice shift. *Journal of Social and Personality Psychology, 42*, 273–280. Laughlin, P. R. and Ellis, A. L. (1986). Demonstrability and social combination processes on mathematical intellective tasks. *Journal of Experimental Social Psychology, 22*, 177–189.
5. Steiner, I. D. (1972). *Group Process and Productivity*. New York: Academic Press.
6. Mulder, M. and Wilkie, H. (1970). Participation and power equalization. *Organizational Behavior and Human Performance, 5*, 430–448.
7. Janis, I. L. (1972). *Victims of Groupthink*. Boston, MA: Houghton Mifflin.
8. Latane, B. (1986). Responsibility and effort in organizations. In P. S. Goodman (ed.), *Designing Effective Work Groups*. San Francisco: Jossey-Bass, 277–304.
9. Schwenk, C. R. (1984). Cognitive simplification processes in strategic decision-making. *Strategic Management Journal, 5*, 111–128.
10. Pfeffer, J. (1981). *Power in Organizations*, Boston, MA: Pitman.
11. Johnson, D. W. and Johnson, R. T. (1989). *Cooperation and Competition: Theory and Research*. Edina, MN: Interaction Book Company.
12. Deutsch, M. (1985). *Distributive Justice: A Social–psychological Perspective*. New Haven, CT: Yale University Press. Deutsch, M. (1980). Fifty years of conflict. In L. Festinger (ed.), *Retrospections on Social Psychology*. New York: Oxford University Press, 46–77. Deutsch, M. (1973). *The Resolution of Conflict*. New Haven, CT: Yale University Press. Deutsch, M. (1949). A theory of cooperation and competition. *Human Relations, 2*, 129–152. Johnson, D. W. and Johnson, R. T. (1989). *Cooperation and Competition: Theory and Research*. Edina, MN: Interaction Book Company. Johnson, D. W. and Johnson, R. T. (1985). Motivational processes in cooperative, competitive, and individualistic learning situations. In C. Ames and R. Ames (eds), *Research on Motivation in Education 2*, New York: Academic Press. Johnson, D. W., Johnson, R. T. and Maruyama, G. (1983). Interdependence and interpersonal attraction among heterogeneous and homogeneous individuals: a theoretical formulation and a meta-analysis of the research. *Review of Educational Research, 53*, 5–54. Johnson, D. W., Johnson, R. T., Smith, K. and Tjosvold, D. (1989). Training managers to engage in constructive controversy. In B. Sheppard, M. Bazerman and R. Lewicki (eds), *Research in Negotiations in Organizations, 2*, Greenwich, CT: JAI Press. Johnson, D. W., Maruyama, G., Johnson, R. T., Nelson, D. and Skon, S. (1981). Effects of cooperative, competitive, and individualistic goal structures on achievement: a meta-analysis. *Psychological Bulletin, 89*, 47–62. Lanzetta, J. T. and Englis, B. G. (1989). Expec-

tations of cooperation and competition and their effects on observers' vicarious emotional responses. *Journal of Personality and Social Psychology,* **56,** 543–554. Tjosvold, D. (1986). Dynamics of interdependence in organizations. *Human Relations,* **39,** 517–540. Tjosvold, D. (1984). Cooperation theory and organizations. *Human Relations,* **37,** 743–767. Tjosvold, D. (1986). *Working Together to Get Things Done: Managing for Organizational Productivity.* Lexington, MA: D.C. Heath.

13. Bennis, W. (1969). *Organizational Development.* Reading, MA: Addison-Wesley. Kipnis, D. (1976). *The Powerholders.* Chicago, IL: University of Chicago Press.

14. Pfeffer, J. (1981). *Power in Organizations.* Boston, MA: Pitman.

15. Kanter, R. M. (1979). Power failure in management circuits. *Harvard Business Review,* July–August, 65–75. Kanter, R. M. (1977). *Men and Women of the Corporation.* New York: Basic Books.

16. McClelland, D. C. (1976). *Power: The Inner Experience.* New York: Irvington. McClelland, D. C. (1970). The two faces of power. *Journal of Affairs,* **24,** 29–47. McClelland, D. C. and Boyatzis, R. E. (1982). Leadership motive pattern and long-term success in management. *Journal of Applied Psychology,* **67,** 737–743.

17. Tjosvold, D. (1985). The effects of attribution and social context on superiors' influence and interaction with low performing subordinates. *Personnel Psychology,* **38,** 361–376. Tjosvold, D. (1981). Unequal power relationships within a cooperative or competitive context, *Journal of Applied Social Psychology,* **11,** 137–150. Tjosvold, D. (in press). Power in cooperative and competitive organizational contexts. *Journal of Social Psychology.*

18. Tjosvold, D. (1985). Power and social context in superior–subordinate interaction. *Organizational Behavior and Human Decision Processes,* **35,** 281–293.

19. Dahl, R. P. (1957). The concept of power. *Behavioral Science,* **2,** 201–218. Emerson, R. M. (1962). Power–dependence relations. *American Sociological Review,* **27,** 31–41. Pfeffer, J. (1981). *Power in Organizations.* Boston, MA: Pitman.

20. Tjosvold, D. (1987). Participation: a close look at its dynamics. *Journal of Management,* **13,** 739–750. Tjosvold, D. (1985). Implications of controversy research for management. *Journal of Management,* **11,** 21–37.

21. Maier, N. R. F. (1970). *Problem-solving and Creativity in Individuals and Groups.* Belmont, CA: Brooks/Cole.

22. Wanous, J. P. and Yountz, M. A. (1986). Solution diversity and the quality of group decisions. *Academy of Management Journal,* **29,** 149–159.

23. Hall, J. (1971). Decisions, decisions, decisions. *Psychology Today,* November, 51–54, 86, 88.

24. Cosier, R. A. (1978). The effects of three potential aids for making strategic decisions on prediction accuracy. *Organizational Behavior and Human Performance,* **22,** 295–306. Cosier, R. A. and Schwenk, C. R. (1990). Agreement and thinking alike: ingredients for poor decisions. *Academy of Management Executive,* **4,** 69–74.

25. Tjosvold, D. (1982). Effects of the approach to controversy on superiors' incorporation of subordinates' information in decision making. *Journal of Applied Psychology,* **67,** 189–193. Tjosvold, D. and Deemer, D. K. (1980). Effects of controversy within a cooperative or competitive context on organizational decision making. *Journal of Applied Psychology,* **65,** 590–595. Tjosvold, D. and Field, R. H. G. (1983). Effects of social context on consensus and majority vote decision making. *Academy of Management Journal,* **26,** 500–506. Tjosvold, D. and Field, R. H. G. (1984). Managers' structuring cooperative and competitive controversy in group decision making. *International Journal of Management,* **1,** 26–32. Tjosvold, D. and Field, R. H. G. (1985). Effect of concurrence, controversy, and consensus

on group decision making. *Journal of Social Psychology*, **125**, 355–363. Tjosvold, D. and Johnson, D. W. (1977). The effects of controversy on cognitive perspective taking. *Journal of Educational Psychology*, **69**, 679–685. Tjosvold, D. and Johnson, D. W. (1978). Controversy within a cooperative or competitive context and cognitive perspective taking. *Contemporary Educational Psychology*, **3**, 376–386. Tjosvold, D., Johnson, D. W. and Fabrey, L. (1980). The effects of affirmation and acceptance on incorporation of an opposing opinion in problem solving. *Psychological Reports*, **47**, 1043–1053. Tjosvold, D., Johnson, D. W. and Lerner, J. (1981). The effects of affirmation and acceptance on incorporation of an opposing opinion in problem-solving. *Journal of Social Psychology*, **114**, 103–110. Tjosvold, D., Wedley, W. C. and Field, R. H. G. (1986). Constructive controversy, the Vroom–Yetton model, and managerial decision making. *Journal of Occupational Behaviour*, **7**, 125–138.

26. Tjosvold, D. (1987). Participation: a close look at its dynamics. *Journal of Management*, **13**, 739–750.
27. Kaplan, M. F. (1987). The influencing process in group decision making. In C. Hendrick (ed.), *Group Processes*. Newbury Park, CA: Sage, 189–212. Levine, J. M. (1989). Reaction to opinion deviance in small groups. In P. B. Paulus (ed.), *Psychology of Group Influence*. Hillsdale, NJ: Erlbaum, 2nd edn, 187–231.
28. Tanford, S. and Penrod, S. (1984). Social influence model: a formal integration of research on majority and minority influence processes. *Psychological Bulletin*, **95**, 189–225.
29. Sheriff, M. (1936). *The Psychology of Social Norms*. New York: Harper.
30. Kaplan, M. F. (1987). The influencing process in group decision making. In C. Hendrick (ed.), *Group Processes*. Newbury Park, CA: Sage, 189–212.
31. Laughlin, P. R. and Earley, P. C. (1982). Social combination models, persuasive arguments theory, social comparison theory, and choice shift. *Journal of Social and Personality Psychology*, **42**, 273–280.
32. Maas, A., West, S. G. and Cialdini, R. B. (1987). Minority influence and conversion. In C. Hendrick (ed.), *Group Processes*. Newbury Park, CA: Sage, 55–79.
33. Nemeth, C. (1986). Differential contribution of majority and minority influence. *Psychological Review*, **93**, 23–32.
34. Tjosvold, D. and McNeely, L. T. (1988). Innovation through communication in an educational bureaucracy. *Communication Research*, **15**, 568–581.
35. Tjosvold, D. (in press). Making a technological innovation work: collaboration to solve problems. *Human Relations*.
36. Tjosvold, D. (1990). Cooperation and competition in restructuring an organization: the role of interdependence dynamics. *Canadian Journal of Administrative Sciences*, **7**, 48–54.
37. Tjosvold, D. (1990). Flight crew coordination to manage safety risks. *Group and Organization Studies*, **15**, 177–191.
38. Tjosvold, D. (1988). Cooperative and competitive interdependence: collaboration between departments to serve customers. *Group and Organization Studies*, **13**, 274–289.
39. Tjosvold, D. and Wong, C. (1990). *Marketing relationship: Goal interdependence approach*. Unpublished manuscript, Simon Fraser University.
40. Tjosvold, D. and Halco, J. A. (1989). *Performance appraisal: goal interdependence and future responses*. Manuscript, Simon Fraser University.
41. Etherington, L., Tjosvold, D. and Young, L. (1989). *Roles and goal interdependence: a study of accountants and managers*. Manuscript, Simon Fraser University.
42. Tuckman, B. (1965). Developmental sequence in small groups. *Psychological Bulletin*, **63**, 384–399.

43. Pritchard, R. D., Jones, S. D., Roth, P. L., Stuebing, K. K. and Ekeberg, S. E. (1988). Effects of group feedback, goal setting, and incentives on organizational productivity. *Journal of Applied Psychology*, **73**, 337–358.
44. Thomas, K. W. and Schmidt, W. H. (1976). A survey of managerial interests with respect to conflict. *Academy of Management Journal*, **19**, 315–318.
45. Argyris, C. and Schon, D. (1978). *Organizational Learning*. Reading, MA: Addison-Wesley. Janz, T. and Tjosvold, D. (1985). Costing effective vs. ineffective work relationships: a method and first look. *Canadian Journal of Administrative Sciences*, **2**, 43–51.
46. Bergmann, T. J. and Volkema, R. J. (1989). Issues and strategies in organizational conflict. In M. A. Rahim (ed.), *Managing Conflict: An Interdisciplinary Approach*. New York: Praeger, 7–19.
47. Tjosvold, D. (in press). The goal interdependence approach to communication in conflict: an organizational study. In M. A. Rahim (ed.), *Theories and Research in Conflict Management*. New York: Praeger.
48. Deutsch, M. (1973). *The Resolution of Conflict*. New Haven, CT: Yale University Press.
49. Van Berklom, M. and Tjosvold, D. (1981). The effects of social context on engaging in controversy. *Journal of Psychology*, **107**, 141–145.
50. Deutsch, M. (1980). Fifty years of conflict. In L. Festinger (ed.), *Retrospections on Social Psychology*. New York: Oxford University Press, 46–77. Deutsch, M. (1973). *The Resolution of Conflict*. New Haven, CT: Yale University Press. Tjosvold, D. (1989). Interdependence and conflict management in organizations. In M. A. Rahim (ed.), *Managing Conflict: An Interdisciplinary Approach*. New York: Praeger, 41–50. Tjosvold, D. (in press). Rights and responsibilities of dissent: cooperative conflict. *Employee Rights and Responsibilities Journal*.

# 4 Perspectives on Organizational Groups

'I liked reading the articles on the team organization model,' Miles began the meeting of the TLC. 'It's good to know that there is some substance behind it. We have so many fads in manufacturing that it can be hard to distinguish what's real from what sounds good.'

'I like it that the idea has been tested,' Art said. 'It is not just more words.'

'Me, too,' Scott said. 'But it certainly isn't the only way to think of groups. I still have questions. Is this model really the right one—the one we should be using?'

'I agree with Scott,' Kyle said. 'We should be using the right approach.'

'But Marian's model is right,' Miles said. 'Look at the research behind it.'

'Other approaches could be better,' Scott said.

'What's the team organization's competitive advantage?' Kyle asked.

'There are different ways to look at groups,' Marian said. 'Researchers have developed different perspectives.'

'Is the team organization the right one?' Scott asked.

'I wouldn't put it that way,' Marian said. 'It is not a matter of which is the one right way to look at groups, or even which one is best. Each way has some uses and advantages, but also limitations.'

'Isn't that what the researchers are trying to do—prove their ideas are right?' Scott said.

'They gather evidence to demonstrate how much confidence we should have in the usefulness of the ideas,' Marian said. 'Research helps us see the extent the approach can help us analyze and influence groups. Studies build up our common experience in using the perspective.'

'But then why do they go through all the trouble of research design, controls, and analysis of data?' Kyle asked. 'Wouldn't it be easier to ask managers if the approach works or not?'

'That kind of evidence helps,' Marian said. 'However, researchers want to test the idea as carefully as possible. Sometimes a manager is successful using an approach with a group because he's used procedures outside of the approach. Success may also be due to very favorable conditions: any approach would have worked. Similarly, failure may be because the approach was not carried out well, or was done under very adverse circumstances. So researchers want to test the approach several times in a number of situations to build up our confidence that the idea is useful.'

'How come social scientists can't get together and agree on the best model?' Scott asked rhetorically.

'It is not so different in the physical sciences,' Marian said. 'Theorists have developed different ways to understand energy, light, black holes, the origin of the universe. Researchers then try to see the extent the theory is consistent with evidence and how accurately it predicts reality.'

'But we seem to have more agreement than the soft sciences,' Scott remarked.

'Research has been going on for centuries in the physical sciences, and much more progress has been made,' Marian said. 'But they too have their skirmishes and revolutions.'

'Groups are pretty complex things, too,' Art said. 'I can see where there'd be many ways to think about them.'

'But I still think we could take a look at other approaches,' Kyle said.

'Agreed,' Marian said. 'Looking at them can help us understand groups. Studying other approaches can also help us know the advantages and limitations of the team organization model.'

# EXAMINING ALTERNATIVE APPROACHES

Researchers are making progress in documenting the value of groups for organizations and in identifying the structures and conditions that make groups successful.[1] Studies have shown that groups can contribute to organizational success. They have identified the conditions under which groups can be useful and the nature of group leadership.[2] Researchers have developed a number of useful perspectives to understand and influence groups in organizations.

This chapter overviews major perspectives on understanding groups in organizations and contrasts them with the team organization model. It distinguishes three major approaches to research on groups in organizations. Much work has focused on identifying the *components of effective organizational groups*. Researchers have developed general models that stipulate how these components interact to produce effective groups. Researchers have also examined these components individually to identify how they contribute to groups. A second major research stream investigates organizational *groups managing themselves*. Semi-autonomous work teams have been examined since the 1950s. Interventions to team build have also been much explored. A third research perspective emphasizes the critical role of the *organizational context*, and identifies how it impacts on group work and performance.

The team organization model is not argued to be superior in all respects to other approaches. The review of the literature does highlight, however, important characteristics of the model. The team organization model is social–psychological in its origin and outlook. It identifies underlying conditions of vision, cooperative goals, empowerment, exploration, and reflection that promote group effectiveness. It is not restricted to manufacturing or service company, profit or nonprofit, the shop floor or the corporate boardroom. Its psychological nature also allows a great deal of research conducted by social scientists as well as management researchers to be drawn upon to support and develop the model.

However, this power and research base comes at a cost. As the model is abstract and psychological, it does not so much specify what groups and leaders should do as help them decide how they are going to manage themselves. *Managers and employees have to use the team model to develop and implement procedures appropriate for their situation.*

## COMPONENTS OF EFFECTIVE GROUPS

Researchers have specified components that make groups within an organization effective. Much of the attention has focused on developing models that outline how group structure, organizational context, group process, and effectiveness are related to each other. A related, more fine-grained approach is to document empirically how tasks, group composition, performance strategies, and other components are related to group success.

### MODELS OF GROUP EFFECTIVENESS

Nieva, Fleishman and Rieck,[3] Hackman,[4] Gladstein,[5] Gist, Locke, and Taylor,[6] and others have proposed models that classify the major components that contribute to effective groups. These models map how various aggregates of variables relate to each other and predict effective groups. They are potentially powerful in that they are expected to be relevant to many different kinds of groups and because they summarize a great deal of diverse research conducted over several decades.

These models have used different terms and categorized variables into different components, but behind the differences in terminology and classification there is a great deal of consensus on substance.[7] Task characteristics, group composition, and organizational context all play prominent roles in the models. (See Figures 4.1 and 4.2.)

Hackman,[7] for example, proposed that facilitating group design, appropriate organizational context, and group synergy together impact on effective group work which, when combined with sufficient materials, results in task success as measured by acceptance of significant others in the organization, strengthened work relationships, and satisfied group members. In Gladstein's model, major inputs are the composition and structure of the group and the resources and structure of the organizations. These inputs together impact group process that, depending on the nature of the task, determines the performance and satisfaction of the group.

The models specify the variables that make up these major components. In Hackman's model,[8] a facilitating group design consists of the appropriate structure of the task, composition of the group, and group norms about performance processes. A supportive organizational climate reinforces work by reward, education, and information systems. Gladstein's model identifies specific variables similar to Hackman's, but, as are the major components, these variables are arranged and labelled in different ways.

In addition to summarizing research, these models also suggest the implications of research for organizational action. For example, Hackman and Walton[9] argued that managers can lead small groups by establishing and maintaining favorable performance conditions. They should take a contingency perspective to make their interventions appropriate to the situation. After they provide a clear, engaging direction for the team, leaders can use Hackman's model to identify major ways they can observe and intervene with groups.

Specifically, managers should structure the task, group composition, and norms and provide a supportive organizational context that rewards, educates, and informs team members so that they exert effort, apply their knowledge, and use appropriate task strategies. The leader then provides the needed material support that the group uses to complete the task and strengthen itself.

## Issues

The breadth and scope that give the models the power to summarize research also present limitations. The models and the major links between their com-

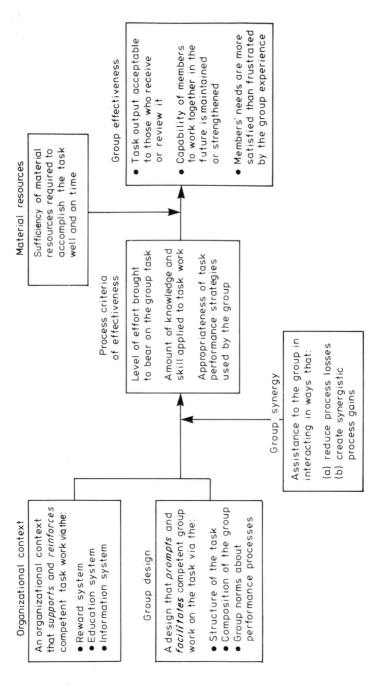

**Figure 4.1**  Hackman's model of group effectiveness. Reproduced by permission from Hackman, J. R. (1983). A normative model of work team effectiveness. *Technical Report No. 2, Research Program on Group Effectiveness*. Yale School of Organization and Management

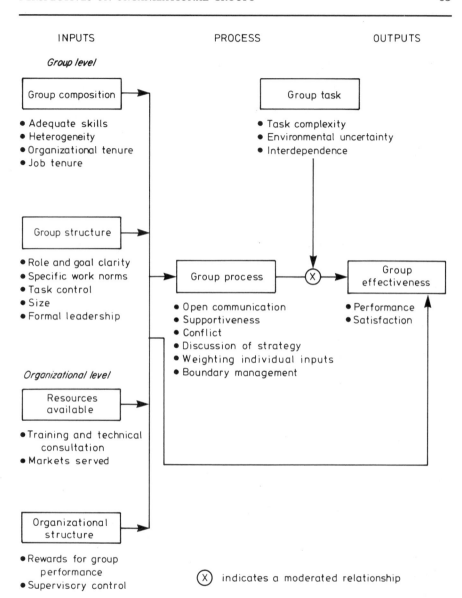

**Figure 4.2**  Gladstein's model of group behavior. Reproduced by permission from Gladstein, D. (1984). Groups in context: a model of task group effectiveness. *Administrative Science Quarterly*, **29**, 499–517

ponents have proved very difficult to test directly.[10] The models assert that some variables are central, but while studies may suggest these variables have a role, we do not know whether the models have identified the most critical variables. For example, a clear, engaging direction is probably very important for an effective team,[11] but is not explicitly highlighted in the models. Nor do we know why the variables selected have a major impact, or the conditions under which they are likely to be critical.

Evidence is also needed to support the stipulated relationships among the variables. Undoubtedly, the variables are interactive so that they each cause the other. Group process is usually stipulated as an outcome of group and organizational inputs, but synergistic interaction within the team is also likely to clarify roles and tasks, support norms for working on the task, and so on. Research is needed to clarify these interactions.

## RESEARCH ON COMPONENTS

Although the models of effective groups have proved difficult to test directly, they are based on considerable research on group composition, group size, leadership, group cohesion, communication, decision-making techniques, and other variables believed to impact group performance and satisfaction. There are a number of recent reviews that consider this literature in depth and detail.[12] This section examines research on group tasks to suggest how these studies can help us understand groups in organizations and the limitations of this approach.

Studies have demonstrated that tasks can affect group functioning and performance. However, the impact of tasks does not seem direct and straight-forward. Hackman,[13] for example, argued that whole, meaningful tasks have considerable motivational potential in that they will engage people to exert effort to complete them. Relatedly, challenging tasks that are possible but not easily accomplished have been found to engage achievement needs.[14]

Yet whole, challenging tasks do not always motivate, and they can evoke stress and avoidance.[15] Achievement research suggests that challenging tasks evoke the most fears of failure and actual avoidance of the task.[16]

Tasks are usually considered in terms of a contingency perspective: the type of task affects the appropriate kind of group and performance. Group strategies and ways to coordinate are appropriate for certain kinds of tasks but not for others. For example, large groups can efficiently complete tasks that can be done in parts that are later added together. However, size may interfere when people must pool and integrate their ideas and efforts to complete the task.

The task and needed performance strategies may affect the appropriate kind of interdependence and coordination. Competition interferes with task completion when team members have to coordinate and combine their individual efforts, but it can be useful for task completion when team members work independently to contribute to group success.[17]

Perhaps the most explored issue is the contingency theory relating group structure and technology and tasks. It postulates a fit between structure and task in that the greater the task uncertainty the less should performance be standardized and decisions made centrally. Consistent with this perspective, Argote[18] found that programmed ways to coordinate were more useful when inputs in a hospital emergency room were certain but tht nonprogrammed ways were more useful when inputs were unpredictable. However, other studies have not found such clear relationships.[19]

## Issues

An elusive problem for this research is that there are so many components to groups, and each component can come in many different shapes and sizes. For example, researchers have used a number of classification systems to distinguish tasks. McGrath[20] proposed that groups can do four things: generate ideas, choose among alternatives, negotiate conflicts, and execute activities. Yet these tasks are not distinct. Certainly, group members negotiate as they choose among alternatives and execute their decisions.

Goodman[21] has argued that even organizational tasks that are called the same, such as continuous mining, may be made up of different kinds of tasks in different organizations. He proposed that tasks and technologies should be described in detail, a proposal that McGrath[22] argued disrupts research progress. It is also likely that it is not so much the inherent characteristics of the task as how these tasks are experienced that affects group behavior.[23] A useful, widely accepted classification scheme seems like a long way off, and, until then, accumulating evidence linking tasks to other components and to effectiveness will be difficult.

Models of effective organizational groups have powerful implications, but how critical their variables are and the links among them, have not been tested and documented empirically. Studies on tasks and other specific components seem, on the other hand, to provide scattered findings difficult to integrate and use. The next section examines research investigating the impact of groups' having the opportunity, and learning how, to solve problems and manage themselves.

# SELF-MANAGING GROUPS

Research on self-managing groups can be divided into autonomous groups and team building. Research on autonomous groups has documented the value of groups determining their own priorities, dividing up their work, and in other ways dealing with problems and obstacles. Team-building research has developed procedures for groups to identify frustrations and barriers and use this feedback to strengthen their group work.

## AUTONOMOUS GROUPS

Autonomous work groups (also called semi-autonomous) grew out of the socio-technical approach to organizational change, and appear to be increasingly used in a number of industrial countries.[24] Usually carried out on the shop floor, these groups give workers considerable authority to determine their day-to-day work. They usually decide the pace of work, division of labor, breaks, recruitment, and training of new members.[25] Typically, the work team members have related sub-tasks that require coordination, diverse skills needed to complete the task, and feedback and evaluation on the performance of the entire group.

The underlying rationale for autonomous work teams is that workers will find the self-determination intrinsically motivating and satisfying. This self-determination in turn improves group performance, strengthens mental health, and reduces turnover.

A number of case studies as well as correlational analyses have found that autonomous work groups can be productive. In addition, several well-documented quasi-experiments also support this method. Recently, Wall, Kemp, Jackson, and Clegg[26] found that autonomous work groups at a new plant in a British confectionery company had a long-lasting impact on employee intrinsic job satisfaction.

A new plant was designed to allow from 8 to 12 people to work in groups, all of whom were expected to carry out all the jobs necessary to produce candy. They collectively allocated jobs, reached production targets, and met quality and health standards, solved local problems, and recorded production data for the company information system, organized breaks, ordered and collected raw material, delivered finished goods to the warehouse, called for engineering support, and trained new recruits and participated in their selection. Each production group was responsible for its own product line. In addition to informal discussions, members met formally once a week. No supervisors were hired because the work teams carried out all supervision functions.

Results indicate that autonomous work groups, compared to control groups at established sites within the same company, had specific rather than general impact on attitudes and outcomes for the company. Workers clearly appreciated these groups and indicated a high degree of involvement and intrinsic job satisfaction. The company also benefited in that supervisors did not have to be hired. However, autonomous work groups were not found to improve employee job motivation, commitment to the organization, work performance, or turnover. In fact, there was higher turnover in the autonomous groups. Managers also experienced more stress in overseeing these groups.

Other studies indicate that autonomous work groups can have a positive impact on attitudes and behavior. Autonomous work groups have been found to improve productivity, commitment, worker attitudes, and safety, but that these groups increase stress for managers.[27] Overall, research has found that autonomous groups and socio-technical interventions more generally improve productivity.[28]

## Issues

Though called autonomous, these groups are highly dependent upon the organization. Indeed, evidence from several studies has documented that they challenge and frustrate management. To make autonomous work groups effective, organizations must change their values, managerial skills, and compensation systems.[29] The nature of these changes has not been clearly identified.

As noted by researchers,[30] giving workers the leeway to manage their own groups does not assure that they can effectively do so. Workers, like managers, need encouragement, guidance, feedback, and other support to manage themselves. Poorly run self-managing groups can be oppressive, and undermine individual initiative and self-autonomy.[31] Workers must develop the skills to lead themselves. It is unlikely that the opportunity to manage insures the capacity to do so. Indeed, team building is designed to help groups manage themselves.

## TEAM BUILDING

Team building has a prominent place in the group and organization development literature, with McGregor, Likert, Blake and Mouton, and Lewin considered its intellectual pioneers. It developed out of the sensitivity training groups designed to stimulate individual awareness and interpersonal skills. Individuals received feedback on how they interacted and affected others. Team building has shifted its emphasis to examining and improving the processes within ongoing organizational groups.

Team building attempts to provide groups with the information and incentives they need to manage themselves effectively. It argues that by discussing how they are working together and sharing thoughts on the major issues and dilemmas they are facing the members of the group will be able to knock down barriers and improve its functioning. Typically, outside consultants structure team-building activities. They emphasize the need for the group to improve problem solving, and assist the team to generate relevant information, identify problems, and create and implement solutions.[32] Within this paradigm, consultants may use managerial grid, role clarification, or other framework to analyze group interaction.

For example, in a study in mining, Buller and Bell[33] tried to improve the skills of mining work groups and to solve problems that interfered with the quality and quantity of ore and the safety of the operations. They were expected to generate ideas concerning the cause of the problems, plan action, and implement and evaluate plans.

The consultant kept asking how could they do the job better and make the mine a better, safer place to work in. Between meetings, the consultant condensed issues raised earlier, and fed back their results via handouts to the crew and management. They identified four issues: poor coordination, working conditions, repair, and an unfair pay and bid system. They decided to have daily work group meetings, and sessions with opposite shifts to improve coordination, to repair tracks, to clean and sort tools and materials, and to take better care of drilling equipment. With management's help, they initiated changes. Results suggest these interventions had a positive, though modest, impact on the quality of the ore produced.

Taken together, studies document that team building can be useful for enhancing relationships and promoting productivity. In Woodman's[34] review, 19 of 30 studies showed a positive impact for team building. In nine studies with an objective measure of productivity, six reported positive effects for team building.[35]

### Issues

Team building is a practical, flexible approach to strengthen organizational teams. Though not invariably effective, team building has demonstrated that many groups can benefit from identifying problems and coping with them. Groups must have skills and experience in order to know how to manage themselves.

Team building is based largely on the idea that feedback will unlock the potential of groups. However, feedback does not insure that teams have the capacity to apply the feedback to improve performance. Teams must develop the relationships and abilities to use the feedback to solve pressing problems, and, ideally, to identify future issues and resolve them. Team building needs to be supplemented with additional theory on group effectiveness. What are the relationships and the conditions in which team members make use of feedback and generate additional feedback?

## ORGANIZATIONAL CONTEXT

Organizational teams operate within the context of the company's mission, values, expectations, and resources.[36] The organization affects the task, motivation, and success of its groups. Groups are open systems given a mandate and resources, but expected to return benefit to the organization. Groups must adapt and respond to significant others. Indeed, a group's very success depends upon these significant others' accepting and recognizing its achievements; a task force is not successful if its recommendations are not accepted and implemented. Even proponents of autonomous work groups understand that teams are not to be independent but must develop a constructive interdependence with the organization.

Groups must negotiate with the organization about their purpose and resources. Though its original mandate might be clear, a team may change its understanding of what it should do as it explores the issues; top management may revise its expectations. Groups must be prepared to request and justify the resources and time needed to be successful. Groups are often more effective if they are able to utilize the ideas and perspectives of people outside their groups.[37]

Bushe[38] identified several organizational characteristics that support teamwork. The organization recognizes and rewards the group, is responsive to its requests, legitimates its tasks and procedures, and expects it to succeed. Relatedly, McCormick[39] argued that organizations should send consistent messages to their groups and reduce the groups' dependence upon the organization.

## Issues

Given the importance of the organizational context, it is surprising how little empirical work has been directed to understanding the links between organizations and their groups. The organization's mission and values, the openness of prospective consumers of the team's output, and the compensation and training practices would all appear to impact groups. Team members need to collaborate with people outside as well as inside their team to obtain and use resources effectively to accomplish organizational purposes.

# THE TEAM ORGANIZATION MODEL

Significant progress has been made in developing the theory and empirical work for approaches to organizational groups. However, based on different assumptions, they have proceeded largely independently. The model of the team organization attempts to incorporate major features of these approaches. Specifically, team organization, like models of organizational groups, is a comprehensive way to examine and influence groups, and like studies on specific components of groups, it is based squarely on research. It holds that teams must have the leeway to manage themselves, and focuses on how teams can learn to manage themselves. Team organization also recognizes the pervasive impact of the organizational context.

The model argues that effective interaction within teams and between them and their organizations is critical for team success. Then teams are able to use their resources and negotiate for additional ones, keep in touch with changing organizational requirements, and complete tasks and develop solutions desired by the organization. Values, rewards, tasks, and training should support this productive interaction.

The model summarizes research on the conditions that can help team members work effectively together so that they can manage themselves. It guides creating the social–psychological situations and characteristics that will empower teams to regulate themselves, identify issues, and make decisions about composition, tasks, design, leadership style, and other issues. Moreover, these conditions also empower teams to negotiate and work with their organization.

An inspiring vision, a unity that commits to cooperative goals, an empowerment that bestows confidence, exploring issues through constructive controversy, and ongoing reflection promote group self-management, development, productivity, and links with the organization. The team model itself does not answer specific issues for teams, such as how large the group should be, what performance strategy the group should use, or how much leeway it needs from the organization. It does identify interaction that can help groups solve these and other issues so that they can manage themselves. It also suggests the conditions that facilitate this productive interaction. Chapters in Part III describe procedures managers and their teams can use to develop successful cooperative teams. In Part II, chapters review how cooperative teams can innovate for their organizations and be valuable for people.

# REFERENCES

1. Levine, J. M. and Moreland, R. L. (1990). Progress in small group research. In M. R. Rosenzweig and L. W. Porter (eds), *Annual Review of Psychology*, **41**, 585–634. Sundstrom, E., De Meuse, E. P. and Futrell, D. (1990). Work teams: applications and effectiveness. *American Psychologist*, **45**, 120–133.
2. Goodman, P. S. (ed.) (1986). *Designing Effective Work Groups*. San Francisco: Jossey-Bass. Goodman, P. S., Ravlin, E. C. and Schminke, M. (1987). Understanding groups in organizations. In B. M. Staw and L. L. Cummings (eds), *Research in Organizational Behavior*, **9**, Greenwich, CT: JAI Press. Pritchard, R. D., Jones, S. D., Roth, P. L., Stuebing, K. K. and Ekeberg, S. E. (1988). Effects of group feedback, goal setting, and incentives on organizational productivity. *Journal of Applied Psychology*, **73**, 337–358.

3. Nieva, V. F., Fleishman, E. A. and Rieck, A. (1978). *Team dimensions: their identity, their measurement, and their relationships*. Final Technical Report for Contract No. DAHC19–78–0001. Washington, DC: Advanced Research Resources Organizations.
4. Hackman, J. R. (1983). *A normative model of work team effectiveness*. Technical Report No. 2, Research Program on Group Effectiveness, Yale School of Organization and Management.
5. Gladstein, D. L. (1984). Groups in context: a model of task group effectiveness. *Administrative Science Quarterly*, **29**, 499–517.
6. Gist, M. E., Locke, E. A. and Taylor, M. S. (1987). Organizational behavior: group structure, process, and effectiveness. *Journal of Management*, **13**, 237–257.
7. Goodman, P. S. (ed.) (1986). *Designing Effective Work Groups*. San Francisco: Jossey-Bass.
8. Hackman, J. R. (1983). *A normative model of work team effectiveness*. Technical Report No. 2, Research Program on Group Effectiveness, Yale School of Organization and Management. Hackman, J. R. and Walton, R. E. (1986). Leading groups in organizations. In P. S. Goodman (ed.), *Designing Effective Work Groups*. San Francisco: Jossey-Bass, 72–119.
9. Hackman, J. R. and Walton, R. E. (1986). Leading groups in organizations. In P. S. Goodman (ed.), *Designing Effective Work Groups*. San Francisco: Jossey-Bass, 72–119.
10. Goodman, P. S. (ed.) (1986). *Designing Effective Work Groups*. San Francisco: Jossey-Bass.
11. Hackman, J. R. and Walton, R. E. (1986). Leading groups in organizations. In P. S. Goodman (ed.), *Designing Effective Work Groups*. San Francisco: Jossey-Bass, 72–119.
12. Goodman, P. S. (ed.) (1986). *Designing Effective Work Groups*. San Francisco: Jossey-Bass. Nieva, V. F., Fleishman, E. A. and Rieck, A. (1978). *Team dimensions: their identity, their measurement, and their relationships*. Final Technical Report for Contract No. DAHC19–78–0001. Washington, DC: Advanced Research Resources Organizations.
13. Hackman, J. R. (1976). Group influences on individuals. In M. D. Dunnette (ed.), *Handbook of Industrial and Organizational Psychology*. Chicago: Rand McNally.
14. Atkinson, J. W. (1984). *Introduction to Motivation*. New York: Van Nostrand.
15. McGrath, J. E. (1976). Stress and behavior in organizations. In M. D. Dunnette (ed.), *Handbook of Industrial and Organizational Psychology*. Chicago: Rand McNally.
16. Atkinson, J. W. (1984). *Introduction to Motivation*. New York: Van Nostrand.
17. Okun, M. A. and DiVesta, F. J. (1975). Cooperation and competition in groups. *Journal of Personality and Social Psychology*, **31**, 615–620.
18. Argote, L. (1982). Input uncertainty and organizational coordination in hospital emergency units. *Administrative Science Quarterly*, **27**, 420–434.
19. Schoonhoven, D. B. (1981). Problems with contingency theory: testing assumptions hidden within the language of contingency. *Administrative Science Quarterly*, **26**, 349–377.
20. McGrath, J. E. (1984). *Groups: Interaction and Performance*. Englewood Cliffs, NJ: Prentice-Hall.
21. Goodman, P. S. (1986). Impact of task and technology on group performance. In P. S. Goodman (ed.), *Designing Effective Work Groups*. San Francisco: Jossey-Bass, 120–167.
22. McGrath, J. E. (1986). Studying groups at work: ten critical needs for theory and

practice. In P. S. Goodman (ed.), *Designing Effective Work Groups*. San Francisco: Jossey-Bass, 362–391.

23. Mintzberg, H., Raisinghani, D. and Theoret, A. (1976). The structure of 'unstructured' decision processes. *Administrative Science Quarterly*, **21**, 246–275. Salancik, G. and Pfeffer, J. (1977). A social information processing approach to job attitudes and task design. *Administrative Science Quarterly*, **23**, 224–253. Tjosvold, D. (1984). Effects of crisis orientation on managers' approach to controversy in decision making. *Academy of Management Journal*, **27**, 130–138.

24. Pasmore, W., Francis, C., Haldeman, J. and Shani, A. (1982). Sociotechnical systems: a North American reflection on empirical studies of the seventies. *Human Relations*, **35**, 1179–1204.

25. Goodman, P. S., Devadas, R. and Griffith Hughson, T. L. (1988). Groups and productivity: analyzing the effectiveness of self-managing teams. In J. P. Campbell and R. J. Campbell (eds), *Productivity in Organizations: New Perspectives from Industrial and Organizational Psychology*. San Francisco: Jossey-Bass, 295–327.

26. Wall, T. D., Kemp, N. J., Jackson, P. R. and Clegg, C. W. (1986). Outcomes of autonomous workgroups: a long-term field experiment. *Academy of Management Journal*, **29**, 280–304.

27. Goodman, P. S. (1979). *Assessing Organizational Change: The Rushton Quality of Work Experiment*. New York: Wiley–Interscience. Walton, R. E. (1982). The Topeka work system: optimistic visions, pessimistic hypotheses, and reality. In R. Zager and M. P. Rosnow (eds), *The Innovative Organization: Productivity Programs in Action*. Elmsford, NY: Pergamon Press.

28. Guzzo, R. A., Jette, R. D. and Katzell, R. A. (1985). The effects of psychologically based intervention programs on worker productivity: a meta-analysis. *Personnel Psychology*, **38**, 275–291.

29. Goodman, P. S., Devadas, R. and Griffith Hughson, T. L. (1988). Groups and productivity: analyzing the effectiveness of self-managing teams. In J. P. Campbell and R. J. Campbell (eds), *Productivity in Organizations: New Perspectives from Industrial and Organizational Psychology*. San Francisco: Jossey-Bass, 295–327.

30. Goodman, P. S., Devadas, R. and Griffith Hughson, T. L. (1988). Groups and productivity: analyzing the effectiveness of self-managing teams. In J. P. Campbell and R. J. Campbell (eds), *Productivity in Organizations: New Perspectives from Industrial and Organizational Psychology*. San Francisco: Jossey-Bass, 295–327. Wall, T. D., Kemp, N. J., Jackson, P. R. and Clegg, C. W. (1986). Outcomes of autonomous workgroups: a long-term field experiment. *Academy of Management Journal*, **29**, 280–304.

31. Manz, C. C. and Sims, H. P., Jr (1987). Leading workers to lead themselves: the external leadership of self-managing teams. *Administrative Science Quarterly*, **32**, 106–128. Manz, C. C. and Angle, H. (1986). Can group self-management mean a loss of personal control: triangulating a paradox. *Group and Organization Studies*, **11**, 309–334. Manz, C. C. and Sims, H. P., Jr (1982). The potential for 'groupthink' in autonomous work groups. *Human Relations*, **35**, 773–784.

32. Dyer, W. G. (1987). *Team Building: Issues and Alternatives*. Reading, MA: Addison-Wesley.

33. Buller, P. F. and Bell, C. H., Jr (1986). Effects of team building and goal setting on productivity: a field experiment. *Academy of Management Journal*, **29**, 305–328.

34. Woodman, R. W. and Sherwood, J. J. (1980). The role of team development in organizational effectiveness: a critical review. *Psychological Bulletin*, **88**, 166–186.

35. Buller, P. F. and Bell, C. H., Jr (1986). Effects of team building and goal setting on productivity: a field experiment. *Academy of Management Journal*, **29**, 305–328.

36. Ancora, D. Gladstein (1987). Groups in organizations: extending laboratory

36. Ancora, D. Gladstein (1987). Groups in organizations: extending laboratory methods. In C. Hendrick (ed.), *Group Processes and Intergroup Relations.* Newbury Park, CA: Sage, 207–230.
37. Katz, R. (1982). The effects of group longevity on project communication and performance. *Administrative Science Quarterly, 27,* 81–104. Katz, R. and Tuchman, M. (1979). Communication patterns, project performance and task characteristics: an empirical evaluation and integration in an R&D setting. *Organizational Behavior and Human Performance, 23,* 139–162.
38. Bushe, G. R. (1986). *Managing groups from the outside: a model of cognitive task-group types.* Paper, Western Academy of Management Meetings. Bushe, G. R. and Johnson, A. L. (1989). Contextual and internal variables affecting task group outcomes in organizations. *Group and Organization Studies, 14,* 462–482.
39. McCormick, D. W. (1985). Environmental relations and group effectiveness in planned changed projects. Ph.D. dissertation. Case Western Reserve University, Cleveland, OH.

# Part II: Teamwork for Effective Organizations

> To the extent that we continue to celebrate the traditional myth of the entrepreneurial hero, we will slow the progress of change and adaptation that is essential to our economic success. If we are to compete effectively in today's world, we must begin to celebrate collective entrepreneurship, endeavors in which the whole of the effort is greater than the sum of individual contributions. We need to honor our teams more, our aggressive leaders and maverick geniuses less.
>
> Robert B. Reich

Teams are the vehicles for continuous improvement and innovation necessary to remain competitive in today's marketplace. Through teamwork employees improve the quality of products, and strengthen the way they are organized and work together. But teams must be good for people if they are going to engender the passion and persistence necessary to innovate. Chapter 5 reviews research on how teamwork facilitates continuous improvement and Chapter 6 shows how teamwork is valuable for people, creates a sense of justice, and instills commitment. But teams are not invariably productive and enhancing. Chapter 7 examines the imperative for leadership, argues that leaders develop relationships, and identifies the leader's role.

# 5 Teams for Continuous Improvement

He that will not apply new remedies must expect new evils: for time is the greatest innovator.

Sir Francis Bacon

Achievement is a *we* thing, not a *me* thing, always the product of many heads and hands.

John W. Atkinson

'I like the idea of making our vision rational,' Kyle said as the TLC meeting began. 'It was good to look at other ways to analyze teams in organizations, and get a better idea of the strengths and limitations of the team model approach.'

'The team organization model does have its power, and it does talk about creating the right climate for a group to be successful,' Art said. 'Managing is not having the right answers, but helping others come up with answers.'

'I like its flexibility,' remarked Kyle. 'I've always been skeptical of approaches that say do step one and then step two.'

'Yet, we're practical people,' Miles said. 'We need step 1, step 2 up to step 100. We've got to act. We all said that before. Just talking about teamwork and doing little will backfire. Less credibility I don't need.'

'We'll have to work together to develop those plans,' Marian said. 'But that is not to say there are not some procedures that can be generally used and modified to develop teams.'

'Wait a minute,' Scott said. 'I still have my doubts. One thing that has long disturbed me—even when my boss first proposed these new product teams —is how can a group really be innovative. Don't independent-minded, far-sighted individuals create new products, not a mealy-mouse group?'

Kyle said, 'Thomas Edison was not a group.'

'A camel is a horse created by a committee,' Miles reminded everyone.

'We talk about a rational vision, certainly we have to know whether teams can pay off for Savory,' Scott said.

'But Thomas Edison did not do it alone,' Art said. 'I read where he was just as much a managing genius as a technological one. He saw the need to create an organization to develop and implement all the other things necessary to make electric lighting a reality.'

'Even in scientific investigation the lone independent pioneer is less and less likely,' Marian pointed out. 'The winners of Nobel prizes in physics seem to turn out to lead a team of 10, perhaps 20, researchers, and lots of technicians.'

'I just read the other day that 75 people co-authored a paper on the location of the gene for some kind of muscular dystrophy,' Kyle said.

'But do groups really drive innovation in a company?' Scott asked. 'The rest of you don't have to worry that much about it, but we in R&D do.'

'I don't agree with that,' Art said. 'Like our CEO said, we're all going to have to respond to the new challenges; we're either moving ahead or we are falling behind.'

'Food processing is not a sleepy business,' Miles said. 'There are new machines, new ways to organize, new attitudes, and new pressures. The CEO is talking about each production facility getting very expensive equipment and then specializing in making a few items to be shipped around the world. We've got to be concerned about innovation.'

'It hits us as well,' Art said. 'We've got to develop a new international perspective and skill. And that is much more than knowing what to order at an Egyptian restaurant.'

'You have to know what to order at a Parisian one, a Prague one . . . ,' Miles joked.

'We accountants have to get with it as well,' Kyle said. 'There are lots of fancy information systems, and we need one or two. But more basically, all your changes mean we will have to change with you.'

'And that's the same with us in human resources,' Marian said. 'We have to be with you, or we will be left behind as irrelevant.'

'I think that it can be safely said that keeping abreast of changes, being able to innovate is everyone's "bottom line," ' Art said. 'Profits this quarter do not insure profits in the future. There are just too many competitors out there who are more than eager to take your market away from you. And you don't have to fall down, just don't keep up.'

'Nicely put, Art,' Scott said. 'You know, I've heard our CEO talk like that before but perhaps I was not really listening. You really got the point across to me.'

'Now how can we get the point across to people below us?' Kyle asked.

'Getting together and talking like we are would help,' Miles offered.

'These sessions have brought home that everyone in the company needs to innovate,' Scott said.

'Innovation is really central to everyone's vision for their teams,' Miles said. 'Marian, everyone wants to lead a team that will not just swim along, but really challenge the present and take charge of its future.'

'Yet I still have my question: can teams really drive innovation in companies —in our company?' Scott asked.

'Teams certainly seem to,' Art said. 'I keep reading about how this team created this product in record time, how that team developed a new software package. Don't those big computer companies use a team approach to marketing, so that they can coordinate how they approach and serve a client?'

'Don't most of those lunch speakers talk about teamwork and innovation, about 3M and all its new products?' Kyle said.

'I have some articles on how different companies are using teams in the workplace successfully to help them change and innovate,' Marian said.

'Let's read them,' Scott said.

'I think we should visit some companies who are using teams. That would be fun,' Miles suggested.

'But we wanted this vision to be rational,' Scott said. 'Where is the evidence that teams, even ones that follow the model, can really innovate?'

'I'm pleased to announce that I am in a position to empower you,' Marian said.

'Sounds great,' Miles said with a laugh.

'I think she means she has more articles,' Kyle said.

'Right,' Marian said.

'What are these articles going to say?' Scott asked.

'The basic argument is that there are a number of obstacles to innovating in an organization,' Marian said. 'Having a neat idea is not enough. The idea has to be developed, accepted, and implemented. No one person can really do it. Teams are concrete ways to channel the intelligence, creativity, and persist-ence necessary to innovate in companies. Studies show that teams can create ideas and persist to implement them.'

## THE NEED TO INNOVATE

The traditional image of innovation is high tech. Bright, eccentric, creative people in a company in California discover a new way to harness biological processes to repair the heart, and the next month they find a way to use the computer to predict heart failures. But innovation is part of, and is increasing-ly required, for all organizations. Waste disposal, health care delivery, den-tistry, municipal services, food processing, and steel production are all under-going transformational change.

It is difficult to identify any business not under pressure to change. In the world-wide competitive marketplace, customers have many choices, and demand high-quality products and services. Technological advances make new products and manufacturing processes possible, and make others obsolete. The speed and diffusion of these advances are increasing rapidly. A computer innovation in North America soon sees its way to the production facilities in the Pacific Rim and South America. Industrial robots developed in Japan are quickly used in North America and Europe.

Governments have stimulated change by promoting trade, forming free trade zones, and demanding efficiency and cutbacks on funds for health care and other services. Health care organizations have joined forces to integrate into one business hospitals, medical and dental clinics, life-long care centers, nursing homes, diagnostic laboratories, and hospices for the terminally ill.

Innovations build upon themselves. Creation of a new product makes refinements and new products possible. Innovations in communication, shipping, and finance make it more feasible for companies to use foreign suppliers and form international joint ventures.

There can be no contentment with the status quo, no going through the motions. If a company and its people are not growing and developing, if they are not committed to innovate, they are falling behind. Striving for competi-tive advantage, managing change, the commitment to continuous improve-ment, and the drive for excellence are not simply slogans, but address the reality of opportunities and threats.

The 1990s will be, according to Jack Welsch, CEO of General Electric, the 'white knuckle decade . . . fast . . . exhilarating.' Standing still is not a viable option for organizations. Without innovation, they risk getting out of touch with their increasingly demanding and savvy customers. Even companies with the luxury of a product with a long life-cycle must still find ways to manufacture and market it in cost-efficient, attractive ways. Or they may be prey for hungrier companies on the prowl for profits and market share.

## COMMUNICATION FOR CONTINUOUS IMPROVEMENT

Communication within and between groups is needed for innovation in organizations.[1] Continuous improvement occurs when people within teams and across them are identifying issues, sharing information, influencing each other, and putting ideas together.[2] Varied, full communication is needed to combine ideas to be greater than the sum of any one.[3]

In several studies, Katz[4] has found that communication patterns have distinguished effective and ineffective R&D teams. For example, teams with long tenure often isolate themselves from sources of critical information, evaluation, and feedback, and this isolation undercuts their effectiveness.

Rosebeth Kanter[5] has strongly argued that communication within and between organizations drives innovation, whereas segmentation is the bane of innovation. Collaboration and integration are needed to generate ideas, develop the coalition to realize the idea, and transfer and diffuse the idea to the marketplace.

Kanter urged organizations to break down divisions that interfere with diverse people working together, and promote contact with those who take new angles on problems to generate ideas. Innovators should see their charge broadly, and gain the perspective of users and others. They should have the freedom to work around and across the organization. Small teams of diverse people focus on developing new products and processes. Flexible funding controlled at the local level supports idea generation and development.

Communication with others outside the organization also stimulates innovation. A skilled, cosmopolitan workforce, a flow of new ideas from R&D centers, and a heterogeneous community setting all increase the mix and clash of various viewpoints. Ambassadors for innovation teams transmit ideas to others, sentries regulate the communication that comes to the group, and guards control how information is communicated.

Communication and coalition building are needed to turn ideas into reality. Creation is an intensive process, whereas diffusion is an extensive process of reaching out and including others beside the product champions and sponsors. It can be useful to have a group who have formal responsibility to move an idea into active use. 3M and Honeywell have 'idea fairs' to connect ideas with those who can use them and help take them to the next step.

For Kanter, relationships, contact between specialists, exchange with users, new product teams (skunkworks), and links to diffuse ideas underlie innovation in organization. Specialists, scientists, managers, and marketers are by themselves limited and restrained. Their integration can generate and market ideas.

Innovation is something that employees, managers, and executives do together. Creative, independent geniuses do not drive innovation in organizations; supportive teamwork and communication do.

## STRIVING FOR QUALITY AT 3M

3M's Decorative Products Division embarked on a broad-based quality improvement program in 1977. According to Kenneth L. King,[6] the division's quality manager, the program has made quality an important competitive advantage. Ford gave the division a 'Q1' award for excellence in supplying; Germany's Adam Opel named it its 'Supplier of the Year' three times; the division received Nissan USA's first 100% score in its Supplier Quality Assurance System survey.

3M uses elements of Deming's statistical control, Juran's Quality Training and Vendor/Supply Management, Crosby's Model-Quality Emphasis, and Ishikawa's Model-Quality Circle/Quality Action Teams. *Teams were critical of the program's implementation and success.* An early survey had indicated that poor communication was the major cause of poor quality. 3M created teams committed and equipped to improve quality continuously.

The eight Area Quality Improvement Teams were responsible for implementing 3M's 'Right the First Time' philosophy. Quality Circles and Quality Action Teams capitalized on the knowledge and skills of employees by involving them in reducing errors. Customer survey teams monitored the quality of the division's products. Teams improved how vendors used 3M's products: e.g. quality and technical service specialists measured how automobile assembly plants were applying the division's products on cars. They reported data on the assembly plant's performance, compared it with other facilities, and helped employees get training to apply 3M's products effectively.

The 'Right the First Time' philosophy was an engaging, shared *vision* for the division. Its tenets: it is cheaper to do it right the first time; every job is to be organized with a goal of no errors; the majority of errors are caused by management; every error has a cause which can be identified and eliminated; there is a goal of planned, measurable improvement toward error-free performance.

The division committed considerable resources so that employees felt *united and empowered* behind this goal. Over 250 people were trained in data analysis and statistics, and over 400 employees and 200 vendors in quality education. Employees also had courses in Juran Quality Management, Rennsselaer Polytechnic color, and corrective action training. Teams were structured to encourage individuals to find new ways to reduce errors.

The teams *explored* how to make it right the first time. They audited suppliers and suggested ways they could supply higher-quality products to 3M. Employees used their training in statistical methods of quality control to *measure and reflect* on their performance. Teams have become instrumental in Decorative Products' ongoing improvement in product quality.

# INNOVATION IN ORGANIZATIONS

Innovation is the process of initiating, adopting, and implementing an idea, procedure, practice, program, or product considered new by the organization.[7] Sometimes these innovations are invented by the company itself; often they have been invented elsewhere, and the company innovates by adopting and modifying them. Companies can innovate by acquiring new machinery, devising new uses for old machinery, implementing new management practices, acquiring skills to make old practices work, developing products, and finding new markets for old ones. They may require a total refocusing of the organization, or slight modification.

Innovations can occur in the technical systems and in management.[8] Technical innovations involve the primary work activity and maybe a new product or new technology to produce it. Management or administrative innovations are changes to the organization's structure and design, management style, corporate culture, and the human resource systems of compensation, training, and development.

# OBSTACLES TO INNOVATION

Innovation tests a company's mettle. Although often chaotic, innovation does not happen by chance. It needs to be nurtured and managed. Continuous improvement requires competence, commitment, determination, and daring.

Innovation in an organization is not simply a quick flash of inspiration, although that is at times a vital part. It is much more than a bright insight. Problems must be found and turned into opportunities. They must be discussed and seen from a new perspective, and ideas must be combined into a new solution. The solution needs to be evaluated and tested, and persistence and commitment are required to implement it.

*Innovators must find problems and situations and turn them into opportunities.* They cannot just throw up their hands in frustration, but need to use this frustration to dig into the situation and to think of alternatives.

Once the issue is understood, people must *create alternative solutions.* Typically, modifications of old approaches are first discussed but found unsatisfactory. Feeling blocked and frustrated, people may feel pessimistic and withdraw. During this period of frustration and doubt, ideas incubate as they consider the problem from several perspectives. Sometimes the solution comes in a great illumination. The 'Aha!,' 'I've got it!' experience. Then the solution is elaborated and selected for more careful testing.

Creative solutions by their very nature can be highly damaging and costly. They must be *vigorously tested and evaluated.* Prototypes, field tests, demonstration projects, focus groups, and surveys collect data. People debate and challenge each other's conclusions and implications they draw from the data.

Well-tested ideas and insights are necessary for innovation in organizations, but so is *persistence.* People must be motivated to make the effort and bear the frustration and tension that usually accompany innovation and change. They need to believe that they have the courage and imagination and find working on innovations rewarding and exciting.

Innovation requires organizational *concurrence and commitment.* In addition to top management, union, workers, middle management, departments, and others will all have a role in implementing the innovation. Resistance is almost inevitable, because people are comfortable with the status quo, have been rewarded for reliable, stable performance, and will want good reasons for why they should go through the effort to make changes. They may suspect that the innovation will work against their interests, power, and status. They want to be convinced that the innovation is cost-effective, fair, has acceptable risks, does not stretch resources too far, and promotes long-term interests.

## THE TEAM MODEL AND INNOVATION

Groups have been found to be the central force behind innovation in organizations.[9] Teams are a practical way to structure and encourage the communication between diverse people and coalition building that are at the heart of innovation. Teams help *employees and managers work together to overcome barriers and negotiate steps to innovate.* Formal and informal groups can share hunches, doubts, and misgivings and discuss emerging ideas and practices to find problems. Their mutual support encourages them to consider these problems as opportunities to exploit. They exchange ideas and suggestions that give them a fresh perspective, together withstand frustration, and integrate ideas in unique, effective ways.[10] They share the work of collecting data on their solution, and together debate the virtues and pitfalls.

Because they have challenged the idea from several perspectives they have the confidence they can be successful and believe they have the resources and strength to see the idea through. Teams can involve and gain the commitment of representatives from the groups and departments who must implement the innovation.[11] It is thus more likely that the innovation makes sense from the various perspectives within a company.

But it is not just any team that can accomplish innovation.[12] Teams can suppress independent thought and stifle initiative. Successful teams are committed to a *vision* of innovation and experiment, feel *united* and cohesive behind this vision, and believe that the organization itself wants continuous improvement and will respond openly to the team's recommendations. Individual skills and competence help the group feel *empowered*. Diversity of approaches openly *explored* and integrated are critical for innovation.

Cooperative goals and constructive controversy have been found to contribute directly to innovation. Retail store personnel who discussed their opposing views openly yet felt united in their goals, solved problems, and implemented new laser-scanning technology successfully.[13] Faculty and support staff who developed cooperative goals, spoke their minds, and integrated their views were able to reform their educational bureaucracy.[14] Cooperative teamwork also helped employees adjust to their organization's restructuring and use the new opportunities of restructuring to be productive.[15] Teams, committed to their cooperative goal to innovate, feeling confident they can overcome the many obstacles, willing to explore alternative solutions, and able to renew themselves, negotiate the difficult steps to innovate in organizations.

## CONCLUDING COMMENTS

Teamwork is an ultimate competitive advantage. By working together, marketing, engineering, and production specialists create a new product. Supervisors and workers invent ways to reduce costs and improve product quality. The top management team hammers out a strategy to exploit emerging opportunities and joins managers and workers to implement it. Teams overcome resistance to new technology and create ways to use it effectively. Teamwork facilitates management as well as technical innovations. Employees, for example, must be able to work together to implement changes if employee ownership is to contribute to business success.[16]

Teams are practical, effective ways to stimulate organizational innovation.

They encourage both the voicing of diverse perspectives and their integration to exploit opportunities, create useful solutions, and gain the persistence necessary for continuous improvement.

# REFERENCES

1. Drucker, P. (1985). *Innovation and Entrepreneurship: Practices and Principles*. New York: Harper & Row.
2. Van de Ven, A., Angle, H. and Poole, M. S. (eds) (1989). *Research on the Management of Innovation*. Cambridge, MA: Ballinger. West, M. A. and Farr, J. L. (1989). Innovation at work: psychological perspectives. *Social Behaviour*, **4**, 15–20.
3. Van de Ven, A. H. (1986). Central problems in the management of innovation. *Management Science*, **32**, 590–607.
4. Katz, R. (1982). The effects of group longevity on project communication and performance. *Administrative Science Quarterly*, **27**, 81–104. Katz, R. and Allen, T. J. (1985). Project performance and the locus of influence in the R&D matrix. *Academy of Management Journal*, **28**, 67–87. Katz, R. and Tuchman, M. (1979). Communication patterns, project performance and task characteristics: an empirical evaluation and integration in an R&D setting. *Organizational Behavior and Human Performance*, **23**, 139–162.
5. Kanter, R. M. (1988). Three tiers for innovation research. *Communication Research*, **15**, 509–523. Kanter, R. M. (1983). *The Change Masters*. New York: Simon & Schuster.
6. King, K. L. (1987). How 3M melds Deming's, Juran's, and Crosby's techniques. In Y. K. Shetty and V. M. Buehler (eds), *Quality Productivity and Innovation: Strategies for Gaining Competitive Advantage*. New York: Elsevier, 303–313.
7. Lin, N. and Zaltman, G. (1973). Dimensions of innovation. In G. Zaltman (ed.), *Processes and Phenomena of Social Change*. New York: Wiley.
8. Damanpour, F. (1987). The adoption of technological, administrative and ancillary innovations: impact of organizational factors. *Journal of Management*, **13**, 675–688.
9. Andrews, F. M. (1979). *Scientific Productivity: The Effectiveness of Research Groups in Six Countries*. Cambridge: Cambridge University Press. Coch, L. and French, J. R. P., Jr (1948). Overcoming resistance to change. *Human Relations*, **1**, 512–532.
10. Michaelsen, L. K., Watson, W. E. and Black, R. H. (1989). A realistic test of individual versus group consensus decision making. *Journal of Applied Psychology*, **74**, 834–839.
11. Hollenbeck, J. R., Williams, C. R. and Klein, H. J. (1989). An empirical examination of the antecedents of commitment to difficult goals. *Journal of Applied Psychology*, **74**, 18–23. Orive, R. (1988). Group consensus, action immediacy, and opinion confidence. *Personality and Social Psychology Bulletin*, **14**, 573–577.
12. Pinto, J. K. and Prescott, J. E. (1987). Changes in critical success factor importance over the life of a project. *Academy of Management Proceedings*, New Orleans, 328–332. West, M. A. and Farr, J. L. (1989). Innovation at work: psychological perspectives. *Social Behaviour*, **4**, 15–20.
13. Tjosvold, D. (in press). Making a technological innovation work: collaboration to solve problems. *Human Relations*.

14. Tjosvold, D. and McNeely, L. T. (1988). Innovation through communication in an educational bureaucracy. *Communication Research*, **15**, 568–581.
15. Tjosvold, D. (1990). Cooperation and competition in restructuring an organization. *Canadian Journal of Administrative Sciences*, **7**, 48–54.
16. Klein, K. J. (1987). Employee stock ownership and employee attitudes: a test of three models. *Journal of Applied Psychology*, **72**, 319–332.

# 6 Teams for Commitment

'People make the organization work,' Miles said. 'It's fun to talk about such nice sounding abstractions as innovation and creativity, but it is people who make a company go. Those articles we looked at tell us that teams can be innovative, but if teams are not good for people, they won't do.'

'You can tell teams they must persist, create, and liaise with managers, but the people in the team have to be motivated to do it,' Kyle said.

'Now we can get people to do things,' Scott said. 'I can yell and demand and get plenty of activity. But we need people committed to doing the best job, who will give it their best shot. It's clear from reading that material on innovation that we need our people to be motivated from within and willing to perform over the long run.'

'Isn't our system based on competition, individual initiative, people wanting to outdo each other?' Kyle asked. 'Isn't that what turns people on?'

'We do hear a lot about how competition motivates,' Marian said. 'But that's not what the evidence indicates. As the research we talked about last time and the articles you read indicate, we have many, many studies indicating that people are more motivated and are more productive when working cooperatively than competitively.'

'But the whole capitalistic economy is based on people pursuing their self-interest,' Scott objected.

'But Adam Smith was a great proponent of cooperation,' Marian said. 'He argued that people can pursue their own self-interest and at the same time pursue the interests of others. That is the heart and soul of cooperation.'

'Yes, but companies compete,' Kyle said.

'They do, but they also cooperate,' Marian said. 'We have to work with our suppliers and our marketing channels, programs to train our employees—schools and universities, and so on.'

'We're always getting together with food-processing people from our competitors at conferences. I regularly talk to the plant manager at Ziem's Foods about improving food-processing techniques,' Miles said.

'So you are saying people can be highly motivated in teams,' Scott said.

'Not only that, but they usually are more motivated and productive than working by themselves or competitively against others.'

'I want to get back to the complicated issue of change,' Miles said. 'We've agreed that our visions call for using teams to innovate. But all the change these groups are supposed to produce may just be their undoing. Here we want teams to change, but we all know that changes really disrupt our people.'

'I certainly know from trying to get these new product teams working,' Scott interjected, 'that people resist change. Now how can we make change into something that's good for people? There must be a Nobel prize in that.'

'That would help my career!' Marian said. 'Of course, I would remember you all made it possible.'

'You would remember our names, *maybe*,' Kyle said.

'We know that there's resistance to change,' Marian said. 'I can remember my history professor saying if the industrial revolution depended upon a vote, it would not have happened. But change does not happen because of majority vote in a free market economy.'

'I guess you can say that we all enjoy the benefits of a dynamic economy because our ancestors had to grapple with all kinds of change, even though they didn't want to,' Kyle said. 'Why is change so disruptive?'

'People feel comfortable with the status quo, and change threatens their sense of security,' Scott offered.

'But there's another side to this coin,' Art said. 'Lots of people seek out change. They move to another part of the country, find a new job, find a new spouse, get the latest computer. Ads talk about new this and new that.'

'Change can be stimulating and exciting,' Marian said.

'Our own visions for our teams include challenging the status quo, and making change continuous and ongoing,' Kyle said. 'We said we wanted to be in charge of change, not have change in charge of us.'

'Change does seem to have two sides,' Miles said. 'We like it but also fear it.'

'Change is a challenge, and I think most of us like challenges,' Marian said. 'But change also threatens, as Scott said, our sense of security. Psychologists say that change can be so threatening because we fear that it may disrupt our links with other people, whom we depend upon for so much.'

'What's this?' Scott asked.

'The idea is that we learned our ideas, values, and skills with other people, and change makes us feel uncomfortable because it implicitly makes us wonder whether these other people would approve,' Marian said.

'We want to do things like we used to because that's the way Dad said we should do it, is that what you're saying?' Scott said.

'Not just Dad, all kinds of people, from our classmates to our boss,' Marian said. 'It's as if we don't want to change by ourselves, because we want the assurance of other people. We learn with other people, and to learn new things we have to learn with people. Then we feel much more confident that our new values and skills are reasonable and useful.'

'So teams can help people cope with the emotions of change,' Art said.

'The unknown can seem exciting and inviting, when we have the confidence that there are others going with us, that they are excited, and they will help us grapple with difficulties and uncertainties,' Marian said. 'Without team-mates, change can seem strange and foreboding.'

'So can we have teams that help us to be productive and innovative, that get things done and help us change, yet are still good for people?' Miles asked.

'There's no real choice,' Marian said. 'We can't have productive teams in the long run without their being good for people. Short-term pressures generate a lot of activity—short-term activity can be done without supporting people, but for productivity and innovation over the long term, you've got to have the people on your side, really believing and committed. You can't expect people to work hard and long for the company unless they see they are getting something in return.'

'That *sounds* good, Marian,' Scott said. 'But can it happen?'

'It can,' Art broke in assuredly. 'I was part of a really great group several years ago for my kids' school. We just clicked as a group—it was fun to work with people from different walks of life. You know, those people who do not live and breathe marketing high-tech food, but regular people like nurses, educators, truck drivers. And did we ever put together a presentation about why the school board should come up with a million dollars to renovate our school! We really showed them that we were a community that cared about its school. We had a ball. It was good for everyone, for the school, the city, the students, the teachers, and us.' Art paused and then said matter-of-factly, 'I wish I had that kind of team at Savory.'

'Seeing is believing,' Kyle said. 'We accountants just don't do that sort of thing very much.'

'Think again,' Marian said. 'Haven't you been part of a sports team, a church committee, or some other group that's been productive, but very good for you as a person?'

'You look alive, Kyle—it must have happened sometime,' Miles teased.

'I can remember people and groups I want to avoid—that's easy. Come to think of it, some of those people may be in this room,' Kyle said with mock seriousness.

'I guess it is experiences like Art was talking about that give "teamwork" such a positive ring,' Miles remarked.

'I know that teams, getting extraordinary things done, and people go together, but it would be good to look at this in more depth,' Art said. 'Not all groups are good for people, and I want to be able to respond to the questions and doubts that I know my people will have when I talk about teamwork in the marketing department.'

'And there are people like me that would like more evidence that teams can be good for people and develop their loyalty,' Scott said.

'We need to have a better idea about how teams can be good for people,' Miles said. 'Then we can have a better idea about what to shoot for, what kind of team to develop.'

'What's so critical for all of this is relationships,' Marian said. 'It may not sound very business-like, but I think we're rediscovering what we have known all along. Good work relationships are much more than nice things, but are central for people to overcome obstacles to innovation and to welcome the challenge of change and be committed.'

'My old boss used to say, "If you feel good about who you work with and for, you feel good about yourself and your job," ' Miles said.

'I think if it got right down to it, most of us would admit that we work for our boss or colleagues more than we work for any company, including Savory,' Kyle said. 'If we didn't feel some loyalty for the people, we wouldn't feel much allegiance to Savory.'

'But why are other people so critical for commitment?' Marian asked.

'You don't want to let your friends down, not when they need you,' Kyle suggested.

'Pride's a big thing,' Art said. 'You feel good about yourself when your group does good.'

'Life's give and take,' Miles said. 'If someone takes care of you, then you should take care of them. It's basic, and people have been like that for thousands of years.'

Scott said, 'What goes around comes around. If you don't help a friend, you can't expect help from someone else.'

'The really important things that have happened to me involve people,' Art said. 'I remember those little things like birthday surprises, and big things, like people taking the time to talk about my problems. It's those little and big times when people really show they care.'

'Other people can make a regular job very rich and rewarding,' Marian declared. 'When we feel we are getting a good, fair deal, we develop commitment to the people, the job, and the company.'

'If you're good to your employees they will be good to you,' Miles said. 'Very basic stuff—too often forgotten.'

'Another process that comes into it is identification,' Marian said. 'That's when we come to define ourselves as an employee at Savory, a manager, or whatever. We see our work as very much an important part of ourselves and our work is a way of expressing ourselves. We want to see the company and group do well to build up our own self-esteem.'

'Again very basic,' Miles said. 'Pride in one's work goes hand in hand with pride in oneself. I can't imagine getting up in the morning and dreading the thought of having to work with people I had no respect for, and having no sense of pride in what we're doing. That would drive me to drink. They couldn't pay me enough.'

'I think that's what happens in some places,' Kyle said. 'Companies try to buy people off for putting up with things rather than pay them for contributing to the firm.'

'Another issue that makes teams and commitment so critical today is that companies don't have the luxury to develop company loyalty over years,' Marian said. 'We need to get people involved and up to speed quickly.'

'The old ways of developing loyalty are less credible today,' Art said. 'When I began work, you could tell people that if they worked for the company, the company would return that loyalty with secure employment to retirement. Now new people are not interested in that so much, and they don't believe a company that tells them that. They know companies might break those promises to restructure.'

'Even if the company keeps you on, you may not be doing the same thing,' Miles added. 'I've lost track of the jobs and places I've been for this company.'

'More pressure,' Marian said. 'People have to develop their relationships much more quickly, and must also know how to step out of them and begin new ones. As Miles said, pride, teamwork, and commitment are very basic, but we have to achieve them in much different circumstances from those of our parents and grandparents. Our challenge is to use something as basic as teamwork to meet our uncommon challenges.'

# NEED FOR COMMITMENT

> We have done a good job in capturing their arms, legs, and minds, but the real secret is in capturing their hearts. Isn't that what employee involvement is all about?
>
> Davey Lui, Manager, Ford Lio Ho plant, Taiwan

Organizations must innovate to survive and prosper; but for innovation to happen, employees must make intense commitments. They must take the long-term view, suffer through frustrations, and master hurdles to help their companies adapt. Fortunately, many people do work long and hard to make their company successful. They feel an internal drive to perform and contribute to the company.[1]

Companies need employee internal commitment. Income, status, and praise are not sufficient to drive needed innovation. People must work to generate new ideas though there is little immediate recognition or reward. Managers and others often cannot appreciate the potential of the work of innovators. More generally, organizations need employees to be good citizens.[2] Not all desired and important behavior is prescribed in job descriptions or stipulated in union contracts. Staying late to deal with a crisis, assisting an overloaded colleague, and listening to a distressed employee all contribute to a successful organization. *Employees must care about the company and each other.*[3]

# VALUE OF TEAMS FOR PEOPLE

> Compared with the contempt of mankind, all other external evils are easily supported.
>
> Adam Smith

To be only for oneself is to be almost nothing.
>
> B. F. Skinner

From the standpoint of everyday life . . . there is one thing we do know; that man is here for the sake of other men—above all, for those upon whose smile and well-being our own happiness depends, and also for the countless unknown souls with whose fate we are connected by a bond of sympathy. Many times a day I realize how much of my own outer and inner life is built upon the labors of my fellow men, both living and dead, and how earnestly I must exert myself in order to give in return as much as I have received.

Albert Einstein

Employees are selective in making their commitments to work long and hard. In some organizations, people shift along, waiting till the end of the day to come alive. Employees become committed to companies because they find their work rewarding and fulfilling, not because of their altruism and selflessness. Rather than feel exploited, they believe their work pays them a fair return. They have the *more for more solution*: they give more to their jobs, and they get more.

Teams develop high commitment that stimulates effort and output.[4] Teams are potentially very rich and rewarding experiences. Through them, people can meet human needs to achieve, be part of a larger effort, and feel accepted. Increasingly people are forming voluntary self-help groups to cope with cancer, divorce, abuse, and death.[5]

Working together is part of our human heritage; we are built for groups. Indeed, *Homo sapiens* was not stronger or faster than other animals, but able to join forces for hunting and protection. The need to coordinate stimulated language and intellectual development. Parents' emotional bond and care allow children to develop their abilities over many years. Our social nature very much contributed to our emerging as the dominating species. Though we live very differently from our ancestors, our underlying needs are similar.

## NEED FULFILLMENT

Psychologists have developed various frameworks to understand human needs, motives, and instincts. There is general agreement that needs to achieve, affiliate, and have power play an important role in our behavior.[6] People want to achieve; they want to complete tasks at a standard of excellence. They like challenging but attainable tasks because they feel an internal sense of accomplishment and realize that it was possible for them to fail. People try to meet achievement needs in a great many ways: building a bridge, climbing a mountain, getting an 'A' on a report card, creating a company, planting a garden, and developing and marketing a new product.

Affiliation involves the desire to associate and feel recognized and accepted by others. People want to be noticed and valued. They will seek the assurance and company of others especially when feeling stressed and anxious. These affiliation needs are particularly strong with significant others, but even the regard of strangers can be important. People have a great many ways of meeting these needs: some demand, some ask, and others hope.

People also have needs for power; they want to have an impact on others and to influence them. It propels some people to try to dominate and control; others want give-and-take collaboration where influence is two-way; some fantasize about great power and recognition.

Researchers have shown that people differ in strength of achievement, affiliation, and power needs, and the ways they try to meet them. However, the more fundamental finding is that everyone has them. Unfortunately, some people have developed unacceptable ways to meet them (e.g. bank robbers, drug lords); other people, demoralized through years of frustration, try to deny their force.

Productive teams are vital ways to meet achievement, affiliation, and power needs. Team members feel internal pride and accomplishment as their team completes challenging tasks they could not do alone. They feel part of a larger effort and accepted as valuable colleagues in their mutual work. Through the give and take of team effort, they meet their needs to influence and have an impact on others.

## SOCIAL SUPPORT

*A friend is one*
*to whom one may pour*
*out all the contents*
*of one's heart,*
*chaff and grain together*
*knowing that the*
*gentlest of hands*
*will take and sift it,*
*keep what is worth keeping*
*and with a breath of kindness*
*blow the rest away.*
　　　　　Arabian proverb

Feeling connected to other people, having meaningful relationships, being able to rely on others, having other people to turn to for assistance, and feeling satisfied with one's friends provide social support.[7] This support helps people be productive and achieve, avoid distressing feelings of isolation, and live longer lives, recover from illness and injury faster, and experience fewer threatening illnesses.

Isolation runs counter to our nature. Loneliness is one of the most painful human experiences. Feeling estranged undermines psychological well-being and the quality of life; it even shortens life itself.[8] Sadly, surveys indicate that depression is growing rapidly in the United States; there has been a tenfold increase in the rate of depression in the last two generations.[9] It is likely that the breakdown of relationships in families and communities has created unprecedented feelings of loneliness, hopelessness, and self-rejection.

A great deal of research indicates that social support provides the care and information necessary to cope with stress, maintain a sense of well-being and self-esteem, and flourish physically and psychologically.[10] Forming links with organizational superiors and more experienced peers through formal and informal mentoring programs can help new employees adjust to the organization.[11] Feelings of being cared for and emotionally valued encourage conscientious work, willingness to be good citizens, and contributions to innovations.[12]

Feeling connected with supportive others provides opportunities to demonstrate one's own compassion and capability by helping others.[13] As Leo Tolstoy, the novelist, wrote, 'We do not love people so much for the good they have done us, as for the good we have done them.' Helping others induces a sense of responsibility and involvement with others.

People also depend upon others to understand and come to terms with reality. They want to be correct in their analysis of their social world.[14] Wanting some assurance that they are experiencing the world in a sensible, sane manner, people turn to others for comparison.[15]

## SELF-ESTEEM

Self-esteem of judging oneself as a worthwhile person very much affects well-being and competence. People who value themselves, for example, make more favorable impressions on job recruiters and get more job offers; they also more effectively cope with job loss.[16] Low self-esteem leads to emotional problems, poor achievement, awkward social relations, susceptibility to influence, and rejection of others.[17]

Personal attitudes about oneself are grounded in relationships. People develop their own sense of self and self-esteem by considering how others see and treat them.[18] They see themselves through the mirror of others' eyes; if others tell them they are understanding, people tend to see themselves as understanding. Our innermost thoughts about ourselves depend upon the actions of others. To the extent others value us, we find it easier to value ourselves.

## IDENTIFICATION WITH THE COMPANY

Rich rewards and warm acceptance can, over time, result in a psychological identification. Employees define themselves as a member of the organization; belonging to Savory has become part of their self-concept. They see themselves as an 'IBM' person; they want to do it the 'Hewlett-Packard way'; they have incorporated the values of James C. Penney. Working for the company and for themselves are integrated; they take pride in the company's achievement as their own. Their own interests and identity are advanced when the company's are.

Company values also affect identification. Most people want to see themselves as fair and compassionate as well as competent achievers. They will find it difficult to identify with a company that acts contrary to these values. For example, dismissing employees in an impersonal way can undermine the morale and commitment of those who remain.[19]

Identification is powerful. People will work hard and well for the company for its success rebounds directly to their own sense of accomplishment and self. They will work for company values of honesty, fairness, and caring because that reinforces their view of themselves. Furthering the company strengthens their self-concept.

However, identification is two-sided and makes demands on the company. If the company violates central values, employees are apt to feel personally betrayed and dismayed, and demand redress.

## SUMMARY

Through teams, people can feel fulfilled by superior achievement, see themselves as part of a larger effort, feel supported, and strengthen their self-esteem. These teams must be well-structured before their potential is realized. A commitment to challenging vision and goals, feeling united behind this vision, and exploring issues are needed to meet achievement needs.

Team members who empower and recognize each other's resources and share the credit for their success help each other feel powerful and worthwhile. Employees receive the support and feedback that increase self-awareness and enhance self-esteem. They are open to accept the interpretation that their job, their team's work, and the organization's vision are significant. On the basis of this grounding and security, they further their own and the company's interests.

# STRIVING FOR JUSTICE

Fairness and justice are prerequisites for commitment. Employees want their worklife to be rich and fulfilling, but they must also see that their rewards are just. Their organizations, their colleagues, and they themselves should be fair-minded. They will not identify with a company they believe treats people unfairly.[20]

But how can a company be fair? Justice is a complex idea, and much more research is needed on the individual, group, organizational, and cultural conditions that create a sense of fairness. This section argues that group rewards are often seen as fair and reasonable, and that teams provide opportunities to resolve conflicts and issues so that people believe they have been treated justly.

## FAIRNESS OF GROUP REWARDS

A common rule is that rewards should be distributed equitably: what one receives relative to others should be determined by one's relative contributions. People who give more should get more; high performers get high rewards; winners should be celebrated and losers left with little. Yet equity is not the only possibility. Equality is often employed, even by the most conservative of companies. Everyone is entitled to enroll in the health care plan by virtue of their membership in the organization. Rewards are also distributed according to the needs of individuals, even in companies that see themselves as highly capitalistic: many organizations support treatment for alcoholic employees.

In contrast to the popular belief that equity is highly fair and productive, people have been found to react very positively to group rewards.[21] As already noted, cooperative rewards induce much greater individual and group productivity, social solidarity, self-esteem, and responsibility toward others than competition or independence. Nor is there consistent evidence that people accept and work more effectively when they expect to be rewarded according to their individual efforts in contrast to being rewarded as a group or on the basis of needs. Group rewards lead to caring and social solidarity; people who care about each other want rewards to be distributed equally.

Rewarding people based on their team's performance rather than on their individual one has important practical advantages. To reward effectively, a manager must select meaningful rewards, communicate useful standards, and measure performance accurately. Managers find it easier to do that for three teams, for example, than for 15 individuals.

Rewarding individuals for their performance relative to others in competition often happens, especially in marketing organizations. But, it is difficult to do fairly or effectively. Fair competition implies a level playing field. But selling copying machines is much easier in an expanding area than in a contracting one; the construction of a large office tower assures the sales person in that area of victory. Not surprisingly, many employees are often going to find competitive rewards unfair and stressful.[22]

Competitive contests also have the potential to focus representatives only on improving short-term sales, at the expense of developing marketing relationships that may prove highly profitable for future years. Competition also works against representatives sharing information and leads and helping each other develop the complex skills of selling. Group-based rewards, even in marketing organizations, are often both fair and practical.

## CONFLICT FOR JUSTICE

Justice is not so much an abstract ideal as something to be worked out and negotiated. People want justice, but recognize that it entails much more than following a simple recipe. No organization can be perfect and respect all needs and interests. Even if people were able to agree that equity should determine wages, they would still need to measure the relative input of the president, middle manager, worker, and janitor. Inevitably, people will be well aware of their own inputs and value them, and be less knowledgeable about the contributions of others. *Team organization encourages people to work out their differences, participate in developing a fair organization, and deal directly with injustices.*

Procedures and processes that involve and give people a voice are extremely important for establishing justice.[23] Indeed, people sometimes value being involved more than how rewards are distributed, even to getting rich rewards for themselves. Having a voice and listening to others helps people understand the reasoning behind agreements, feel their questions have been addressed, and believe they have had some control and influence over the outcome. They have directly confronted different interests and discussed opposing positions. They understand the rationale behind the decision.

People, removed from deciding the issue, easily second guess the decision and suspect its rationale. They are apt to be insensitive to conflicting, legitimate interests and points of view. When workers are uninformed about the financial state of the company and its need to attract investors, they focus on their own claims for higher wages, not company profits. Uninvolved people often feel they have been unjustly treated, and angrily want compensation.

It is through the give and take, the back and forth of team discussion that people come to understand everyone's contributions and needs and accept the rules that should be used and how they should be applied. People are willing to accept less than they hoped, if they come to see why the present agreement is mutually acceptable and to the extent possible that it satisfies the legitimate interests of all.

Effective teams also promote justice by providing the social support for people to discuss their frustrations and sense of injustice openly. Unexpressed conflict and frustrations are great threats to a group or organization. Without giving voice to the issues, people harbor their sense of grievance, feel unfairly treated, and want to leave.[24]

As they regularly reflect on their workings as a group and their progress, teams provide a structured forum for discussing frustrations before people feel highly aggrieved. Team members know that they cannot be highly productive unless everyone feels empowered and motivated. Their cooperative goals encourage open discussion of differences and the use of conflict to find mutually agreeable solutions.[25]

Involvement in deciding how rewards should be distributed, determining rules, and settling disputes promotes fairness and justice in organizations. Belonging to a team that manages itself, reflects on its experiences, and deals with conflicts openly convinces employees they are not suckers being exploited, but their contributions are fairly compensated and their concerns responded to. They believe they work for a company that represents their own ideals.


## INNOVATION AND COMMITMENT DILEMMA

> Love is loyalty. Love is teamwork. Love respects the dignity of the individual. Heartpower is the strength of your corporation.
>
> Vince Lombardi

Contemporary organizations confront a dilemma. Though innovation is a necessity and requires commitment, the very need to innovate has undermined traditional ways to develop commitment. Job security and long-term employment are less desirable and less credible bases for commitment. Companies have had to restructure their businesses and lay off long-service employees to adapt to the changing marketplace and shareholder demands for higher returns. Values have also shifted. Changing jobs is no longer seen as disloyalty, but a sign that people want new challenges and opportunities to grow. The idea that people may need and want to change careers is also gaining currency.

Job changes and short-term assignments also mean that people often work with others they do not know well. They will have less time to develop friendships and networks to help them do their tasks and feel integrated and committed. Working with people who remain strangers results in distancing from one's work and organization.

Companies are told to innovate to attract today's savvy consumer, but employees are also demanding and selective. Companies must experiment with how they are managed in order to engender the commitment and caring needed to prosper in the contemporary environment. Strong relationships, though more difficult to develop in the changing workplace, are increasingly important to integrate employees with each other and with their work. Investing in relationships through positive teams pays off in ongoing improvement and innovation.

## CONCLUDING COMMENTS

Today's employees, surveys suggest, want the traditional economic benefits of job security, opportunities to make as much money as they can, and good retirement programs. But they want more: their work should be intrinsically meaningful.[26] In one survey, 88% of US employees said it was personally important to them to 'work hard and to do their best on the job.' In another survey, the majority of respondents agreed with the statement, 'I have an inner need to do the very best job I can, regardless of pay.' Only one out of four thought a job was just an economic necessity or simply an economic transaction. Employees want their companies to be successful, to give them well-paying jobs, and their work to be meaningful and rewarding.

Teamwork melds organizational requirements to be successful and human needs for achievement and solidarity. Teams assigned to complete projects, especially complex, challenging ones like innovating, can be highly rewarding and fulfilling. People meet their individual achievement needs to accomplish tasks, but at the same time influence others and gain their support, companionship, and esteem. They strengthen their own self-esteem as competent, compassionate, and fair by furthering the values and success of their team and company. But teams must be well-structured and cooperative to integrate people and productivity.

Teams give innovation a human face. Employees in well-run teams have the challenge to succeed, the support of colleagues, and the opportunities to influence and be a part of a larger effort. These incentives propel them to persist, overcome hurdles, and generate and implement changes. There is distress and worry as well as challenge and discovery in change. People are charting new ground, but team members need not do it alone. They can feel reassured and rely on the stability and security of working with trusted others.

## GAINING COMMITMENT AT DAEWOONG PHARMACEUTICAL COMPANY (KOREA)

The energy and commitment of employees are thought to be powerful forces behind the incredible economic growth of Asian countries like Korea. But companies there too have to earn the respect and commitment of employees.

Daewoong Pharmaceutical struggled in the 1970s.[27] Employees were uncommitted, and even stole from the company and each other. But since 1978 it has been ranked in the top class for growth, safety, and profitability. In 1981 it ranked first in Korea in sales and profit growth.

Teamwork has been critical for this transformation. The company has promoted employee ownership and involvement. Its labor–management consultation council hears disputes and deals with conflicts. It discusses common issues of productivity, worker welfare, training, and grievances. Some 89% of the employees own 32% of the stock.

The company has a motivating *vision* that speaks directly to the needs and interests of employees. Its motto is 'You can get without fail what you endeavor for' and recruits new employees with 'Let's meet in the Daewoong Paradise.' Its philosophy emphasizes basic values of honesty, faith, gratitude, and creativity. Mr Yoon, the principal owner, says, 'If you plant a soybean, don't expect a redbean to grow from it.'

Employee ownership helps *unite* the company. In addition, company-wide bonuses are given employees based on company performance. Employees are *empowered* through extensive education and health programs, and their suggestions are used to improve work. They use the labor–management council and other work groups to *explore* issues and resolve problems. Conflicts and grievances are *reflected* upon and dealt with, not swept under the rug, and employees work for continuous improvement.

# REFERENCES

1. Meyer, J. P., Paunonen, S. V., Gellatly, I. R., Goffin, R. D. and Jackson, D. N. (1989). Organizational commitment and job performance: it's the nature of the commitment that counts. *Journal of Applied Psychology*, 74, 152–156. O'Reilly, C., III and Chatman, J. (1986). Organizational commitment and psychological attachment: the effects of compliance, identification, and internalization on prosocial behavior. *Journal of Applied Psychology*, 71, 492–499.
2. Organ, D. W. (1988). *Organizational Citizenship Behavior: The Good Soldier Syndrome*. Lexington, MA: Lexington Books. Organ, D. W. and Konovsky, M. (1989). Cognitive versus affective determinants of organizational citizenship behavior. *Journal of Applied Psychology*, 74, 157–164.
3. Eisenberger, R., Fasolo, P. and Davis-LaMastro, V. (1990). Perceived organizational support and employee diligence, commitment, and innovation. *Journal of Applied Psychology*, 75, 51–59.
4. Walton, R. E. and Hackman, J. R. (1986). Groups under contrasting management strategies. In P. S. Goodman (ed.), *Designing Effective Work Groups*. San Francisco: Jossey-Bass, 168–201.
5. Jacobs, M. K. and Goodman, G. (1989). Psychology and self-help groups: predictions on a partnership. *American Psychologist*, 44, 536–545.
6. McClelland, D. C. (1987). *Human Motivation*. New York: Cambridge University Press.
7. Johnson, D. W. and Johnson, R. T. (1989). *Cooperation and Competition: Theory and Research*. Edina, MN: Interaction Book Company.

8. Tjosvold, D. and Tjosvold, M. (1983). *Working with the Elderly in Their Residences*. New York: Praeger.
9. Seligman, M. (1988). Boomer blues. *Psychology Today*, **22**, October, 50–55.
10. Kirmeyer, S. and Lin, T. (1987). Social support: its relationship to observed communication with peers and superiors. *Academy of Management Journal*, **30**, 138–151.
11. Fisher, C. D. (1985). Social support and adjustment to work: a longitudinal study. *Journal of Management*, **11**, 39–53.
12. Eisenberger, R., Huntington, R., Hutchison, S. and Sowa, D. (1986). Perceived organizational support. *Journal of Applied Psychology*, **71**, 500–507. Eisenberger, R., Fasolo, P. and Davis-LaMastro, V. (1990). Perceived organizational support and employee diligence, commitment, and innovation. *Journal of Applied Psychology*, **75**, 51–59.
13. Jecker, J. and Landy, D. (1969). Liking a person as a function of doing him a favor. *Human Relations*, **22**, 371–378.
14. Kaplan, M. F. (1987). The influencing process in group decision making. In C. Hendrick (ed.), *Group Process*. Newbury Park, CA: Sage, 189–212.
15. Wood, J. V. (1989). Theory and research concerning social comparisons of personal attributes. *Psychological Bulletin*, **108**, 231–248.
16. Ellis, R. and Taylor, M. (1983). Role of self-esteem within the job search process. *Journal of Applied Psychology*, **68**, 632–640. Shamir, B. (1986). Protestant work ethic, work involvement and the psychological impact of unemployment. *Journal of Occupational Behavior*, **7**, 25–28.
17. Johnson, D. W. and Johnson, R. T. (1989). *Cooperation and Competition: Theory and Research*. Edina, MN: Interaction Book Company.
18. Mead, G. H. (1934). *Mind, Self and Society*. Chicago, IL: University of Chicago Press. Brockner, J. (1988). *Self-esteem: Theory, Research, and Practice*. Lexington, MA: Lexington Books.
19. Brockner, J. (1988). *Self-esteem: Theory, Research, and Practice*. Lexington, MA: Lexington Books.
20. Eisenberger, R., Huntington, R., Hutchison, S. and Sowa, D. (1986). Perceived organizational support. *Journal of Applied Psychology*, **71**, 500–507. Fryxell, G. E. and Gordon, M. E. (1989). Workplace justice and job satisfaction as predictors of satisfaction with union and management. *Academy of Management Journal*, **32**, 851–866. Tyler, T. (1989). The psychology of procedural justice: a test of the group-value model. *Journal of Personality and Social Psychology*, **57**, 830–838.
21. Deutsch, M. (1985). *Distributive Justice: A Social-psychological Perspective*. New Haven, CT: Yale University Press. Johnson, D. W. and Johnson, R. T. (1989). *Cooperation and Competition: Theory and Research*. Edina, MN: Interaction Book Company. Pfeffer, J. and Langston, N. (1988). Wage inequality and the organization of work: the case of academic departments. *Administrative Science Quarterly*, **33**, 588–606.
22. Cespedes, F. V., Doyle, S. X. and Freedman, R. J. (1989). Teamwork for today's selling. *Harvard Business Review*, March–April, 44–53.
23. Folger, R. and Konovsky, M. A. (1989). Effects of procedural and distributive justice on reactions to pay raise decisions. *Academy of Management Journal*, **32**, 115–130. Greenberg, J. (1987). A taxonomy of organizational justice theories. *Academy of Management Review*, **12**, 9–22.
24. Withey, M. and Cooper, W. H. (1989). Predicting exit, voice, loyalty, and neglect. *Administrative Science Quarterly*, **34**, 521–539.
25. Deutsch, M. (1980). Fifty years of conflict. In L. Festinger (ed.), *Retrospections on Social Psychology*. New York: Oxford University Press, 46–77. Tjosvold, D. (in

press). Rights and responsibilities of dissent: cooperative conflict. *Employee Rights and Responsibilities Journal.*

26. Hundley, J. (1987). J. C. Penney relies on people power. In Y. K. Shetty and V. M. Buehler (eds), *Quality Productivity and Innovation: Strategies for Gaining Competitive Advantage.* New York: Elsevier, 81–101.

27. Euh, Yoon-Dae (1989). Daewoong Pharmaceutical Company. In Dong-Ki Kim and Linsu Kim (eds), *Management behind Industrialization: Reading in Korean Business.* Seoul: Korea University Press, 540–578.

# 7 Leadership

'You social science types are tricky and cagey,' Scott said, looking at Marian as the meeting of the TLC began.

'I'm a tiger in a cage, you said,' Marian shot back. She felt more comfortable mixing it up with the group.

'I'm sure he meant a beautiful Bengal tiger,' Art said.

'Now we know why you're in marketing, Art,' Miles said.

'As I was seriously exploring the issues so that we would all better understand our vision and feel more empowered . . . ,' Scott joined in the fun.

'So you have been listening,' Kyle said to Scott.

'But now I'm talking, or trying to!' Scott said to general laughter. 'Seriously, we've talked a lot about how groups can be good for the company to keep it on top of changes, and for the people as well. We've said that teams reconcile the requirements of organizations and the needs of people. Let's say I buy that. But there's a strong catch to all of this. This little word "can." Groups can innovate and involve, but they don't always.'

'That's true,' Art agreed. 'We've all been in groups that abuse people and fritter away opportunities.'

'Groups can sink to the lowest common denominator,' Miles said.

'People sometimes just don't care, and everyone lets the other guy do it. Guess what? Nothing gets done,' Scott said.

'What also seems a part of all this is our role as leaders,' Kyle said. 'We might give our teams this power and responsibility, and we become very dependent upon them, but if they don't come through, how are we supposed to deal with that?'

'It seems to me that we're giving up a lot to these groups,' Scott said. 'It's the classic case where we're held accountable but we don't have the power and authority to do it. These groups are responsible and are supposed to do things, but we're blamed if they don't come through.'

'We'll be held accountable, no doubt about that,' Miles said. 'Then we should have the control, not these groups.'

'I've been thinking along different lines,' Art said. 'These groups would give us more control and power in the sense that they would help us accomplish our objectives and vision. We're not going through all the trouble to develop teams if they aren't going to be useful to us.'

'The teams should extend our influence and reach, not limit us,' Marian said. 'We might be giving them some autonomy and decision-making responsibility, but that's so they can be more successful—more empowered—to accomplish your group's vision.'

'But won't they make us more dependent and, thus, vulnerable?' Kyle asked.

'Look around, Kyle, we're already dependent,' Art said. 'You can't lead by yourself—you have to have followers, and when you have followers you depend on them, and they depend upon you.'

'The issue is not whether as leaders we will give up something to our employees or be dependent upon them, that's a reality,' Marian said. 'Our challenge is to set up our relationships with them so that we can all be successful. Teams can help us do that.'

Scott remarked, 'There's the word "relationship" again.'

'That's the heart of leadership—developing productive links with followers. And relationships are by nature two-way streets,' Marian said.

'You're telling us that great leaders establish relationships,' Kyle said. 'That's news to me. I thought they were inspiring, charismatic transformers with high impact.'

'I read where leaders were effective influencers, Kyle said.

'But leaders must inspire . . . must influence someone else,' Marian said. 'If your people aren't inspired and influenced, then you aren't much of a leader. And you can't influence someone very much if they mistrust you.'

'How come you see these guys in business magazines with articles talking about how they single-handedly, against great odds, turned bankruptcy into success?' Scott asked.

'Sells magazines,' Marian said. 'But read those articles carefully. Usually, the leader will talk about how he couldn't do it without the team around him, without everyone in the organization pitching in. Granted, you might not read about it till the end of the article.'

'But you're talking about relationships among employees, not just with us as leaders,' Scott said.

'The beauty of teams is that people are helping the leader by encouraging colleagues to work well and hard on the group task,' Marian said. 'Leaders do not have to try to supervise and coach everyone by themselves, but get help from team members.'

'But using teams to strengthen relationships among employees—that is a different way of looking at leadership,' Art said.

'It may sound foreign, but you guys already believe it,' Marian said. 'I've heard you talk about good communication being so important. That's another way of saying the same thing. Open, two-way communication and influence between you and your employees and among your employees are vital to a good leader relationship; they are essential to being a leader.'

'An interesting idea, and I want to think more about leaders and relationships,' Scott said. 'But getting back to my basic issue of "can". Teams can innovate and involve, but they may not. So what is to assure that our team "will" do these things?'

'Leadership, for one thing,' Marian answered. 'You need to work with your people to make the groups into teams that work.'

'We can't just throw our people together, and tell them be effective,' Art said. 'We have to work with them.'

'That's where the team organization model comes in,' Marian said.

'What happens, though, if the group is just not motivated?' Kyle asked. 'All the talk is not going to help that.'

'To me, lack of motivation usually means a number of things,' Marian said. 'Remember, the team members must themselves envision, feel united, feel empowered, explore alternatives, and reflect on their experiences. They have to buy into and then do it. It is not enough for you to want them to, *they* must want to.'

'So you are telling us that it is their choice really, we don't control that,' Scott said. 'Be how are we supposed to lead when we don't have the proper authority?'

'I could say that you have the authority and power to make them believe,' Marian said. 'But that's not true. It's not me saying that you don't have the clout to force them—that's just the nature of people. But you still have power and authority. You can work with your people so that they understand and have the skills to be an effective team. They have to decide for themselves, but you can help them make this decision.'

'That relates back to your ideas about leadership being a relationship,' Art said. 'The success of any team, then, should be credited both to the leader and the team.'

'Right,' Marian said. 'Leadership is a "we" thing, something leaders and followers do together. Their successes and failures should be shared.'

'Let's look at our own leader, Allan,' Art suggested. 'He can talk all he wants about teamwork, but if we don't believe and carry through, it's not going to happen.'

'So you are going to tell me that the CEO does not have a lot of clout, that he's dependent upon us,' Scott said. 'I'll take that kind of dependence, especially at his salary.'

'But he's dependent,' Art said. 'I remember his talking about how he felt dependent upon everyone.'

'Look at when there's an oil spill or chemical leak, the company's CEO is given all kinds of flack,' Marian said. 'I bet the CEOs didn't realize how dependent they were on the pilot of the ship, on the engineer at the chemical plant, but they do after the disaster.'

'It does seem like CEOs are the ones that really get the heat,' Kyle said. 'I guess the public holds them responsible for the company.'

'If our food gets people sick,' Miles said, 'the CEO and all of us will be held responsible.'

'The CEO gets it because he's supposed to have developed the kind of organization that does not walk into a disaster,' Scott said.

'That's my point,' Marian put in. 'Allan needs to work with us, and us with him. We should share the glory and the heat that goes with that.'

'Some more things to think about,' Kyle said. 'But what are we supposed to *do* with our teams?'

'That's the question that we should start to answer over the next weeks,' Marian said. 'My short answer is that we and our groups can use the team organization model to become more effective and overcome the obstacles that stand in our way. But using the model requires planning and experimenting. We have challenges ahead.'


# TEAM LEADERSHIP

Leaders listen, take advice, lose arguments, and follow . . . I didn't turn the company around. I presided over it. The people in this company turned it around. I was the captain of the ship, but they were doing all the rowing.

Irwin Fedries, President and CEO, Monolithic Memories

The reason we were so good, and continued to be so good, was because he [Joe Paterno] forces you to develop an inner love among the players. It is much harder to give up on your buddy, than it is to give up on your coach. I really believe that over the years the teams I played on were almost unbeatable in tight situations. When we needed to get that six inches we got it because of our love for each other. Our camaraderie existed because of the kind of coach and the kind of person Joe was.

Dave Joyner

What are leaders in organizations about and how are they successful? Managers and researchers have over the years come up with a great range of answers. Some successful leaders are driven visionaries, some are tough and demanding, and others caring and supportive. Researchers have concluded that leadership depends upon the circumstances: an approach effective in one situation is not effective in another.

The team organization model argues that leaders take their goals from the requirements of the organization and the needs of employees. They strive to create the productive teamwork necessary to gain the commitment of employees for continuous improvement and innovation.

Team leaders consistently focus on designing the team organization and breathing life into it. According to Steve Jobs, the founder of Apple Computer, 'Leaders are keepers of the dream.' But they do much more, for they are 'keepers of the team.' They work to have employees passionate about their vision, feel united and purposeful, be empowered to get things done, explore alternatives, and reflect and keep on learning.

Though focused on developing teamwork for innovation and commitment, leaders are highly flexible in their methods. They work on aspects of teamwork most critical for success. Some teams can benefit most from a sharpening of the vision, some by boosting confidence and power, and others by reflecting on the anger and conflict in the group. And leaders will use many approaches and strategies in dealing with these critical issues.

But leaders do not create a team single-handedly. They work with and through others so that everyone is committed to making their group innovative and involving. Like developing a new product, making a new technology work, or implementing a new organization design, leadership to create a team is a "we" thing done by managers and employees together.

## THE LEADERSHIP CHALLENGE

Leadership appears to be the art of getting others to want to do something that you are convinced should be done.

Vance Packard

The few projects in my study that disintegrated did so because the manager
failed to build a coalition of supporters and collaborators.

Rosabeth Moss Kanter, The Change Masters

Teamwork requires passion and persistence. *Leaders must be courageous* to
look to the future, and break away from old habits and outworn ideas. *Employees have to take risks* to learn new ideas and skills and overcome suspicions.
Leading and working in a team is not a simple, automatic process, but
challenges us to use our central abilities.

Researchers have documented what every manager knows: groups face a
number of obstacles that can undermine their success. Indeed, some researchers have concluded that defective interaction among groups will inevitably
result in process losses that prevent the group from utilizing its full resources.[1]
Groups confront threats that frustrate their ability to envision, unite,
empower, explore, and reflect.


## THREATS

Team members are not automatically committed to a vision. They can easily
feel they are going through the motions without much purpose. Groups can
even gang up against the assigned task and work against it.[2] Groups have been
observed to pressure people to restrict their productivity to maintain an easy
pace of work.[3] Inspiring commitment to a company vision is particularly
difficult when divisions have worked at cross-purposes with a sense of
superiority and competition.

Silence, nodding heads, and talk of teamwork do not themselves mean that
a team is united behind common goals. Team members often conclude that
their goals are independent, even opposing. Competition and independence
can seem appealing for they do not require the time and skill to collaborate.
Competition is stronger when the organization rewards and promotes people
for outperforming others. Impersonal attitudes and ineffectively handled
conflict undermine cooperative goals.

The organization may not provide the mandate and resources the group
believes it needs to get the job done. Team members may lack confidence in
themselves and each other; their sense of powerlessness undermines motivation and success.[4] The group may fail to develop a useful division of labor:
'I'm the thinkist, and you're the typist.'[5] Expecting a free ride and not held
accountable, individuals do not pitch in; others retreat because they do not
want to be 'suckers' who are exploited. As a result, no one feels responsible
and committed.

Teams often fail to investigate issues comprehensively, create a range of
alternatives, and select an effective solution.[6] Teams have been found to fall
into 'groupthink' in which opposing views are systematically suppressed.

Social psychologists assume that people often want to reduce dissonance and reach premature closure rather than explore various options.[7]

Self-serving biases can prevent an accurate assessment of performance. People have been found to take credit for success, but not for failure.[8] Sensitive and aware of their own contributions, they devalue others. Argyris and Schon[9] found that managers use a great deal of energy and time trying to avoid discussing conflicts. Without a way of reflecting on doubts about others' commitment and discussing their frustrations, teams will either explode or wither.

## LEADERSHIP OPPORTUNITIES

> Whenever anyone asks me [how to develop leaders] I tell them I have the secret to success in life. The secret to success is to stay in love. Staying in love gives you the fire to really ignite other people, to see inside other people, to have a greater desire to get things done than other people. A person who is not in love doesn't really feel the kind of excitement that helps them to get ahead and lead others and to achieve. I don't know any other fire, any other thing in life that is more exhilarating and is more positive a feeling than love is.
> Army Major General John H. Stanford

What are leaders to do? Leaders are more than visionary thinkers; they are doers who get things done. Yet they do not 'make' things in the traditional sense but rather oversee, identify and break down barriers, engage and involve, and in other ways help employees succeed. Leaders create the conditions under which employees get things done and make the organization productive and innovative.

Leaders are critical to stimulate the ongoing revitalization teams need. Teams have to update their vision, renew their unity, feel confident they can meet present challenges, openly solve problems, and honestly assess themselves. Teams will look for knowledge and inspiration from their leaders to overcome obstacles and improve their performance.

There is always the threat of 'process losses' and decline. But there is also the possibility of 'process gains' and rejuvenation. However, creating a team is much more than identifying people, finding a convenient time to meet, and giving a speech on the value of teamwork. *It takes persistent, joint work by leaders and employees to make individuals into a team.*

Leaders form and rally the team and help members get excited about the vision and task, feel together and powerful, able to explore and solve issues, and maintain momentum by celebrating successes and dealing with problems. Groups inevitably stumble and confront obstacles. Leaders do not dismiss the group as unmotivated and find a scapegoat to blame, but hold the whole group, including themselves, accountable and work together to overcome barriers.

It is not enough that managers want their teams to perform. Employees must want to and have the skills and opportunity to be effective. The team organization model identifies the conditions for high performance. Leaders must work diligently and skillfully so that team members themselves become committed to the vision, feel united, have a sense of power, explore alternatives, and reflect in order to improve continually.

# RESEARCH: LEADERSHIP AS RELATIONSHIP

In the process of work many of us are outstanding pitchers, able to throw the telling fastball, but it is also true that those pitchers can only be effective if there are many of us who are outstanding catchers.
                              Max De Pree, Chairperson and CEO, Herman Miller

Decision making proceeds not by 'recommendations up, orders down,' but by development of a shared sense of direction among those who must form the parade if there is going to be a parade.
                                        Harlan Cleveland, former US Ambassador

Traditionally, researchers have investigated the ways managers persuade, direct, and influence employees.[10] However, progress in identifying these strategies and documenting which ones are effective is disappointing.[11] A major limitation is that the impact of any strategy depends upon the relationship the leader has with the employee. A command may induce compliance and commitment with one employee, but resentment and resistance with another. To lead requires employees who want to be led.

## THE MYTH OF THE COMPETITIVE LEADER

Robert Helmreich and his associates[12] investigated how differences in the desire to achieve affected individuals' success. They proposed that the desire to achieve had three parts: competitiveness as the desire to win in interpersonal situations in which others must lose, mastery as the desire to take on challenging tasks, and work as positive attitudes toward working hard. To their surprise, they found that male Ph.D. scientists who were most successful as measured by citations of their work were high on mastery and work, but low on competitiveness. Competitive scientists apparently get distracted by attempts to outshine others and produce research that is more superficial and less sustained than that of less competitive ones.

Subsequent studies confirmed the basic findings. Successful (as measured by salaries) businessmen in large corporations had lower competitiveness and higher mastery and work scores than less successful ones. Similarly, less competitive airline pilots, airline reservation agents, supertanker crews, and students were all more effective than more competitive ones. The researchers were unable to identify any profession in which more competitive persons were more successful. Taking on challenges and hard work are not synonymous with competition. Indeed, it is when competitiveness is low that the desire for challenges and hard work results in success.

## LEADERSHIP AND COOPERATIVE GOALS

Recent studies document the central role of the relationship between the leader and employee. One hundred and ten medical laboratory workers identified the extent their leaders had developed cooperative, competitive, or independent relationships with them.[13] Leaders who had cooperative relationships, results suggest, inspired commitment and were considered competent. Competitive and independent leaders, on the other hand, were seen as obstructive and ineffective.

In a follow-up study, managers and employees were interviewed on specific incidents in which they worked together.[14] From the standpoint of both managers and employees, cooperative goals, in contrast to competitive goals, were found to improve the communication, exchange, and influence between them; this interaction in return resulted in progress on the job, efficient use of resources, strengthened confidence in future collaboration, and positive affect. Employees found independent managers obstructive.

The study also identified interactions that helped and interfered with productive work. In effective situations, leaders and employees assisted each other by sharing resources and expertise, integrated different points of view and ideas to solve problems, discussed issues to reach a mutually satisfying agreement, showed initiative, consulted with others, and followed proper procedures. Unproductive work was characterized by being unwilling to help and giving the task low priority, viewing the problem only from one's own perspective, refusing to discuss problems, strictly following job descriptions, ignoring advice, working in isolation, and failing to follow procedures.

The consequences of managerial styles and strategies depend upon the nature of the relationship that leaders and employees develop. Cooperative relationships foster collaborative, effective influence; competition leads managers to use tough, forceful strategies that backfire.[15]

## POWER AND AUTHORITY

The traditional view of power is that it is zero-sum: the more power the leader has, the less power employees have. The contemporary view is that power is expandable; the total amount of power can be enlarged so that leaders and employees both feel more powerful and influential.

Kanter,[16] an ardent champion of the value of power for organizations, proposed that employees prefer powerful managers who are able to protect them from unwanted interference and obtain organizational resources. Powerful managers are also thought to be more confident and willing to be helpful.

Studies have documented that leaders and employees who develop cooperative relationships are able to put power into constructive use. In a variety of situations, cooperative compared to competitive goals created higher expectations of assistance, more assistance, greater support, more persuasion and less coercion, and more trusting and friendly attitudes in power relationships.[17] Evidence collected in various organizations indicates that these dynamics and outcomes of cooperation occur in ongoing relationships.[18] Within cooperative relationships, employees and leaders are able to exchange resources and be productive.

As with power, authority can be buttressed and made more effective when it is shared. Leaders who used a collaborative, participative approach to using their authority were found to inspire commitment.[19] In contrast, both supervisors who wanted to control major decisions and supervisors who abdicated decision-making responsibilities were considered ineffective and frustrating.

The participation of employees in solving problems and making decisions can improve the quality of solutions and commitment to implement them.[20] However, a cooperative relationship is needed for employees to voice their opposing views, participate fully, and use the potential of shared decision making.

Successful leaders have various styles and personalities, and flexibly use different ways to influence others. What they have in common are interpersonal abilities and sensitivities.[21] They develop strong, cooperative relationships within which they influence, are open to influence, and work productively and together with employees.

*A leader without followers is not a leader.* Leaders develop relationships in which they are seen as powerful, authoritative, far-sighted, credible, capable, and trustworthy. These relationships also make employees powerful, far-sighted, and trustworthy. Leaders flexibly use methods and procedures appropriate for the situation, but consistently pursue cooperative relationships.

## THE LEADER'S ROLE

Managers have indicated that they spend their time managing groups and coordinating between them and see their role as designing and implementing effective group and intergroup work.[22] They develop group level performance indicators, diagnose and resolve problems within and between groups, negotiate with peers and superiors, and design and implement reward systems that support cooperative behavior. Executives, in addition, foster collaboration between the organization and its environment.

Leaders take the initiative for their groups to become a team. As discussed in the Introduction, the leader works with employees to develop a shared conviction of the value of teamwork, have a common understanding of the nature of productive teamwork, create appropriate, useful norms and procedures, and strive for continuous development. The last chapter discusses becoming a team organization at length. Leaders also need to adopt a role that supports teamwork every day.

## ARTICULATE A VISION AND FORMULATE OBJECTIVES

Leaders search out opportunities, challenge the status quo, and articulate an engaging vision for the team. In addition to sharing this vision, leaders identify tasks, put them into priority, and are prepared to explain their importance and how they relate to the vision of the team and the direction of the organization. Leaders use teams to complete complex tasks that require high-quality solutions; the benefits of using a team clearly outweigh the costs.

## UNITE BEHIND THE GROUP TASK AND REWARDS

Leaders identify the team's direction and tasks, and state their expectations and requirements. Employees and leaders together discuss the vision and tasks and use their different opinions to appreciate their priority and rationale. They may modify the project so that everyone understands its importance and is committed to completing it.

Leaders structure cooperative goals. They ask the team for a single product, and point out how they must collaborate to use their resources effectively. They indicate that individuals will be rewarded to the extent the team succeeds, and the group as a whole will be held responsible for failure. Leaders reveal their expectations that employees develop good work relationships in which they trust and care about each other and deal openly with problems and conflicts.

## EMPOWER, MONITOR, AND INTERVENE

They select employees with relevant information and expertise, and various views and backgrounds that can help the group succeed. Representatives from groups and departments with a stake in the task and its solution and people who are skilled at working with others are also included. They recognize that no one team size is best for all situations. The group should be large enough to include the resources and abilities needed to accomplish the task, but small enough so that people can coordinate without great costs.

Leaders and employees keep in touch and negotiate so that the team has needed information and assistance. Leaders observe meetings and interview employees to collect information about team functioning. They encourage them to deal with conflicts openly and mutually. They intervene actively when needed to teach skills and help the team solve problems.

## EXPLORE, COMMIT, AND IMPLEMENT

Leaders structure controversy by including people with different perspectives, assigning someone to be a devil's advocate, and forming sub-groups with opposing views. They have the team use consensus decision making to the extent appropriate so that all employees understand and, at least to some extent, agree with the team's decisions. They encourage communication with others inside and outside the organization to help them solve problems and implement their plans. Employees publicly commit themselves to carry out the group's plans.

## REFLECT, EVALUATE, AND PROCESS

Leaders compare the team's output with expectations and praise success and challenge failures. They distribute rewards for joint success and hold the whole group accountable for failure. With the team, they reflect on its work to identify strengths and weaknesses. Employees discuss their differences openly to promote their common objectives and plan how to deal with them to be more productive in the future.

Leaders recognize that working hard and together is stressful and taxing as well as valuable. They encourage the heart: they cheer on employees, 'find someone doing something right,' recognize individual contributions to the common vision, celebrate their joint successes together, and provide emotional support.[23]

## LINK WITH THE ORGANIZATION

Leaders work to develop teamwork among their employees, but to do that within an organization requires acting as an ambassador for the team. They work to have the team's vision connected and contributing to the organization's vision. Managers keep their team appraised of the agenda of executives and other managers; they show executives how the team's efforts contribute to the organization's success. In this way, executives and other managers value and respect the team and provide it with resources.

## CONCLUDING COMMENTS

Research has constructed conflicting images of managers in organizations. Managers have been observed to live in a highly interpersonal world in which they are continually interrupted; their work is fragmented rather than goal-oriented and contemplative.[24] But managers have indicated that they see themselves as focused on promoting teamwork within and across groups.[25] Researchers have also given conflicting advice. Leaders are advised to speak and act consistently, for credibility and trustworthiness are essential for successful leadership.[26] On the other hand, researchers remind leaders that they must be flexible; the strategies they take must be appropriate to the situation.[27]

The team organization model reconciles these apparently inconsistent images and advice. Leaders persist tirelessly to develop strong relationships with employees, and relationships among employees. More specifically, they are committed to work with their employees to develop a team, united behind an engaging vision with a deep sense of confidence and the ability to explore and reflect. Yet the specific methods they take to develop these teams are varied. The way they work, indeed, the very nature of the vision itself, will depend upon circumstances and the needs of the team. A leader works closely with a newly formed team, for example, but lets a developed one be more self-managing.

The team organization model is not an easy, quick fix to managing well or a blueprint for action, but it provides an integrated framework to understand leadership and to lead. Part III describes ways that leaders and employees can together create a team that serves them and their organization.

## REFERENCES

1. Steiner, I. D. (1972). *Group Process and Productivity*. New York: Academic Press.
2. Salomon, G. (1981). *Communication and Education: Social and Psychological Interactions*. Beverly Hills, CA: Sage.
3. Roethlisberger, F. J. and Dickson, W. J. (1939). *Management and the Worker*. Cambridge, MA: Harvard University Press.

4. Langer, E. and Rodin, J. (1976). The effects of choice and enhanced personal responsibility for the aged: a field experiment in an institutional setting. *Journal of Personality and Social Psychology*, **34**, 191–198.
5. Sheingold, K., Hawkins, J. and Char, C. (1984). 'I'm the thinkist, you're the typist': the interaction of technology and the social life of classrooms. *Journal of Social Issues*, **40**, 49–61.
6. Simon, H. A. (1976). *Administrative Behavior*. New York: Free Press.
7. Wood, J. V. (1989). Theory and research concerning social comparisons of personal attributes. *Psychological Bulletin*, **108**, 231–248.
8. Leary, M. R. and Forsyth, D. R. (1987). Attributions of responsibility for collective endeavors. In C. Hendrick (ed.), *Group Processes*. Newbury Park, CA: Sage, 167–188.
9. Argyris, C. and Schon, D. (1978). *Organizational Learning*. Reading, MA: Addison-Wesley.
10. Campbell, J. (1977). The cutting edge of leadership: an overview. In J. G. Hunt and L. L. Larson (eds), *Leadership: The Cutting Edge*. Carbondale, IL: Southern Illinois University Press, 221–234. Stogdill, R. M. (1974). *Handbook of Leadership*. New York: Free Press.
11. Davis, T. R. and Luthans, F. (1984). Defining and researching leadership as a behavioral construct: an idiopathic approach. *Journal of Applied Behavioral Science*, **20**, 237–252.
12. Helmreich, R. (1982). *Pilot selection and training*. Paper presented at the annual meeting of the American Psychological Association, August, Washington, DC. Helmreich, R., Beane, W., Lucker, W. and Spence, J. (1978). Achievement motivation and scientific attainment. *Personality and Social Psychological Bulletin*, **4**, 222–226. Helmreich, R., Sawin, L. and Carsrud, A. (1986). The honeymoon effect in job performance: temporal increases in the predictive power of achievement motivation. *Journal of Applied Psychology*, **71**, 185–188. Helmreich, R., Spence, J., Beane, W., Lucker, W. and Matthews, K. (1980). Making it in academic psychology: demographic and personality correlates of attainment. *Journal of Personality and Social Psychology*, **39**, 896–908.
13. Tjosvold, D., Andrews, I. R. and Jones, H. (1983). Cooperative and competitive relationships between leaders and their subordinates. *Human Relations*, **36**, 1111–1124.
14. Tjosvold, D. (1988). Interdependence and power between managers and employees: a study of the leader relationship. *Journal of Management*, **15**, 49–64.
15. Tjosvold, D., Johnson, D. W. and Johnson, R. T. (1984). Influence strategy, perspective-taking, and relationships between high and low power individuals in cooperative and competitive contexts. *Journal of Psychology*, **116**, 187–202.
16. Kanter, R. M. (1979). Power failure in management circuits. *Harvard Business Review*, 67–75. Kanter, R. M. (1977). *Men and Women of the Corporation*. New York: Basic Books.
17. Tjosvold, D. (1981). Unequal power relationships within a cooperative or competitive context. *Journal of Applied Social Psychology*, **11**, 137–150. Tjosvold, D. (1985). The effects of attribution and social context on superiors' influence and interaction with low performing subordinates. *Personnel Psychology*, **38**, 361–376. Tjosvold, D. (1985). Power and social context in superior–subordinate interaction. *Organizational Behavior and Human Decision Processes*, **35**, 281–293.
18. Tjosvold, D. (1988). Interdependence and power between managers and employees: a study of the leader relationship. *Journal of Management*, **15**, 49–64. Tjosvold, D. (1988). Cooperative and competitive interdependence: collaboration between departments to serve customers. *Group and Organization Studies*, **13**,

274–289. Tjosvold, D. (1988). The goal linkage approach to interaction between organizational groups. *International Journal of Management*, **5**, 201–208.

19. Tjosvold, D., Andrews, I. R. and Jones, H. (1985). Alternative ways leaders can use authority. *Canadian Journal of Administrative Sciences*, **2**, 307–317.

20. Richter, F. and Tjosvold, D. (1981). Effects of student participation in classroom decision-making on attitudes, peer interaction, motivation and learning. *Journal of Applied Psychology*, **65**, 74–80. Tjosvold, D. (1987). Participation: a close look at its dynamics. *Journal of Management*, **13**, 739–750. Tjosvold, D. (1985). Dynamics within participation: an experimental investigation. *Group and Organizational Studies*, **10**, 260–277.

21. Ellis, R. J. (1988). Self-monitoring and leadership emergence in groups. *Personality and Social Psychology Bulletin*, **14**, 681–693. McClelland, D. C. and Boyatzis, R. E. (1982). Leadership motive pattern and long-term success in management. *Journal of Applied Psychology*, **67**, 737–743.

22. Kraut, A. I., Pedigo, P. R., McKenna, D. D. and Dunnette, M. D. (1989). The role of the manager: what's really important in different management jobs. *Academy of Management Executive*, **3**, 286–293.

23. Johnson, D. W. and Johnson, R. T. (1989). *Leading the Cooperative School*. Edina, MN: Interaction Book Company. Kouzes, J. M. and Posner, B. Z. (1987). *The Leadership Challenge*. San Francisco: Jossey-Bass.

24. Mintzberg, H. (1973). *The Nature of Managerial Work*. New York: Harper & Row.

25. Kraut, A. I., Pedigo, P. R., McKenna, D. D. and Dunnette, M. D. (1989). The role of the manager: what's really important in different management jobs. *Academy of Management Executive*, **3**, 286–293.

26. Kouzes, J. M. and Posner, B. Z. (1987). *The Leadership Challenge*. San Francisco: Jossey-Bass.

27. Stogdill, R. M. (1974). *Handbook of Leadership*. New York: Free Press.

# Part III: Creating Teamwork

Working together in a democratic fashion on a day-to-day basis proved to be the hardest thing most of us had ever done. It gets easier as trust grows and mutual respect deepens—and as all can see the payoff.

Patricia Carrigan, Plant Manager, General Motors

The challenge is to create spirited, productive, and enhancing teamwork. How can divisiveness, mistrust, and rivalry be replaced with a conviction of shared destiny and community? The chapters in this section describe the ingredients of teamwork and identify how managers and employees can envision an engaging direction, feel united and empowered, explore alternatives to solve problems, and reflect on progress to grow.

# 8 Envision

A compelling shared vision directs and energizes an organization and a group. People not only understand where the organization is headed and why, but feel a sense of urgency and adventure toward it. They are confident they can move the organization to where it wants to go. Without this engaging common direction, they feel detached and retreat to pursuing private agendas.

A company vision should define both its business mission and its organization culture. A strategy, regardless of how elegant, requires organizational effort to be realized. A viable business strategy in turn unites and empowers people to work together. When the business strategy and organization framework are in sync, then the company vision inspires.

Yet there is no blueprint for what this common vision should be. Each company must create its own business mission and strategic thrusts that capitalize on its particular strengths and market opportunities. Each company must also develop its own organization framework that fits its personality and situation. The team organization model suggests major characteristics of that framework, but the particular procedures, norms, and styles to facilitate collaboration need to be created.

## VISION AT J. C. PENNEY'S

The Penney Idea, formulated in 1913, aspires:

1. To serve the public, as nearly as we can, to its complete satisfaction.
2. To expect for the service we render a fair remuneration and not all the profit the traffic will bear.
3. To do all in our power to pack the customer's dollar full of value, quality, and satisfaction.
4. To continue to train ourselves and our associates so that the service we give will be more and more intelligently performed.
5. To improve constantly the human factor in our business.
6. To reward men and women in our organization through participation in what the business produces.
7. To test our every policy, method, and act in this wise: Does it square with what is right and just?

Though the language may be a little old-fashioned, the message is up to date. The Penney Idea focuses the whole company on the challenge of competitive advantage by creating value for customers so that the company can remain prosperous. It recognizes the need for continuous development in the skills of people and in how they work together to improve service. The vision also speaks to the values and needs of employees. Men and women are to share in the rewards of a successful company, strengthen their abilities, and be treated fairly.

The Penney Idea, of course, must be lived and translated into action. It is not enough to be recited at company functions or displayed in employee lunch rooms. Ongoing teams that involve associates are an integral part of the company and consistent with its vision of productive partnership.[1] Teams have shared responsibility for operating results: the company recognizes that no one person can make the company successful. After senior management identifies issues, *ad hoc* teams are used to bring pertinent viewpoints and information to bear before a decision is made. The company uses pay to support these teams. All managers have a sizeable portion of their income based on how well their teams perform. Many of the 70 000 sales associates are rewarded on the performance and performance improvement of their teams.

The Penney Idea and teamwork integrate the company requirements to serve both customers and employees. The vision, though, does not straitjacket the company into one particular strategy; it has recently repositioned itself in the competitive retail marketplace.[2] Its values and teamwork will, it appears, continue to serve the company well into the future.

# AN ENGAGING VISION

*A vision portrays an uplifting and ennobling future.*[3] By challenging the status quo and taking risks, leaders and employees create a forward-looking ideal of where they should be. Their ideal is possible, but stretches the imagination and abilities of the team. The vision shows the people how they are unique, and indicates how they can meet their own interests.

A vision is much more than lofty sounding ideals ground out by the public relations department. Managers and employees working together have to forge a vision that fits the company's own particular situation and become committed to it. Both the business strategy and the organization frameworks need to be rational, meaningful, and challenging.

Visions are to inspire and direct people, but they first must be *rational and realistic*. People are not going to get fired up about ideas and plans that will not pay off. They must believe that the company has the strengths, abilities, and wherewithal to move toward realizing the business strategies and organization framework. The vision must 'fit' the company's environment in that it takes advantage of opportunities and wards off threats. It must be realistic in that it recognizes how competitors and legal restrictions may try to create barriers. The organization framework should be based on sound management ideas developed through empirical research.

To be motivated, people themselves must be convinced that the vision has value. *The vision has personal meaning.* They know that the vision will promote their own values and needs. They want the company recognition and monetary rewards that they will earn if their new product is successful in the marketplace. They want to feel proud and enhance their self-image by being part of a team that respects and appreciates people's racial diversity and personal individuality.

*An engaging vision has social significance.* Team members believe that people the group cares about will appreciate their efforts. They work hard to develop international marketing opportunities because their friends in the company will feel more secure and productive with more orders. The people at Savory want to see themselves as part of a company that brings highly nutritional affordable food to infants in developing countries. The work team takes pride in that their state's governor regularly buys their products.

*A motivating vision challenges.* Team members stretch their abilities to become more effective.[4] Difficult, but achievable, goals energize people to demonstrate to themselves that they can succeed.[5] They break out of the humdrum of the known to seek the excitement of furthering and demonstrating their competence. The members of the accounting group challenge themselves. 'We can, if we pull together, do what it takes to provide timely, useful information managers need to make decisions.'

*The vision is both stable and flexible.* The vision must adapt to emerging conditions, but it is not changed whimsically. The business mission and strategy provide ongoing direction, but must also be updated in light of new opportunities and threats. The organizational framework outlines the basic values and procedures for the company that keep people on the same wavelength. However, the ways the values are expressed and the specific procedures used must respond to the needs of employees and the strategy and objectives of the business.

Employees must know and understand the overall mission of the organization to work hard to realize it. *The vision must be shared.* All employees, not just top management, must believe. It can be useful to have team members help the leader formulate the vision so that they can adjust and modify it to fit their own particular needs. More basic is that employees are involved enough so that through discussion they come to understand the vision clearly and see how it is rational, promotes their personal aspirations, stretches their abilities, has value to significant others, and guides them to know where they are going.

# PITFALLS TO ENVISIONING

Groups and organizations are not inevitably committed to a shared direction. Indeed, *they may 'gang up against' official goals and tasks*.[6] They see the direction the leader wants as an incursion against them, and sabotage it. Highly cohesive groups are particularly able to withstand pressure from supervisors and work for their own objectives.[7]

*Visions can divide.* A group may be committed to its vision, but not the organization's. Groups in organizations easily adopt a competitive attitude toward each other, and soon see their goals in terms of outgoing and outperforming other departments.[8] They assume outsiders are on the 'other' side. Their internal cohesion may be based on distinguishing themselves and seeing the other groups as the 'enemy.' A vision can also split a company between those who believe and those who do not. A common danger is for top management to be keen, middle management doubtful, and employees suspicious.

Success, as well as failure, threatens. A prosperous company that stagnates encourages rivals to attack and penetrate its markets. Success can lull a company into rigid commitment to its strategy and framework, and leave it unprepared to change when circumstances warrant. *Complacency can turn the company's dream into a nightmare.*

# CREATING A VISION

> A loyal constituency is won when people, consciously or unconsciously, judge the leader to be capable of solving their problems and meeting their needs, when the leader is seen as symbolizing their norms, and when their image of the leader (whether or not it corresponds to reality) is congruent with their inner environment of myth and legend.
>
> John W. Gardner, *On Leadership*, NY, The Free Press, 1990

Four key principles guide creating an engaging, uniting common direction. First, managers and employees set the stage by developing their relationships so that they can begin work on a vision. Second, they challenge the accepted ways of working and proactively seek out the adventure to change rather than wait for a crisis that demands action. Third, the process of developing the vision models the kind of organization framework that the company aspires to: creating the vision itself furthers the desired team organization. Fourth, forging a vision is an ongoing process, not a one or two step quick fix.

## SETTING THE STAGE

What are the conditions that help managers and employees create an engaging vision? Dissatisfaction and pain have often been proposed as needed for an organization to make an effort to evaluate and try to form a more united approach.[9] Yet much pain and pessimism can lead to denial that there is much at stake and change is needed. They also can create a paralyzing sense of powerlessness and withdrawal. Both *incentives to change and the confidence that change can be implemented* are needed.

A company that has lost money, customers, and support has ample incentives for developing and refocusing the vision. Losing more money than any other company in history in 1981 was clear evidence for Ford management and employees that they should act![10] Yet even a company that is blessed with abundant customers and a healthy bottom line can develop an urgency by ascribing to excellence and taking the long-term view. Boeing in 1989 enjoyed tremendous business in commercial aviation, but might not that market attract not only European AirBus but Japanese competition, especially if the company does not maintain innovativeness and quality?

In addition to the business mission, people must see the need to revitalize how they are organized and managed, and believe they can. Here too, painful conditions can motivate but also debilitate. If people are highly suspicious and hostile, then discussing common goals may well seem at best abstract, and may cause great cynicism as people realize the discrepancy between talk and reality. *A central dilemma is that visions are expected to unite people and groups, but there must be some basic unity in their relationships before work toward a vision will succeed.*

(1) *Assess the business mission* Discussion with customers and industry experts and examination of the competition provide concrete tests of the strengths and weaknesses in the company's business strategy. Employees must consider the long-term viability and risks of the present course of action.

(2) *Reflect on the organization framework* Team members discuss the nature of productive teamwork and compare their work relationships to the team organization model. Are they united and empowered behind a common vision? Do people speak out and explore issues in depth?

(3) *Confront relationship issues* Managing long-standing conflicts may be necessary before serious work on a vision can begin. Once top management is able to convince employees that grievances and injustices will be considered and dealt with, then employees feel the need both to forge a vision and believe it is possible. Such direct dealing with conflicts also models the team organization leaders want as part of the company vision.

(4) *Take first steps* Incentives to sharpen the vision must be complemented with at least some confidence that the company can succeed. Beginning to improve the quality of the products, strengthening internal communication, dealing with conflicts, and taking other first steps convince people that the company is serious in that it has both the incentive and the wherewithal to move forward.

## CHALLENGING THE STATUS QUO

Leaders and employees continually search out opportunities to innovate and improve.[10] They understand that, even without any immediate danger, companies must continually revitalize and update. They will be better off if they strive for excellence rather than wait until forced to act. Crises catch people off guard, and while they compel action, that action may not be well-considered.[11] A crisis gives incentives for change, but may undercut confidence that meaningful change will happen. One of two crises can unite people as they recognize that they must pull together to survive. However, continual crises lose that motivational value and create a sense of powerlessness and despair.

(1) *Search for opportunities to initiate change, innovate, and grow* New assignments become challenges to turn around. People wonder if things could be done differently and better, and, rather than wait for a crisis to hit, find something that is 'broken' that they can fix. They break out of the routine and usual, and consider their work an adventure to enjoy.

(2) *Use frustrations and conflict* Employees talk about their concerns about the business strategy, and what bugs and annoys them about their jobs and work environment. They let each other know what they would like to change.

(3) *Take risks and learn from mistakes* People gather new ideas, try little experiments, model risk taking, and turn stress into excitement. People recognize that no new effort is risk-free and, while perfection can be striven for, it cannot be assumed or reached.

(4) *Present a short vision statement* A leader or task force evokes images and metaphors in describing the business mission and organization framework of the company. The leader persuasively and credibly communicates central values and aspirations in a five-minute speech.

## A TEAM APPROACH

It is a long-standing truism that organizational change does not happen unless the people at the top are committed to change. But it is also true that an inspiring vision is not going to happen unless people at the middle and low levels of the organization are also committed. A vision cannot inspire by itself; managers and workers have to want to be inspired. The vision of team needs to be reinforced by a team approach to developing it. Forcing cooperation is a contradiction.

(1) *Dialogue* Team members discuss opposing views to explore the vision and its potential significance for them and the organization. They are convinced by the reasoning behind it, and appreciate the risks of not changing and the opportunities the vision holds.

(2) *Include* The ideas and suggestions of team members are used to modify the vision to make it as motivating and uniting as possible. The business strategy and organization framework must make sense to employees before they will be committed to them.

## ONGOING

Rapid advances in technology, shortened life-cycles for products, and the globalization of markets are transforming the business landscape. Strategies must be continually updated to remain current and fresh. Companies realize that to keep on top of changes they need to form strategic alliances and joint ventures to pool resources. New business thrusts require new organizational frameworks. The professional and diverse workforce, employee demands for rights and participation, and changing notions of leadership make traditional management styles obsolete.

The team recognizes that no strategy or organization design can be assumed to be continually successful. They regularly re-examine their vision in light of new data and opportunities. In this way, they feel in control of their destiny, not overwhelmed by events.

(1) *Update* Periodically, the team revises its vision in light of change in and out of the group.

(2) *Confront complacency* Success is tempered with the recognition that future success is not guaranteed. The team again hears customers' ideas and complaints, and the predictions of industry experts, and reviews the competition.

(3) *Appreciate accomplishments* The team celebrates its capacity to change and rewards progress toward its vision.

Visions of the highest quality product and working together as a team are not costly, but are not easily established. It may be necessary to deal with an underlying distrust before talk about a vision becomes credible. The vision must be worked on, lived, and institutionalized. People will be tempted to fall back on old ways of thinking and working, and inevitably there will be bumps along the way that must be weathered and overcome. Business missions and team organizations are ongoing journeys, not destinations.

## VISION TO INTEGRATE AN ORGANIZATION

Setting the stage, challenging the status quo, dialoguing, and working toward ongoing development are much easier to do with a team of 10, than an organization of hundreds and thousands. But team development just focused on the department can very much interfere with organizational effectiveness. The team is united, but in a direction that does not complement, and even works against, other groups in the organization. The teams feel they are motivated and contributing, and self-righteously denounce other teams for not getting on board. What is needed is for groups within a large organization to be committed to common vision and seeing their roles as complementary.

Gary Jusela and his associates[12] developed an approach at Ford and Boeing for departments and groups to develop a system vision. In the early 1980s, Tom Page, executive vice president at Ford's Diversified Product Operations (DPO), whose eight divisions made automobile parts for Ford assembly plants, wondered how to get all managers behind the quality and teamwork vision outlined by Ford executives. How can 70 000 employees become committed to moving in one direction? How can middle managers be open to employee input and suggestions?

A team of consultants and managers interviewed potential participants and worked out a design, not to teach participative management, but to build a team around the actual business issues DPO confronted. They invited the top four levels of managers in each division, which ranged from 80 to 200 people, to attend a five-day seminar, usually broken into a three-day and a two-day part separated by several weeks. People worked with those up and down the hierarchy and across departments on the critical business issues of quality, cost containment, and need to be responsive.

Managers discussed with Tom Page and other executives their hopes and visions. They got feedback from their customers about their products and found out how their errors frustrated assembling quality cars and trucks. They heard testimonies from owners of Japanese cars. They examined the quality of the competition, and could see for themselves their weaknesses. Many groups got fired up about their preferred future state of affairs, and began taking first steps to improve their products for their customers.

The groups also examined how they worked together. They sent 'valentines' to reveal their 'sads,' 'glads,' and 'mads' about each other and publicly declared how they would respond to this feedback.

This system approach to envisioning reinforces the message of teamwork. Executives dialogue with managers about their vision, and involve them in shaping and implementing the vision. In this way, executives prepare managers to work as a team with their employees.

## GETTING GOING AT SAVORY

The TLC had discussed leadership as a 'we' thing for some time. They also reviewed the leadership steps of articulating a vision, uniting behind group task and rewards, empowering an intervening, exploring and implementing, reflecting and evaluating, and linking with the organization.

'We sure have spent a lot of time getting ready and talking about our hopes,' Miles said. 'But we have to act.'

'I've already been talking to my people about teamwork,' Art said. 'I like to give them as much lead time as possible. But I agree we should get going.'

'But planning is important,' Marian said. 'I often think that most managers know how to work with colleagues pretty well. They realize that impersonal competition really doesn't work. But when it comes to structuring work for other people or when there's a crisis, then ideas and ideology become very important. And many managers think, if competition is good for the economy, it must be good for our company too, and start pitting employees and groups against each other.'

'There're lots of managers who think an organization is a machine,' Kyle added. 'They think each person should do his job and not be bothered with or by others.'

'I've often thought it ironic that executives always want to be talking and interacting, but will set up organizations that expect workers to work in isolation,' Marian said.

'You could even say it's hypocritical,' Miles said with a laugh.

'As we're learning, just wanting teamwork is not enough; we have to know how to get it,' Kyle said.

'I think we are getting a good fix on just what our visions are for our teams, and how we need to involve them so that we can all get committed,' Art said.

'It is reassuring to know that our vision about teamwork is a rational one, that it does not just sound good,' Scott said. 'That will help us be credible.'

'We need to dialogue with our teams and help them fill our vision out,' Kyle reminded them.

'Just like Allan,' Marian said. 'He talks about teamwork and becoming a global company, but he needs us to take up the challenge, expand upon it, and go for it.'

'I would like to get Allan on the shop floor, and say those things,' Miles said. 'That would help us get this started.'

'Why not?' Art said. 'I think he would be very genuine and believable.'

The meeting ended with Art indicating that he planned to get his team plans working, and would report back at the next meeting.

# REFERENCES

1. Hundley, J. (1987). J. C. Penney relies on people power. In Y. K. Shetty and V. M. Buehler (eds), *Quality, Productivity and Innovation: Strategies for Gaining Competitive Advantage*. New York: Elsevier, 81–101.
2. Saporito, B. (1989). Retailing's winners and losers. *Fortune*, December 18, 69–78.
3. Kouzes, J. M. and Posner, B. Z. (1987). *The Leadership Challenge*. San Francisco: Jossey-Bass.
4. Argyris, C. (1970). *Intervention Theory and Method: A Behavioral Science View*. Reading, MA: Addison-Wesley.
5. Atkinson, J. W. (1984). *Introduction to Motivation*. New York: Van Nostrand.
6. Salomon, G. (1981). *Communication and Education: Social and Psychological Interactions*. Beverly Hills, CA: Sage.
7. Seashore, S. E. (1954). *Group cohesiveness in the industrial work group*. Ann Arbor, MI: Survey Research Center, Institute for Social Research.
8. Blake, R. R. and Mouton, J. S. (1989). Lateral conflict. In D. Tjosvold and D. W. Johnson (eds), *Productive Conflict Management: Perspectives for Organizations*. Minneapolis, MN: Team Media, 91–150. Friedkin, N. E. and Simpson, M. J. (1985). Effects of competition on members' identification with their subunits. *Administrative Science Quarterly*, **30**, 377–394.
9. Beckhard, R. and Harris, R. T. (1987). *Organizational Transitions: Managing Complex Change*. Reading, MA: Addison-Wesley.
10. Kouzes, J. M. and Posner, B. Z. (1987). *The Leadership Challenge*. San Francisco: Jossey-Bass.
11. Tjosvold, D. (1984). Effects of crisis orientation on managers' approach to controversy in decision making. *Academy of Management Journal*, **27**, 130–138.
12. Jusela, G. E. (1989). Personal communication. Jusela, G. E., Chairman, P., Ball, R. A., Tyson, C. E. and Dannermiller, K. D. (1987). Work innovations at Ford Motor. In Y. K. Shetty and V. M. Buehler (eds), *Quality, Productivity and Innovation: Strategies for Gaining Competitive Advantage*. New York: Elsevier, 123–145.

# 9 Creating Unity

> . . . man has almost constant occasion for the help of his brethren, and it is in vain for him to expect it from their benevolence only. He will be more likely to prevail if he can interest their self-love in his favour, and shew them that it is for their own advantage to do for him what he requires of them. Whoever offers to another a bargain of any kind, proposes to do this. Give me that which I want, and you shall have this which you want, is the meaning of every such offer; and it is in this manner that we obtain from one another the far greater part of those good offices which we stand in need of. It is not from the benevolence of the butcher, the brewer, or the baker, that we expect our dinner, but from their regard to their own interest. We address ourselves, not to their humanity but to their self-love, and never talk to them of our own necessities but of their advantages.
>
> Adam Smith, *Wealth of Nations*

A team united behind a vision into a shared purpose and destiny is in position to accomplish the extraordinary. It combines talents, examines problems from different perspectives, and achieves creative solutions. It fosters a family feeling, energizes and enlivens people, and makes them feel integrated into the organization.

*Unity must be forged; it cannot be assumed.* Putting people into a room and calling them a team do not make a unified force. Team members will not automatically be committed to their vision and willing to work together. They may well believe that their real interests compel them to work independently with little regard for others, or even that they should try to show up and outdo others. Competition and independence are real alternatives to cooperation.

How can leaders and members work together to attain unity? *Common goals* convince team members that they can only be successful together. They realize that they will *share their rewards;* either all of them will be rewarded or no one will be rewarded. The *task requires coordination.* They have *complementary roles* so that for one to be effective others have to fulfill their responsibilities. *Resources are distributed* among the team members. They develop a sense of *community membership* that gives them a common identity. Their *trusting attitude* makes them confident that their contributions will be reciprocated.

# FEELING UNITED

The feeling of unity remains special, though it is a common experience. People talk about how they are operating on the same wavelength, have a good relationship, and can communicate well. They believe they are operating in sync, moving in the same direction, and have common hopes and values. They understand what is good for one is good for all; they have found their common ground. They are part of the same community, celebrate each other's victories, and share each other's defeats. They have a 'we are in this together' feeling and believe they will 'swim or sink together.'

Unity derives from the belief team members have that their goals, aspirations, and interests are positively linked. They have concluded that, for one to be successful, others have to succeed. For Marian to accomplish her goal of promoting teams at Savory, then Kyle, Miles, Scott, and Art must know how to structure teams. For them to do so, they need to understand Marian and learn from her and each other. As discussed in Chapter 3, in cooperation, as one person moves toward goal attainment, others move toward reaching their goals.

## EXPERIENCE OF COOPERATION

The results of the perception of cooperative goals are profound. Team members strive for *mutual benefit* so that all gain from their group experience.[1] They recognize that what helps one helps others; one's productivity helps others be productive. They share a common destiny where they all gain or lose depending on the team's overall performance.

Team members recognize that their performance is *mutually caused* so that they have a *mutual investment* in each other and are *mutually responsible*. No team member works alone, but persons encourage and support each other. They realize that their own performance is a function not only of their own efforts, but also of the assistance of team members. People view themselves as instrumental in the productivity of others, and others instrumental in their own productivity. They feel a mutual obligation to assist and support each other.

The unity of goals creates a *shared identity*. Group members see themselves as individuals, and as part of the team. This identity binds people together emotionally. Feeling a part of the team results in camaraderie and belonging.

Team members expect to *share rewards*. The team's success is mutually caused, and its credit needs to be jointly celebrated. Team members take pride in the achievements of individual team members.

Unity is derived from a commitment to shared purpose and success. It is not based on altruism of giving without thought of getting. Rather, cooperative unity is based on the recognition that self-interests can be jointly pursued and enjoyed.

## COMPETITION AND INDEPENDENCE

Team members often reach quite different conclusions about how they depend upon each other. They may believe that their interests and goals are *independent*: the success of one neither helps nor interferes with others' success. Employees believe that their completed assignment will be appreciated and valued, and it matters little whether others have completed theirs. Or team members may believe their goals are largely *competitive*: success of one prohibits, or at least makes it more unlikely, that others will be successful. They expect to be appreciated and rewarded to the extent that they outdo and show they are better than others.

People in competition conclude they are working at cross-purposes; what is good for one is bad for the other; if one swims, the other sinks; they need to outshine and outperform others; their purpose is to win. As a consequence, they suspect that others will want them to fail, will avoid helping them, and may even sabotage their work. They use their abilities for their own benefit. They avoid dealing with conflict if possible, but if not, they fight win–lose battles. Faced with unsupportive, hostile colleagues, they feel frustrated and besieged.

Employees with independent goals see themselves as working alone; they are doing their own thing. They use their resources and information to pursue their own agenda; they neither expect help nor offer it. They feel impersonally distant, perhaps estranged and isolated.

Competition and independence are distinct alternatives, and research has shown that, though under most conditions both disrupt relationships, they have different dynamics. Studies also indicate that individuals and groups that compete also try to be independent.[2] People move away from competition to independence to reduce stress and hostility. But independence is impersonal and unrealistic because people in organizations are interdependent and need to interact. Many troubled relationships move back and forth between competition and independence.

Competitive and independent elements are inevitable in teams. Not every interest and goal of everyone will be cooperatively linked. Light competition —who has the best jokes, who can get the most people to donate to a charity —stimulates and adds excitement to group life. Team members will want to work independently on some tasks, especially straightforward ones. However, serious, ongoing competition and independence undermine the unity necessary for teams to be productive for the company and enhancing for people.

# FORGING UNITY

The honor of one is the honor of all.
The hurt of one is the hurt of all.
                              Creek Indian Creed

Team members themselves must believe their goals are cooperative and that they are united in their purpose. Leaders cannot themselves make team members believe their goals are cooperative; team members themselves must decide. The issue is not whether employees should or should not be involved and participate in forging this unity. They have to be. Reaching unity, like other great acts of leadership, is a 'we thing,' done with and for employees.

There is no direct, absolute link between the objective situation and conclusions about cooperation and competition. Scarce resources sometimes result in competition, and sometimes in cooperation. Having to pool outputs may lead to cooperative purpose, or to intense rivalry. Yet there are powerful strategies to strengthen unity. Leaders and team members can use goals, rewards, tasks, roles, membership, and attitudes to be convinced they are united.

## VISION AND GOALS

United employees believe the team has a shared vision and common set of goals that they are all striving to achieve and that success depends upon them all reaching these goals. The team management group is united to learn about teams in organizations, and develop the procedures and skills to put teamwork in place. They recognize that to the extent that they all discuss ideas and work together to implement their plans, they can all be successful together. Ways to structure cooperative goals include:

(1) *Explore the team's vision* All team members know the purpose and value of the team. They understand that no one can fulfill the vision alone; they must work together.

(2) *Analyze critical success factors to achieve vision* The team identifies what needs to be done, lists them in priority, and assigns people to be responsible for accomplishing them.[3]

(3) *Assign a task and ask for one product* The team as a whole is to make a set of recommendations, develop and produce a new product, or solve a problem. The manager wants team members to integrate their ideas and develop one solution. Individual team members sign off on the team's output indicating that they have contributed to and support it.

(4) *Keep track of group productivity* All workers average their individual output to form a group average for each week. Each worker is responsible for keeping their own output up, and for helping others improve theirs.

(5) *Promote group learning* All group members are expected to improve their skills in managing, selling, or operating machinery. The manager will chose at random one team member to demonstrate learning, and the team is rated on that basis. All team members are expected to help each other learn.

## COMMON TASKS

Tasks strengthen unity when team members understand that the work requires them to coordinate. Thompson[4] defined task interdependence in terms of work flow. In sequential task interdependence, one employee must complete a process before others can work on theirs. In pooled interdependence, everyone works on the output of everyone else. The greater the work flow interdependence, the more kinds of coordination procedures team members use.[5] Ways to structure tasks include:

(1) *Structure sequential interdependence* Team members recognize that they must complete the marketing survey before they can develop a marketing plan.

(2) *Structure pooled interdependence* Specialists have to integrate their ideas to develop a product that can be marketed and manufactured profitably.

(3) *Make the task challenging* Team members will be highly motivated to accomplish achievable, but difficult, tasks and will recognize they need everyone's ability and support to do so.

## GROUP REWARDS

Team members understand that their own individual rewards depend upon team progress. If the team is successful, then they will receive tangible and intangible benefits. Either everyone is rewarded or no one is rewarded. If the team is unsuccessful, they are not rewarded, and may suffer a consequence. A sales team has a night on the town or is flown to Hawaii for achieving more than expected. At 3M, members of new product teams enjoy bonuses and recognition as the product meets established targets in sales. Ways to structure cooperative rewards include:

(1) *Praise the team as a whole for its success* The team's accomplishments are recognized in the company newsletter. A party is thrown to honor the team members.

(2) *Reward individuals based on group performance* Each team member receives a monetary bonus based on the team's success. Each one receives 5% of the profits for a new product that the team developed and manufactured.

(3) *Reach a common ground* Team members identify their own particular

interests and agendas, and then negotiate until they decide on goals that promote at least to some extent the interests of all.

(4) *Reward equally* Unequal rewards can induce a feeling of rivalry over who should get the most benefits.[6] However, accepted unequal rewards can still promote unity. Although the task force leader is given 5% of the cost savings from the first year's use of a new inventory system, each member accepts 3% as reasonable for them because the task force leader was required to do much more work.

(5) *Hold an unproductive group accountable* Cooperation does not imply that everyone is rewarded and no one is ever punished. Public humiliation of course is seldom useful. However, managers need to confront unproductive teams, not cover up by rewarding them, and perhaps have them suffer some consequence. Managers avoid the temptation of blaming a few, but hold the group as a whole responsible.

## CONNECTED ROLES

Roles create unity when team members understand that they have complementary and interconnected roles. Each team member has a role that needs to be performed for the team to function properly.[7] Employees recognize that all must fulfill their role obligations. Ways to structure roles for unity include:

(1) *Assign complementary roles* An employee is asked to record ideas, another to encourage full participation, another to be a devil's advocate to challenge common views, and a fourth to observe and provide feedback to help the group reflect on its workings.

(2) *Clarify how roles are complementary* The president, secretary, vice president, and treasurer discuss how their responsibilities supplement each other and how no one can be effective unless others do their jobs.

## SCARCE, COMPLEMENTARY RESOURCES

When each one only has a portion of the information, abilities, and resources necessary to accomplish the task, employees recognize that each person must contribute. Ways to structure resources for unity include:

(1) *Limit the resources to the group* Team members realize that as individuals they cannot each try to accomplish the task, but must pool their resources. Unlimited resources may tempt some people to try to be a hero and do it themselves.

(2) *Highlight everyone's abilities* Team members identify their own individual abilities and talents so that they appreciate how each one can move

the group toward goal attainment. A new product team recognizes that it must blend the skills of marketing, engineering, research, and manufacturing specialists to produce a commercial product.

(3) *Jigsaw materials* Each team member is given a part of the resources necessary to get the job done. For example, each member of a five-member team studies material on one aspect of the team organization model. Then they come together to make sure they all understand the five components and how they are related.

## SENSE OF COMMUNITY

Team members can feel united because they share a common identity and feel they belong to one community. Membership interdependence is particularly strong when the self-concept of employees includes being a member of the team and organization. They see themselves as marketing specialists who are part of the marketing area at Savory. Ways to structure community interdependence include:

(1) *Encourage team identity* Teams devise and publicize their own name and symbol. For example, the members of a quality circle group at Musashi Semiconductor Works called themselves the 'Ten Philosophers' and described their personalities on the bulletin board.[8] Team members focus on their common characteristics and backgrounds.[9]

(2) *Foster a 'caring culture'* People commit themselves to teams and companies in which they feel accepted, valued, and supported.[10] In addition to discussing the importance of acceptance, teams also show they care about individuals by responding to their special needs, celebrating their personal victories, and supporting them in times of crisis.

(3) *Write a philosophy* Team members develop their own value statement. These values emphasize that they belong together and should be helpful 'citizens' to each other.[11]

(4) *Keep history alive* Employees recall stories and examples that illustrate the vision, values, and unity of the team.[12]

(5) *Develop shared norms* Norms are rules regarding how team members are to treat each other. They discuss their present norms and decide the norms they want that will enhance them as individuals and as a team and promote their work. Team members then know what to expect and need less monitoring and influencing.

(6) *Turn physical proximity into psychological unity* The members of the team share an open space and have their offices next to each other, and separated from other groups. The team holds regular meetings and exchanges. Physical contact such as embracing and holding hands are tangible signs of unity.

## TRUST

Trust, attraction, and regard also unite people in a common mission. Trust involves feeling that one can rely on others. Marian and Jerry felt they could trust each other because each believed the other would not use their words against them. They felt that though they may have had a different perspective, they were on the same side. Trust involves disclosing information that leaves one vulnerable in that others could use it exploitatively. People demonstrate trust when they take risks that could leave them worse off than if they had not risked, but they are confident others will aid them. Trust has long been regarded as critical for working together. Indeed, suspicion can undercut goal, task, role, and other kinds of cooperative interdependence. Ways to develop trust include:

(1) *Encourage mutually rewarding interaction* Trust is typically based on previous experience of working together productively. 'Small wins' in which the team successfully achieves a number of well-defined objectives develop confidence among the team members.

(2) *Promote self-disclosure* People trust those they know, and suspect those who remain unknown. Team members can discuss their feelings and values they consider important. 'Small talk' about family and oneself develops personal, trusting relationships.

(3) *Foster warmth and friendliness* People trust others who sincerely express warmth, friendliness, and concern. Social gatherings such as Friday afternoon 'beer busts' and Christmas parties encourage such interaction.

(4) *Pledge to cooperate* Team members begin meetings by all openly declaring that they will cooperate and work together.[13] Trust can be established when team members believe they have all decided to promote common goals.

(5) *Reciprocating* Team members can develop trust by following suit when others work for mutual benefit.[14]

## CREATING UNITY IN JOINT VENTURES

When I try to set up joint ventures, for example, a medical imaging center involving the hospital, physicians, and private investors, the only way to make it work is to demonstrate to each party what they have to gain. And how what they have to gain can *only* happen if they work together.
Bob Phillips, President, Health Business Development Associates

Joint ventures underline the importance, and difficulty, of forging unity. There is no common membership or sense of community that serves as a powerful indicator of cooperative goals. Many joint ventures cross national boundaries and add the complexities of cross-cultural communication.

General Motors and Toyota, fierce competitors in the automobile market, still understood that in some areas cooperation could be highly useful.[15] After preliminary discussions, executives from both companies met in March 1982, and announced plans for a joint venture, New United Motor Manufacturing Inc. (NUMMI). The venture would produce a new sub-compact at GM's old Fremont, California, plant for the US market.

Both companies formed the joint venture for significant self-interests. GM wanted to replace its sub-compact, the Chevette, to respond to competition in that market niche. It needed such a car to meet its fuel standards for the cars sold in the US and to improve relations with united automobile workers (UAW) by employing laid-off workers. It thought that it could use a model Toyota had already developed for the Japanese market. GM also wanted to learn Toyota's production methods that gave it a $1500 to $2000 advantage per car. Such improvement would help win back customers to GM products.

Toyota too saw significant gains in such a plan. Both the Japanese and US governments were pressing it to establish US production to reduce the US trade deficit with Japan. Toyota had reservations about US production and had let Honda and Nissan take the lead. But a joint venture would reduce the costs of determining the feasibility of US production. GM would also give it access to the world's more extensive supplier of automobile parts.

In addition to developing a consensus within each company, participants had arduous, complex negotiating to realize these significant advantages. In April 1982, teams from each company met and assigned such issues as facilities planning, costing, strategic planning, and labor to different working groups. They set September as the target to reach a final agreement.

Though each side was thoroughly prepared, the negotiations were much more complex than anticipated. There were, for example, a great number of parts, and decisions about who was to make them had to be made. The two companies had different styles of negotiating. The Americans liked to get down to specific proposals quickly, whereas the Japanese wanted to discuss broad issues first. The Americans thought that the Japanese were too indirect, and often took silence to mean agreement. The Americans could access information from their organizations more quickly than the Japanese.

Five months late, on February 14, 1983, the companies announced they had reached final agreement that would save capital and share risks. Toyota had eased government pressures, and also had a foothold to compete against Nissan and Honda on US made cars, but at half the cost. GM had a new sub-compact at billions of dollars less than if it had designed the car itself. To make the joint venture pay off by producing quality cars and learning from each other, GM and Toyota would have to continue to negotiate and emphasize their cooperative goals.

# FAILURE TO COMMIT

Team members do not automatically feel united. In addition to believing that their important goals are competitive or independent, team members may fail to commit themselves to cooperative goals. They may understand that the group's mission and tasks make them cooperatively dependent, but never get enthusiastic. They don't give the group much priority, and let other interests in and out of the company dominate their thinking.

The power of cooperation is based on self-interest; people promote their own interests by promoting the interests of others. As argued in Chapter 6, team members can meet many vital utilitarian, social reality, and identity needs through group work. However, for cooperation to be energizing, individual team members must themselves believe that their interests can be served by cooperative work. There are pitfalls that interfere with this conclusion.

## AWARENESS

Cooperation implies that people recognize their own interests and needs. Yet people must work to understand themselves. They have to use previous experiences and self-reflection to try to reach conclusions about that perplexing question, 'What do I really want?' Many people experience a sense of meaningless because they are unaware of their central needs and values, and consequently cannot pursue them effectively.

Cooperation also implies that team members recognize the needs and goals of others. But here too people often can be mistaken. Misjudging people is particularly common when they are little known, but can happen between long-time colleagues. Some people consistently misread others. Suspicious people, for example, quickly assume that others are motivated to harm them.

## COORDINATION

Team members must also solve problems for coordination. They may all be committed to providing social support for each other, but disagree about the now, but the other team members want to get on with accomplishing their task. They may all be committed to getting their assigned task completed, but some want to pursue it now and others next month. They have to work out arrangements to coordinate their activities to promote the interests of all.

Yet coordination itself may alienate. A team member chafes at his role of secretary because it is inconsistent with his own image of himself. Another finds her responsibilities are too inconsequential to be taken seriously. People resent that others try to influence them in strong, controlling ways.[16]

Team members often have to take turns; some group members are served first while others wait. Team members need to take a long-term view to see that everyone's interests will be enhanced, but the short term can seem more real and important.

## COSTS

Cooperation is not free. Team members will want to know whether the costs of scheduling more meetings, getting to know others, and working with people they may not know or like will be fruitful and worth the effort. They also realize that involvement with some groups will mean that they have less time and resources to pursue alternative relationships and opportunities.

Teams pose risks. Members have to assume that their investment will be reciprocated by others and will result in a payoff in the future. They want to believe their actions are reasonable, and they are not being taken for 'suckers.'

Gaining commitment to cooperative goals requires work on several fronts. The team organization model proposes that, in addition to an engaging vision and cooperative goals, team members must be supported so that they feel empowered, are able to solve problems, and can reflect upon their successes, failures, and conflicts to strengthen their teamwork. In this way, team members become increasingly convinced that not only are their major interests cooperatively linked, but they can pursue them enjoyably and profitably together.

## COMPETITION AND INDEPENDENCE

Team members may be highly aware of their goals, even committed to the organization's vision, yet not feel united. Although they undermine team productivity and solidarity, *competition and independence are real, potentially motivating alternatives*. Competition has long been valued. Employees are often expected to prove themselves capable by showing that they are better than others. Business publications and leaders are constantly telling organizations and people that they must be competitive. There is an easy, but false, assumption that because the free market economy demands competition between firms, competition is needed within firms. Indeed, competition is assumed to have made the West more prosperous than the East. Education, even the masters degree in business administration (MBA), has traditionally valued competitive experiences as realistic training for the world of work.

Being a winner, proving that one is right and others wrong can be both intrinsically and extrinsically rewarding. It can feel good that one has won, especially knowing that losing was a real possibility and indeed people did lose. Managers often have competitive interests *vis-à-vis* future promotions. Many companies encourage this competition to motivate managers and because they believe it helps move the best people into more responsible positions.

Independent work also has its rewards, and avoids the costs and inconveniences of coordination. Success can seem sweeter because it is attributed to one's sole effort.

## CONSISTENCY AND CREDIBILITY

> You can go out and preach common goals and work at it. . . . But you can bring your credibility down in a second. It takes a million acts to build it up, but one act can bring it down. . . . People are suspicious because for several thousand years that suspicion was warranted. So it's fragile. And we work very hard to try not to do things that will create distrust.
>
> Howard K. Sperlich, President, Chrysler Corporation

Goals, rewards, roles, tasks, resources, community, and attitudes all can be brought to bear to create unity. Leaders and members have a number of strategies to help them become a highly committed, unified team. These strategies are mutually reinforcing and together can build a positive cycle to strengthen the cohesion and productivity of the team.

However, the variety of sources of information people use to determine they are cooperatively interdependent also means that people have many ways to conclude that they are competitive or independent. People can turn to goals, roles, resources, and attitudes to conclude that they can go it alone, or that they should try to outdo others. Team members need consistent, overlapping cues that they are united.

An interesting issue is the specific dynamics by which people combine different information to make their judgment about how they depend upon others. Typically, there are at least some incomplete or conflicting cues. Their goals are cooperative, but they are unknown to each other, or have some suspicion based on previous experience. People are able to emphasize some aspects while discounting others. Indeed, they may selectively use one kind of information: despite cooperative goals, complementary roles, shared bonuses, and so on, team members may believe that they are really competitive because they expect their boss to remember which team member was the 'best.'

Sometimes people make these judgments very quickly. Expectations and first[17] impressions can impact subsequent interaction. Some conclusions are based on years of experience, and are not easily changed. Yet new information can cause re-evaluation and change: hated enemies one year become the best of friends the next.

Individuals differ as to the ways they draw conclusions about their inter-dependence. Some people rely on attitudes; others on objective outcomes. Culture also affects how conclusions are made. Mexican negotiators have been found to rely very strongly on personal attitudes and community to assess whether there is common ground, whereas US Americans look at the 'bottom line' of financial and tangible rewards.[18]

We need much more research to shed light on these important, complex dynamics. However, the practical issue is *how to structure as many types of interdependence as feasible in order to get as many people united behind the team's vision as possible.* Achievement-oriented, 'bottom-line,' task-oriented people can use common goals and shared rewards; people-oriented employees can use attitudes and community; bureaucratically oriented people can use task and roles to believe they are united in the pursuit of common goals.

People consider goals, rewards, tasks, resources, design, roles, and attitudes together.[19] They expect that if they have a common goal, then they will share the rewards and have complementary roles. If these sources of information are inconsistent, then they are unsure whether they are united. Managers and employees should structure overlapping cues so that people are highly com-mitted to their common vision.

## MARKETING SEEKS UNITY

Art had outlined his vision for the marketing department to his three assis-tants, Harrison Knight, the head of sales for overseas, Ken Ibsen, the head of sales for North America, and Diane Wong, in charge of marketing research. They wanted to be part of a proactive marketing area to transform Savory into a global competitor.

'We will take up the challenge from Allan,' Ken said. 'Let's go after the adult market, buy some brand names, use joint ventures to give us a presence in new parts of the world, improve our franchising. . . . Sounds great to this marketing guy.'

Harrison, who had the longest tenure of the three, liked Ken, but was embarrassed by his emotional displays. 'I think our people will take to the vision, but getting them to work differently is another matter,' he said.

'My people will be skeptical,' Diane said. She and her group were very oriented to their profession, not necessarily the company. 'They will think the sales people are just trying to sell them something.'

'Marketing resistance,' Ken said, only partly joking. 'We're used to overcoming that and closing the deal. No problem.'

'We aren't selling them a product to take home and plug in, but a way of working,' Art said. 'I think they need to be highly involved so they understand and are committed. Another thing is that we, including us, have to feel united, that we are all behind this vision.'

'Selling unity—the politicians try to do it,' Ken quipped.

'At the same time they are going after different groups of voters,' Diane said.

'What I've been learning is that we need to create a vision that people can accept as their own and follow that up with common goals, shared rewards, and overlapping responsibilities that make it clear that they need to work together to accomplish the vision,' Art said. 'But how we go about doing this should reinforce this unity. We can't force it down their throats—we have to establish this unity together.'

'I think I follow,' Ken said.

'We need a plan, though,' Harrison said.

'We have a plan, but we need to make it so that others help us sketch it in and fill it out,' Art said. 'Here is something I got from my management meetings on how to establish unity.' Art handed a summary of the readings from Marian.

They discussed how, in addition to a shared vision, cooperative goals, common rewards, interdependent tasks, the need to exchange resources, complementary roles, a sense of community, and trusting attitudes all contribute to unity.

'So we need some kind of profit-sharing plan,' Ken said.

'Not practical,' Diane said. 'The CEO will never agree to it, and what if we don't have any profits.'

'Exactly,' Harrison said. 'Then we all go without. That appeals to me.'

'I like a bonus plan,' Ken said. 'Then we don't have to get into the accounting games executives like to play.'

'This task interdependence—couldn't we get research and sales people working together on a common task?' Diane suggested. 'There's too much distance between my research people and sales.'

'I can be in charge of trusting attitudes,' Ken said. 'Planning parties, going on trips, fishing together—I've got lots of good ideas.'

'At least, expensive ideas,' Harrison teased his younger colleague. 'I like the idea of giving people just enough resources so they know they have to work together and be efficient. Us old people still know the value of a dollar!'

'My favorite is that we can all learn together by being united in improving our abilities and the success of our area,' Diane said.

'Good thoughts,' Art said. 'But I think we need more people involved, perhaps a representative cross-sample of the marketing area, and let them propose specific ways for us to be united behind our vision. Then we could work with that task force and reach some kind of agreement and then proceed.'

'That will take longer,' Diane said. 'But I see where the method will reinforce the message.'

'But what if the task force comes back with losers, things that won't fly because they're too expensive or whatever?' Ken asked. 'You'll have to go along with it or ruin your unity.'

'We'll make it clear from the onset that the task force will recommend, but we will feel free to disagree and debate,' Art said. 'We promise to be open-minded, but not to rubber stamp. We have to be responsible; we can't agree to things we don't believe in.'

'But that doesn't sound like a team,' Diane said.

'A team disagrees, a team conflicts,' Art replied. 'How can it be a team decision if one part forces its will on another? That would be divisive if we do it, or the task force does it. We want consensus at the end, but we may well disagree before we get there.'

'I think I follow,' Ken said.

'I'm glad to hear you're learning to follow as well as lead,' Harrison teased again.

'Let's brainstorm who we should ask to be on the task force and what their charge should be,' Art said.

# REFERENCES

1. Johnson, D. W. and Johnson, R. T. (1986). *Cycles of Learning*. Edina, MN: Interaction Book Company.
2. Baker, J., Tjosvold, D. and Andrews, I. R. (1988). Conflict approaches of effective and ineffective managers: a field study in a matrix organization. *Journal of Management Studies*, **25**, 167–178.
3. Hardecker, M. and Ward, B. K. (1987). Getting things done: how to make a team work. *Harvard Business Review*, November–December, 112–119.
4. Thompson, J. D. (1967). *Organizations in Action*. New York: McGraw-Hill.
5. Van de Ven, A., Delbecq, R. and Koenig, R., Jr (1976). Determinants of coordination modes within organizations. *American Sociological Review*, **41**, 322–338.
6. Deutsch, M. (1985). *Distributive Justice: A Social-Psychological Perspective*. New Haven, CT: Yale University Press. Schuster, M. (1984). The Scanlon Plan: a longitudinal analysis. *Journal of Applied Behavioral Science*, **20**, 23–38.
7. Cheung, J. L. (1983). Interdependence and coordination in organizations: a role-system analysis. *Academy of Management Journal*, **26**, 156–162.
8. Davidson, W. H. (1982). Small group activity at Musashi Semiconductor Works. *Sloan Management Review*, Spring, 2–14.
9. Kramer, R. M. and Brewer, M. B. (1984). Effects of group identity on resource use in a simulated commons dilemma. *Journal of Personality and Social Psychology*, **46**, 1044–1057.
10. Eisenberger, R., Huntington, R., Hutchison, S. and Sowa, D. (1986). Perceived organizational support. *Journal of Applied Psychology*, **71**, 500–507. Eisenberger, R., Fasolo, P. and Davis-LaMastro, V. (1990). Perceived organizational support and employee diligence, commitment, and innovation. *Journal of Applied Psychology*, **75**, 51–59.
11. Organ, D. W. (1988). *Organizational Citizenship Behavior: The Good Soldier Syndrome*. Lexington, MA: Lexington Books. Ouchi, W. (1981). *Theory Z: How American Business can Meet the Japanese Challenge*. Reading, MA: Addison-Wesley.
12. Deal, T. E. and Kennedy, A. A. (1982). *Corporate Culture: The Rites and Rituals of Corporate Life*. Reading, MA: Addison-Wesley.
13. Orbell, J. M., van de Kragt, A. J. C. and Dawes, R. M. (1987). Explaining discussion-induced cooperation. *Journal of Personality and Social Psychology*, **54**, 811–819.
14. Axelroad, R. (1984). *The Evolution of Cooperation*. New York: Basic Books. Deutsch, M. (1980). Fifty years of conflict. In L. Festinger (ed.), *Retrospections on Social Psychology*. New York: Oxford University Press, 46–77.
15. Weiss, S. E. (1987). Creating the GM-Toyota joint venture: a case in complex negotiations. *Columbia Journal of World Business*. Summer, 23–36.
16. Tjosvold, D. (1979). The other's controlling strategy and own group's evaluation in intergroup conflict. *Journal of Psychology*, **100**, 305–314. Tjosvold, D. and Deemer, D. K. (1980). Effects of control or collaborative orientation on participation in decision-making. *Canadian Journal of Behavioral Science*, **13**, 33–43.
17. McClintock, C. G. and Liebrand, W. B. G. (1988). Role of interdependence structure, individual value orientation, and another's strategy in social decision making: a transformational analysis. *Journal of Personality and Social Psychology*, **55**, 396–409. Tjosvold, D. (1986). *Working Together to Get Things Done: Managing for Organizational Productivity*. Lexington, MA: D.C. Heath.

18. Unterman, I. (1988). *National negotiating style: Mexicans*, Paper, Academy of Management Meetings, Anaheim, CA.
19. McClintock, C. G. and Liebrand, W. B. G. (1988). Role of interdependence structure, individual value orientation, and another's strategy in social decision making: a transformational analysis. *Journal of Personality and Social Psychology*, 55, 396–409. Tjosvold, D. (1986). *Working Together to Get Things Done: Managing for Organizational Productivity*. Lexington, MA: D.C. Heath.

# 10 Empower

Act your part, therein lies the goal.

William Shakespeare

If you want one year of prosperity, grow grain.
If you want ten years of prosperity, grow trees.
If you want one hundred years of prosperity, grow people.

Chinese proverb

Every individual is continually exerting himself to find out the most advantageous employment for whatever capital he can command. It is his own advantage, indeed, and not that of the society, which he has in view. But the study of his own advantage naturally, or rather necessarily, leads him to prefer that employment which is most advantageous to the society.

Adam Smith, *Wealth of Nations*

Unity empowers; a united team is likely to have the confidence it will succeed. Empowering unifies; believing the team members have the abilities and resources to be successful strengthens cohesion. Yet a team, even a united one, can feel demoralized and unmotivated. Employees, though they would like to accomplish the team's vision, conclude their efforts will not pay off. They put their energy and thoughts into other pursuits.

Team members want answers to three related questions before they feel highly empowered:

(1) Does the organization value the team and its vision? Team members want to know whether the company will give them needed resources. They want to believe that placing their hopes on this team is sensible for their future in the company.
(2) Does the team have the wherewithal to be successful? A group without necessary resources will sputter.
(3) Will the team apply itself to be successful? Team members are unmotivated when they suspect they will not all work hard and together to achieve goals.

Team leaders and members can work to answer these questions affirmatively. A clear mandate from the organization shows that 'our team and vision are valued.' Designing the group so that it is well aware of its individual abilities and the team's resources strengthens the feeling that 'we can do it.' Holding individuals accountable and expecting them to apply their skills to work together instills a sense that 'we will do it.'

## DECIDING TO BE MOTIVATED

Many managers make the easy, but false, assumption that an unmotivated employee and team simply do not care. If they wanted to, they would do it. But wanting to is not enough to be motivated. People ask several questions before committing the effort to pursue a task.[1] They want to know whether they have the resources necessary to get the job done and reach their goals. In a team setting, they need to believe that others will also work hard.

In an organizational setting, employees want to believe that their company values their team. Reports of organizational development efforts and task forces are replete with examples of how the failure to secure top management support doomed the program. Teams wonder why they should exert themselves without recognition from top management; indeed, their work may be held against them. They realize that, without top management support, they will be unable to get the resources to complete their tasks or the acceptance needed to implement their recommendations.

Even with a mandate, a team needs to believe it has the skills, resources, and technology to accomplish its task.[2] The most attractive goal does not generate much action without a sense that it is possible to achieve it. Team members would like to devise the dream product to save the company from bankruptcy, but they think it is more reasonable for them to find another job.

Even if they believe that the team collectively has the resources, they may remain skeptical. Researchers have documented that team members can shirk their duties and develop a 'let George do it' attitude.[3] They have argued that groups have a tendency to diffuse responsibilities and encourage social loafing.

Studies underline that groups do not invariably stimulate individual effort, but also document that groups do not inevitably undermine that effort either. Requiring joint work, making tasks interesting,[4] making the contributions of individuals public, having each person's contribution unique,[5] and assigning each person a responsibility[6] have been found to increase individual effort and reduce social loafing.

Team members also want to believe they have the relationships and skills to coordinate and manage conflicts. Although they have cooperative goals, they will still conflict over the way they should proceed, how they should divide the work and rewards fairly and effectively, and how they should treat each other as persons. If they believe they cannot work out of frustrations and move forward, they will not commit themselves fully to the task.

# EMPOWERING

Demonstrating organization support, structuring the appropriate design and sufficient resources, and strengthening confidence through division of labor and holding individuals accountable motivate people and empower teams.

## ORGANIZATIONAL SUPPORT: THE TEAM IS VALUED

The active, consistent support of the top management has long been seen as critical to change organizations, indeed, to get just about anything done. Even changing to participative management, bottom-up planning, and decentralization require visible, consistent effort by top management.

Top management has to be credible as it articulates the organization's vision and proves it can be trusted to stay the course. Ultimately, the team members have to believe the organization not only permits them to work together, but needs them to be successful.

(1) *Relate the team's vision to the organization's* Employees discuss how their team's goals complement and further the business strategy of the organization. They know that top management wants a team organization.

(2) *Attend talks by top management on the company's direction* Employees are apt to believe that executives who commit themselves publicly are serious and will follow through.

(3) *Engage in dialogue* Executives indicate how they see the team's role in the company and informally discuss with employees how they have a common direction. The leader dispels fears that they are just 'doing their own thing,' and shows how they are in step with the current direction of the organization.

(4) *Allocate resources* The company backs up its talk with a budget and an assignment of people.

(5) *Structure team human resource systems* The organization rewards group effort, uses teamwork as a criterion for promotion, provides training in group skills, and makes consultation on teamwork available.

Marian made sure the Team Leaders Corps realized their effort was very much in line with the vision of the CEO. Allan had argued that strengthened teamwork would help Savory meet the challenges of globalization. The team members also knew that their vice presidents were encouraging team development, and strengthening their own team. The managers discussed at length their visions for their own areas and how creating a team organization was central to those visions.

## DESIGN: THE TEAM CAN DO IT

Though a team values its vision and recognizes that top management values it too, employees will still wonder whether they will be able to achieve it. We might think it is glamorous to sing at the Met, but don't bother to take a lesson because it is not going to happen. This cautiousness is very reasonable: why pursue a goal with little chance of success? A challenging task that has the possibility of failure can be highly motivating, but a task with low probability of success is not.[7]

Team members who believe that they have the personal abilities, finances, information, and knowledge are confident.[8] Teams should also believe that they can negotiate to get resources they discover they need.

(1) *Include skilled, relevant people* People who are specialists in technical areas, in facilitating groups, and linking with management help the team accomplish its goals. The more people in the group, the more available resources and knowledge, but the more coordination needed.[9]

(2) *Identify team members' skills and abilities* Team members discuss their previous accomplishments, experiences, and credentials, and in other ways realistically disclose their personal strengths. They point out and recognize how individuals have used their abilities in the service of the team.

(3) *Take inventory of tangible resources* Using preliminary estimates of what the task requires, the team identifies how it can apply its technical skills, money, and other resources to it.

(4) *Negotiate for needed resources* Based on input from the group, the leader approaches top management for more resources.

(5) *Develop abilities* Team members take courses, read books and journals, and discuss ideas to keep current in their specialities. Readings, workshops, and reflection on experiences develop skills in dealing with conflicts and other group issues.

(6) *Structure opportunities to work together* Regular meetings, proximity of offices, electronic mail, and computer systems help team members exchange information and keep each other posted.

The managers in the TLC controlled their own agendas so that they did not need formal authority to meet. They expected they could justify to top management additional resources if need be. Through discussion, they shared their knowledge about teamwork and demonstrated their abilities to foster it. Marian was especially helpful in providing them with ideas to guide their work.

## PSYCHOLOGICAL CONFIDENCE: THE TEAM WILL DO IT!

Having the potential does not mean that it will be put to use. People have to decide to do it. In a team, the decision has to be a joint one: team members believe they will all apply their abilities. They publicly commit themselves, use division of labor, and hold individuals accountable for their part.

(1) *Commit publicly* The team members indicate they are personally motivated to get the group's job done well. Their public announcement convinces themselves and others that the team will apply its collective abilities to get the job done.[10]

(2) *Divide work* Team members accept roles and see how they are needed and complementary to get the job done. The team charts responsibilities. The task is analyzed into its parts, and one or more team members are formally assigned the responsibility to complete each one.

(3) *Hold individuals accountable* Each team member reports on their activities to the group and shows their personal responsibility. Individual performance is compared to role expectations and assignments, and contribution to the team is monitored. Individuals who complete their assignments are recognized. The team confronts individuals who fail to fulfill their obligations, and may decide to encourage and give assistance, or warn, or reprimand and punish the individual. In difficult cases, the team involves their manager in mediating a resolution.

In the TLC, the managers committed themselves to implement teamwork in their areas. As they applied their learning, they clarified their understanding and skills in using teams. They were finding various ways to help each other. The group members also began reflecting on their working together to identify problems and sharpen their skills.

## EMPOWERING AND EMPLOYEE OWNERSHIP

> Believe me, the ESOP works, and it works very well. . . . [But] just creating an ESOP isn't going to make you a better company. It's how you involve the employees, it's how you maintain a dialogue, listen to their input, and use it.
>
> Joe Vittoria, Chairman, Avis Car Rental

Employee ownership and gainsharing are growing. By the end of 1987, there were about 1500 companies that had employee stock ownership plans (ESOP). Employees are expected to share in the risks and the rewards of their common effort, and to be more highly motivated and united to make their company profitable.

However, employee ownership by itself appears to have rather minor impact on company success.[11] What is critical is that employees be empowered by the organization's vigorously encouraging their involvement. Employees need opportunities to contribute by proposing how to reduce costs and improve quality, and then managers must respond by refining and implementing their ideas.

Avis has flourished under ESOP. Shares in the company are allocated to employees in proportion to their salary, and within 18 years all stock will be held by employees.[12] All service indicators have improved since the adoption of the plan. Operating profits rose 35% in the first six months of 1988 compared to 1987; on-time arrival of car deliveries at airport rose from 93% to 96%, and customer complaints dropped 35%. When Westinghouse announced Avis would be its primary car-rental agency, every employee in Pittsburgh where Westinghouse is based signed a letter to travel managers pledging to provide the best possible service. Indeed, Avis uses employee ownership in marketing to convey that customers can be assured of quality service by a motivated workforce.

Avis has used participation to reinforce ESOP. Managers are asked to get their employees involved and interact with them. Monthly, at each of the Avis-owned locations, representatives from each job category have met and developed many valuable ideas. These meetings help employees feel listened to and managers believe that employees want a disciplined, effective work team.

## DIVERSITY: THREAT OR OPPORTUNITY?

If I am [white male] VP, I'm not going to put a million-dollar piece of business in your hands if I don't know you, if I'm uncomfortable with you symbolically or personally.

Barbara Walker, Digital Equipment Corporation

The whole country is moving from being white, Anglo, and Protestant to polyglot, particularly in places like California, Colorado, Texas—places we do business. You have to recognize what's happening and be part of it.

Marion Sandler, Golden West Financial

Diversity has always been part of organizations, but forces are at work to accentuate differences among employees. Companies are using more professionals, and these professionals are in turn more specialized. The workforce in the US, Canada, and many other countries is increasingly female, nonwhite, and immigrant. Estimates are that these groups will make up 85% of the net increase in the US labor pool from 1988 to the year 2000.[13] As jobs are expected to increase faster than the labor supply, companies will compete for female and nonwhite employees.

Ongoing mergers and acquisitions have created more global corporations composed of employees from countries with different social and political traditions. Consumers in booming economies of Asia and increasingly in such traditional markets as California and New York are nonwhite. Global companies seek suppliers and customers in developing and developed, capitalistic and socialistic countries. Today, one's co-worker, boss, subordinate, supplier, and customer may well have different national, racial, and cultural backgrounds.

## DIVERSITY'S POTENTIAL

Differences between groups are potential explosives that can rip apart an organization. Alliances and rivalries based on race, ethnicity, or specialization create a suspicion that paralyzes a company and makes reasonable decisions impossible. What is right and good for the company becomes secondary to supporting one's own group and sabotaging others. Even subtle stereotypes can undermine morale and the ability to work together.

Yet diversity has a very positive potential as well. Heterogeneity has a richness which makes teamwork more productive and personally satisfying. Diversity of opinions and backgrounds induces creativity and new solutions to problems.[14] Discussing issues with people with different perspectives stimulates thinking and cognitive development.[15] People become more sensitive and aware of others and themselves and the complexities of interaction when confronted with the need to coordinate with diverse others. Diversity empowers because a heterogeneous group is likely to have the varied skills and resources necessary to accomplish tasks. Indeed, managers are continually advised to use multi-skilled, diverse groups.

Diversity is two-sided. It can stimulate creativity and growth, or suspicion and decay. What is critical is not diversity *per se*, but how it is managed. Well-managed relations among diverse people are vital to organizational success.

## BARRIERS TO POSITIVE DIVERSITY

Ignorance, anxiety, and low expectations reinforce each other as obstacles to constructive interaction among people of different ethnic, racial, national, and cultural backgrounds. Majority and minority groups quickly develop stereotypes of each other.[16] These stereotypes oversimplify and leave the impression that people in a group share similar characteristics, and that outgroups have much different values and personalities. People further assume that the characteristics they have are generally positive, whereas the traits of other groups are less desirable. This reasoning leads to oversimplified, negative opinions and aggression toward other racial and ethnic groups.[17]

Stereotypes leave majority and minority people ignorant of each other.

Because they are unfamiliar, they often experience strain when they begin to interact, and this anxiety reduces the positive impact of any meeting.[18] Feeling at ease working with people with a common background, they restrict their exposure to diverse others. In this way, ignorance leads to anxiety, anxiety leads to avoidance which reinforces ignorance.

Avoidance reinforces stereotypical thinking. With little interaction, people do not receive much information about the subtleties and complexities of others. Based on the theory of least effort, they tend to think of diverse others in simplistic, rigid ways.[19]

Stereotypes also undermine interaction by inducing low expectations. Stigmatized groups are characterized as having minimal competence and resources. Majority people are doubtful that interaction with less competent people will be rewarding: they have low expectations of task success. Consequently, they try to avoid such interaction, or, if obligated, to put very little effort into their work. Such tentativeness may well be reciprocated by the minority person and, in a self-fulfilling prophecy fashion, their joint work fails for lack of effort.

The traditional view has been that majority attitudes toward minorities could not be changed through social action: 'stateways cannot change folkways.' However, research by a number of social scientists has challenged this view, and supports the 'contact' hypothesis that, through interaction, majority people can know stigmatized people as individuals and accept them as valuable colleagues.[20] However, not all interaction will have a salubrious impact. Even supportive interaction that results in acceptance of specific individuals may not generalize to more positive attitudes toward the stigmatized group as a whole: majority people may accept a minority member as competent and motivated, but still believe the group as a whole is incompetent and lazy.

# TEAM ORGANIZATION FOR POSITIVE DIVERSITY

Managers should take a proactive approach to get diverse groups to work together. The team organization creates opportunities for majority and minority people to know each other and appreciate their abilities. It empowers teams by encouraging people of diverse groups to recognize and value each other's ideas, opinions, and other resources. Yet empowering must be supplemented with cooperative unity, exploration of opposing views, and ongoing effort to create the supportive, effective interaction needed for positive diversity.

## COOPERATIVE GOALS

Research has shown that how people believe they depend upon each other critically affects the dynamics and outcomes of diversity. Specifically, employees with cooperative goals are oriented toward valuing and discussing their differences and using them to promote common interests; as a result, they are able to work productively, strengthen their relationship, and modify their attitudes.

Cooperative goals create an acceptance and appreciation of differences. People in cooperation come to see that an opposing viewpoint stimulates their thinking and brings new ideas so that they can be more successful. Different backgrounds add a richness to the interaction and discussion that is enjoyable, involving, and productive.

In contrast, employees who conclude that their basic interests are competitive suspect diversity and feel that others will work against them. They worry that another's background or idea may make them look like a 'loser'; others will be seen as superior and right, themselves inferior and wrong. They are tempted to derogate others to make sure they appear better themselves. Even if they feel like winners, they expect others want them to tumble. They cannot rely on others for support, but must be on guard to protect themselves. This orientation interferes with exchanging ideas and resources and results in frustration, low productivity, and reinforced prejudices.

## WORKING TOGETHER

These contrasting orientations toward diversity create very different dynamics and consequences. People with cooperative goals are open to each other and integrate their ideas to solve problems. They develop high-quality solutions that help them work productively and help strengthen their work relationships. Employees with competitive goals either avoid collaboration or attempt to impose their ideas. As a result, they fail to develop new solutions or manage their conflicts.

Cooperative goals by themselves are insufficient. Diverse persons must actually interact and discuss their different perspectives open-mindedly. The benefits of opposing opinions and contrasting points of view require that people voice their positions and arguments, and attempt to incorporate and integrate them into more effective solutions.

Open-mindedness is also needed to challenge simplified, rigid attitudes toward minorities. Studies indicate that when people conclude that the stigmatized individual they cooperated with is a competent person able to contribute to team success, is open to receiving assistance, and communicates acceptance of them, then they are willing to challenge their stereotypes.

## EXAMPLES OF RESEARCH

Stuart Cook's[21] research program demonstrated that cooperative goals and experiences can reduce white prejudice toward black Americans. In several studies, white US servicemen from small towns in the South participated in a management training activity called the Railroad Game. Their task was to ship a variety of products between 10 cities in 500 cars of 6 different types. To perform well they had to learn that some cities shipped only certain products, cars had to be kept where they would be needed, and money could be saved by shipping products in cars that would be needed at the station of destination.

The serviceman worked with one white and one black person. After five 15-minute 'work days,' white servicemen developed positive attitudes towards the black Americans with whom they worked cooperatively. The impact of cooperation appears to be stronger when the group succeeds and when people are highly involved. However, whites were found to develop attraction even when the blacks appeared to be less competent, as long as the whites had an opportunity to help the blacks directly. Results of these studies confirm the usefulness of face-to-face cooperation to overcome prejudice.

David W. Johnson and his colleagues used a meta-analysis to summarize 95 studies on the impact of interaction on relationships between people with different ethnic backgrounds or handicapped status.[22] Results, when taken together, indicate that cooperative goals very much strengthen relationships for people with heterogeneous as well as homogeneous backgrounds. It would take hundreds of studies showing no effect to make these results statistically non-significant and to alter the conclusion that cooperative experiences bind diverse people together.

United, cooperative teams composed of diverse people are central to managing diversity in organization. These teams should recognize individual abilities and characteristics, value the competence of all members, create positive expectations of fulfillment and productivity, help people feel relaxed and safe, and anticipate future collaborative work. Especially when the organization as a whole values diversity and employees have high levels of self-acceptance, these teams are productive and explode stereotypes.

## MANAGING DIVERSITY IN THE WORKPLACE

The way to colorblindness is through color-consciousness.
King Ming Young, diversity project, Hewlett-Packard

Several companies have recognized the reality of diversity and the need to manage it, and have begun to tap its positive potential. Top management at US West is committed to creating a pluralistic culture for its companies.[23] It financially supports associations for blacks, women, gays, and other groups so that they can dig into issues and develop mutually rewarding relationships. Recently 68 000 employees completed a two-hour survey to measure how they perceived their company's diversity climate. Results indicate that companies who have been holding seminars and workshops are making progress. The plan is to re-do the survey in two years, and use the results to reward managers who are making their companies more pluralistic-positive.

Intel, Avon, Proctor & Gamble and other companies have joined the valuing diversity effort.[24] Avon has networks of black, Hispanic, and Asian employees to support each other, share their cultural traditions within the company, identify barriers and prejudices, and communicate their concerns to top management. Intel has set up ethnic advisory panels, and put faitas and sushi on the cafeteria menu. Proctor & Gamble provides special career-development programs for black women at its research and development division.

## VALUING DIFFERENCES AT DIGITAL

The Digital Equipment Corporation has for two decades developed an extensive diversity-positive program, now called Valuing Differences.[25] In the 1960s, Digital realized that it was going to become a large, international company and needed to use the abilities and resources of all its people. The company wanted minorities and women to feel very much a part of Digital; they did not want foreign national employees to feel like a minority when they worked for Digital in their own country.

In 1976, Digital with the leadership of Bill Hanson, Vice President Manufacturing, and others began a series of workshops to have managers in manufacturing talk about racism without feeling attacked and guilty and needing to defend themselves. *The idea was that people are victims of racism if they deny it, not if they do something about it.* After very rocky beginnings, they developed successful workshops. Three whites and three blacks met to discuss these issues away from the pressures of everyday work. From 1978 to 1979, they had 18 meetings that involved all senior persons.

Digital hit upon the idea of *small, heterogeneous core groups.* Barbara Walker, a black woman, began a core group that included her boss, Bill Hanson, Linda St. Clair, and others in the department who wanted to talk about their differences and develop strong mentoring relationships. Core groups expanded quickly. They have become the place where people can talk about topics previously considered taboo.

According to Hanson and Walker, Valuing Differences has been a successful personal and organizational development program. Individuals have improved their awareness, skills, and sensitivities. Managing diversity has also helped people of all backgrounds and perspectives feel more included and helped them work together effectively to make Digital successful.

Cooperative teams were instrumental to the success of the program. *Digital learned to develop a strong cooperative context so that people realized they could all benefit from dealing with diversity.* Employees focused on how all people, including white males, were victims and were hurt by racism and other prejudices. They could all learn and they could do so together by listening to each other. They recognized that power is not a zero-sum game, but that they could help each other feel and be powerful. They all benefited when people developed their abilities and confidence, and combined them with others. This collaboration strengthened both the company and its people.

## EMPOWERING IN PRODUCTION

'We're moving slowly, but quickly,' Art reported back to the TLC.

'I can see top management written all over you,' Miles teased. 'You're learning all the right words and moves.'

'What I mean is that we are taking the slow approach of getting people involved in helping to get unity,' Art said. 'But it is paying off with some very sensible ideas that can really make a difference.'

Art reported that the task force recommended a department bonus depending upon the performance of the marketing group as a whole. The more the task force members explored the idea, the more convinced they became of the value of a group rather than an individual bonus. They were now struggling with identifying the standards and targets that would be a true measure of their overall performance. They wanted the targets to reflect actual sales, but also orient them to future sales growth. They asked the accounting group to work with them to develop standards and measures.

'My people were excited about helping,' Kyle said. 'They get enough of keeping score, checking up on budgets, and being told "These numbers are wrong!"'

'Will everyone get a bonus?' Scott asked.

'The task force thought it very important that everyone get a bonus, and perhaps even equal ones,' Art said. 'They would rather have the bonus be modest and everyone get it if we are successful.'

'Sounds good,' Marian said.

Art also reported that the task force charged another group to develop a

'We're Moving Forward' fair. They would like to get as many people as possible together for a day to talk about the company's vision and Marketing's role in it. The CEO and vice president would speak and answer questions. And then groups of people from the different departments would form to explore specific ways that the marketing area should proceed. For example, one group would talk about how they could become more sensitive to working in other cultures; another one on using marketing teams. The fair would both set the stage and suggest ways that marketing people could work toward the vision.

'What happened to the resistance to teamwork?' Scott asked. 'Weren't they thinking you were talking Greek?'

'Language is an apt analogy, Art said. 'Once we understood that we wanted unity that empowers and lets us explore different points of view, much of the resistance disappeared.'

'How did that happen?' Kyle asked.

'Some feared being boxed into having to think alike, some worried about losing their individuality, and others thought we wanted them to sing the company song every morning,' Art said. 'Explaining the team model reduced those fears.'

'What did you do about those suspicions between departments?' Miles asked.

'They are still there.' Art paused. 'I hope this program is breaking them down.'

'One reason I ask is that our suspicions, mostly around color, really make any attempt at teamwork impossible,' Miles said. 'We have had our quality circle groups, and our labor–management groups, but they seem to break down and not get very far.'

'Have you been observing these groups?' Marian asked.

'When we talked about leadership as a "we" thing and how leaders monitor and intervene, I decided to observe our work groups more closely and inter-view some people as well,' Miles replied.

'How did the interviews go?' Marian asked.

'Terrific. After people got over the shock of being asked, they really seemed to enjoy my listening to them talk about their concerns and hopes. It was fun —I recommend it.'

'They might have thought you were prying,' Scott said.

'I didn't ask them to rat on their co-workers or anything like that,' Miles said. 'Several of them said they liked it that I made the effort to listen to them. It was as if interviewing them was a great effort and gesture on my part.'

'Interviewing makes the idea that leadership is two-way very concrete,' Marian said.

'The process was great, but the outcome was sobering,' Miles said. 'That we are very divided on race came up over and over again. It's so corrupting. People fight over new hires, new programs, new promotions not on the basis of what is best, but whether it favors this group or that group. It's more than ugly.'

'It sounds like we have to attack the race issue head on,' Kyle said.

'It's a problem of empowering in terms of our model,' Marian said. 'How can people recognize that others who might be different have the competence and resources to help them accomplish their goals?'

'But it seems to me to also be a problem of unity,' Scott said. 'The groups don't trust each other to help out. Each group is thought to be out for itself and against the others.'

'I agree it's both,' Marian said. 'I'm thinking, though, that Miles may want to put most of his efforts now into empowering.'

'I always thought I had to start with vision and unity,' Miles said.

'The parts of the model are all related and eventually they must all be worked on, but sometimes it makes more sense to begin at different points,' Marian explained. 'And you may want to begin with a program that values the racial and other diversity in production.'

'Unless we do something about race relations, then teamwork will just seem like talk,' Miles said.

'I'm sure that you have already tried to work on this,' Scott said.

'You bet,' Miles said. 'I've bent over backwards to be fair and equal to all groups, and set up a committee to deal with human relations complaints. The unions are onside, and have supported our efforts.'

'How much have you tried to get the groups to value their differences?' Marian asked. 'Getting them to talk openly about being white, being black, and being Chinese . . . having them talk about what it's like to be a woman working in the male world of production?'

'I think that's what we have been avoiding,' Miles said. 'I didn't want to stir things up and emphasize our differences.'

'But acceptance and equality can't be mandated,' Marian said.

'Isn't Marian saying that before people can really accept each other as "equals" they have to know and value each other as people?' Kyle asked.

'And that requires that people know and value my group as well as me,' Marian said. 'Also valuing diverse groups builds self-confidence. As Kurt Lewin used to say, the social esteem of an individual's groups is the secure ground on which they stand.'

'You're saying that when the different groups are all valued, all employees can be proud of their group and themselves,' Miles said.

The team brainstormed with Miles about how to proceed. Based on this discussion, Miles decided that he would ask three supervisors to help him develop a valuing differences program to make the production area more united.

Miles was glad that he had promoted Raymond Cheung to supervisor. Raymond was as hard-working and as conscientious a supervisor as he had been a worker. Miles's fears that he was too passive had not been borne out. He asked Nadine Howe, a black woman, and Doug Huber, a white male, to join Raymond to head up the valuing differences program.

Miles reminded them how the poor race and gender relations undermined the quality of worklife and production. Raymond and Doug were at first skeptical when Miles explained his rationale for celebrating and emphasizing differences between groups. But after some intense discussion, they agreed the idea was worth a good effort.

They met twice without Miles to develop some ideas how they might begin. They proposed that Miles introduce the program at a specially convened meeting of all people in Production and explain the rationale. The racial suspicions and stereotypes would be dealt with head on, but the point was not to blame people but to help everyone recognize how these attitudes hurt everyone. Accepting and appreciating diverse others was not only more productive but more fun as well. The theme of the program would be 'Unity through Diversity.'

The annual picnic usually degenerated into whites talking to whites, Asians with Asians, and blacks with blacks. The next one would focus on all the groups sharing their foods and some of their customs. Families of diverse backgrounds would be grouped together to explain the foods and meet each other.

The supervisors also proposed that development groups be formed where people of different backgrounds and gender could discuss issues and deal with frustrations. These groups could recommend changes to help make the production department diversity-positive. Facilitators would have to be trained to encourage open, win–win dialogue.

'The more we talked about it, the more sense it made to take our diversity out of the closet,' Doug said. 'We have tried for years to pretend we're all the same, but that's not true. Even the whites divide into Italians and Poles, single and married, and whatever.'

'Differences don't divide us,' Nadine said. 'We do that ourselves, but we don't have to.'

# REFERENCES

1. Campbell, J. P. and Pritchard, R. D. (1976). Motivation theory in industrial and organizational psychology. In M. Dunnette (ed.), *Handbook of Industrial and Organizational Psychology*. Skokie, IL: Rand McNally, 63–130.
2. Bottger, P. C. and Yetton, P. W. (1987). Improving group performance by training in individual problem solving. *Journal of Applied Psychology*, **72**, 651–657. Tziner, A. and Eden, D. (1985). Effects of crew composition on crew performance: does the whole equal the sum of its parts. *Journal of Applied Psychology*, **70**, 85–93.
3. Latane, B. (1986). Responsibility and effort in organizations. In P. S. Goodman (ed.), *Designing Effective Work Groups*. San Francisco: Jossey-Bass, 277–304.
4. Kerr, N. (1983). The dispensability of member effort and group motivation losses: free-rider effects. *Journal of Personality and Social Psychology*, **44**, 78–94. Harkins, S. G. and Petty, R. E. (1982). The effects of task difficulty and task uniqueness on social loafing. *Journal of Personality and Social Psychology*, **43**, 1214–1229.
5. Jones, G. R. (1984). Task visibility, free riding, and shirking: explaining the effect of structure and technology on employee behavior. *Academy of Management Review*, **9**, 684–695. Sheppard, J. A. and Wright, R. A. (1989). Individual contribution to a collective effort: an incentive analysis. *Personality and Social Psychology Bulletin*, **15**, 141–149.
6. Maruyama, G., Fraser, S. C. and Miller, N. (1982). Personal responsibility and altruism in children. *Journal of Personality and Social Psychology*, **33**, 178–187.
7. Atkinson, J. W. (1984). *Introduction to Motivation*. New York: Van Nostrand.
8. Bottger, P. C. and Yetton, P. W. (1987). Improving group performance by training in individual problem solving. *Journal of Applied Psychology*, **72**, 651–657.
9. Laughlin, P. R. (1988). Collective induction: group performance, social combination processes, and mutual majority and minority influence. *Journal of Social and Personality Psychology*, **54**, 254–267.
10. Hollenbeck, J. R., Williams, C. R. and Klein, H. J. (1989). An empirical examination of the antecedents of commitment to difficult goals. *Journal of Applied Psychology*, **74**, 18–23.
11. Klein, K. J. (1987). Employee stock ownership and employee attitudes: a test of three models. *Journal of Applied Psychology*, **72**, 319–332.
12. Kirkpatrick, D. (1988). How the workers run Avis better. *Fortune*, December 5, 103–114.
13. Solomon, J. (1989). Firms address workers' cultural variety. *Wall Street Journal*, February 10, 131.
14. Maier, N. R. F. (1970). *Problem-solving and Creativity in Individuals and Groups.*

Belmont, CA: Brooks/Cole. Tjosvold, D. (1985). Implications of controversy research for management. *Journal of Management*, **11**, 21–37.

15. Murray, F. (1982). Teaching through social conflict. *Journal of Educational Psychology*, 7, 257–271.
16. Insko, C. A. and Schopler, J. (1987). Categorization, competition, and collectivity. In C. Hendrick (ed.), *Group Processes*. Newbury Park, CA: Sage, 213–251. Tajfel, H. (1981). *Human Groups and Social Categories*. Cambridge: Cambridge University Press.
17. Struch, N. and Schwartz, S. H. (1989). Intergroup aggression: its predictors and distinctness from in-group bias. *Journal of Personality and Social Psychology*, **56**, 364–373.
18. Wilder, D. A. and Shapiro, P. N. (1989). Role of competition-induced anxiety in limiting the beneficial impact of positive behavior by an out-group member. *Journal of Personality and Social Psychology*, **56**, 60–69.
19. Allport, G. (1954). *The Nature of Prejudice*. Cambridge, MA: Addison-Wesley.
20. Messick, D. M. and Mackie, D. M. (1989). Intergroup relations. In M. R. Rosensweig and L. W. Porter (eds), *Annual Review of Psychology*, **40**, 45–81.
21. Cook, S. (1984). Cooperative interaction in multiethnic contexts. In N. Miller and M. Brewer, *Groups in Contact: The Psychology of Desegregation*. New York: Academic Press, 156–186. Cook, S. (1978). Interpersonal and attitudinal outcomes in cooperating interracial groups. *Journal of Research in Developmental Education*, **12**, 97–113.
22. Johnson, D. W., Johnson, R. T. and Maruyama, G. (1983). Interdependence and interpersonal attraction among heterogeneous and homogeneous individuals: a theoretical formulation and a meta-analysis of the research. *Review of Educational Research*, **53**, 5–54.
23. Fernandes, J., Weller, L. and Selzer, J. (1988). *Pluralism and the competitive edge*. Paper, Academy of Management Meetings, August, Anaheim, CA.
24. Solomon, J. (1989). Firms address workers' cultural variety. *Wall Street Journal*, February 10, 131.
25. Walker, B. A. and Hanson, W. C. (1988). *The design and implementation of the 'Valuing Differences' program at Digital*. Paper, Academy of Management Meetings, August, Anaheim, CA.

# 11  Explore

Conflict is the gadfly of thought. It stirs us to observation and memory. It instigates invention. It shocks us out of sheep-like passivity, and sets us at noting and contriving . . . [C]onflict is a 'sine qua non' of reflection and ingenuity.

John Dewey

It's a serious mistake for any leader to be surrounded by sycophants . . . The stronger and more self-assured a leader is the more likely he or she is to seek diversity of advice. If you are insecure or don't have confidence in yourself, then you're apt to listen to a narrow range of advice. I deliberately chose advisors with disparate points of view.

Jimmy Carter

When two men in business always agree, one of them is unnecessary.

William Wrigley, Jr

A directed, united, confident team is poised to overcome obstacles and reach success. Though preparation is critical, action is necessary. Teams must do. Members must talk, listen, debate, criticize, counsel, and support. They must offer information and ask for assistance; they have to dig into issues and work out solutions. Team members committed to their common goals and believing they have the wherewithal and the desire to accomplish them, many studies document, interact in productive ways. But without an open exchange, unity and empowerment are only reminders of what might be.

Obstacles, issues, and problems test a group. The TLC had decisions to make about its business of developing teamwork and how it was organized. It dealt with conflicting opinions about the impact of groups and how they could be structured. Team members had to devise plans for how they could implement their vision. They also had to decide the kind of leader they wanted Marian to be.

Problem solving is the *sine qua non* of successful teams. Forming a shared vision, dealing with conflicting interests, and developing confidence in each other all demand identifying problems and implementing solutions. Teams that grapple with difficulties, cope with uncertainties, and seize opportunities thrive; those that cannot, feel threatened and at risk.[1]

What distinguishes groups that thrive on problems and those stymied by them? The issue is often reduced to whether groups do or do not solve problems effectively. But groups vary a great deal in how they communicate and deal with issues. The challenge is to understand *the potential and limitations of team problem solving, and identify the conditions that facilitate and the barriers that undermine team decision making.*

Controversy, it is argued, is critical for groups to explore issues and make decisions. When teams discourage the open discussion of opposing views and ideas, individuals feel intimidated and the group suffers. *When controversy brings out ideas and information, the group identifies and grapples with problems fully and integrates views to create new, valuable solutions.* Though the pull to avoid controversy can be strong, constructive controversy is the key to unlocking the power of team decision making.

## THE POTENTIAL OF TEAM DECISION MAKING

Despite misgivings about groups, organizations rely on formal and informal teams to make decisions. Corporate management committees, departmental meetings, and other sessions are used to advise executives and managers. Informally, managers often discuss issues with others and get feedback before they act. Even 'autocratic' bosses usually have confidants to bounce ideas off. Most important issues are discussed over time, and people in different ways express their opinions, give information, and make suggestions.

Does having several persons discuss issues reinforce the biases and simplifications of individuals? Reviewers, although recognizing conflicting findings, have concluded that shared responsibility and discussion have considerable potential for solving problems.[2] Through discussion, *people challenge and correct each other's errors and biases in reasoning, present a variety of information that no one person has or can adequately remember, and combine ideas and perspectives into new solutions not previously considered.* Recent meta-analysis found that people who were able to discuss issues with others made superior decisions than did individuals working alone, especially on complex tasks.[3] Studies when taken together demonstrate that groups make superior decisions than do individuals.

In addition to a superior solution, teams can generate acceptance and commitment to follow through. Consensus and informing others of one's intentions lead to implementation.[4] People who explicitly committed themselves resist attempts to persuade them to lower their efforts to achieve, are receptive to persuasion to increase their efforts, and comply with requests for assistance. Encouraging others and persuading them to work on a task also strengthens one's commitment.

Managers are not, recent research indicates, simple-minded information processors, as traditionally portrayed.[5] They can step out of their framework, use varied criteria, and seek out additional and conflicting information. In fact, well-managed teams are helping organizations nimbly respond to rapid changes in technology, international competition, and consumer preferences. Teams have created new products, strategies, and service delivery systems. Teams are practical ways for organizations to cope with the demands of contemporary decision making. But for teams to explore issues thoroughly and create solutions, they must master the skills and procedures of constructive controversy.

## PITFALLS IN MAKING DECISIONS

Organizational researchers have emphasized that decision makers are hard pressed to process all relevant information and create solutions that respond to emerging conditions.[6] Because of rapid changes in environments and organizations, decision makers often make choices under considerable uncertainty. Their decisions require assimilating novel, partially validated information, and predicting new conditions. Decision making can be emotionally as well as intellectually demanding. The complexity of the problem, difficulty of verifying solutions, and high stakes generate excitement, tension, and stress.

### LIMITATIONS OF INDIVIDUALS

A great deal of research indicates that individuals are poorly equipped to make decisions under these circumstances.[7] In identifying the problem, analyzing it, developing alternatives, considering consequences, and selecting the choice, limitations are thought to operate and potentially interfere.[8]

Individual decision makers have been found to be unwilling to consider much information, especially information that is new and that opposes their perspectives. They use easy to recall, available information to form their opinions.[9] Despite clear evidence indicating their original hypotheses on the relationship between variables were false, people continue to make decisions based on them. They overestimate the importance of confirming information and dismiss opposing data. Decision makers are also anchored to their original positions; final estimates are biased toward their initial estimates. Commitment to a course of action can intensify even when feedback suggests it is failing.[10]

Decision makers often use an analogy to make an unknown situation similar to a well-known, simple one, and reasoning is carried out on the analogous situation. Decision makers assume present and future conditions will be similar to previous ones, and feel more comfortable with traditional solutions.[11]

Decision makers have been found to evaluate information inadequately. With a 'belief in the law of small numbers,' they have made unreasonable conclusions based on very small samples and used early trends to predict final results overconfidently. Correlation and causality are also confused. Decision makers may on the basis of the co-appearance of two variables assume a causal link has been established.[12]

Apparently oblivious to their own faulty reasoning, decision makers have been found to be confident in their conclusions. They form preferences early, and dismiss alternative solutions easily, particularly those that are only partially developed.[13]

Decision makers often fall far short of a thorough, systematic exploration of the problem, development of alternatives, and selection of the optimal solution. They not only avoid digging into the problem and uncovering all relevant information, but they distort and dismiss new information. They have been found reluctant to develop alternative solutions; they become committed to their original one early, fail to see the need to develop new ones, and easily dismiss emerging solutions that are not well defined and defended.

## SHORTCOMINGS OF TEAMS

Many organizational researchers doubt that groups are able to examine issues in depth or create high-quality solutions, but that they enhance the biases and limitations of individuals.[14] The nominal group technique and other procedures have been proposed to protect individual autonomy and minimize the suppressive impact of interaction on the exchange of ideas.[15]

Research has documented barriers for team decision making. Individuals working alone can at times brainstorm more ideas than in a group.[16] Sometimes teams are not able to recognize expertise and the interacting group solves the problems less effectively than the individual expert alone. Teams may be either particularly keen to take risks or conservative. Group members may just discuss already known information and reinforce present positions, not share information.[17] Prestigious, but less informed, people may dominate the discussion and decision.[18] Decision makers may cope with stress and tension by demanding conformity and isolating those who offer contradictory, challenging information and ideas.[19]

# VALUE OF CONTROVERSY

Have you learned lessons only of those who admired you, and were tender with you, and stood aside for you
Have you not learned great lessons from those who braced themselves against you, and disputed the passage with you?

Walt Whitman

We shall not cease from exploration
And the end of all our exploring
Will be to arrive where we started
And know the place for the first time.

T. S. Eliot

Dramatic evidence of the value of controversy for team decision making is that suppressed conflict has resulted in major fiascoes. President John F. Kennedy and his advisors pressed foreign policy experts to suppress their reservations about the invasion of Cuba. The Bay of Pigs fiasco remains a blot on American foreign policy. Learning from this experience, Kennedy insisted on controversy in the Cuban missile crisis, and his actions still earn him high marks.[20]

Suppressed controversy contributed to the Challenger disaster early in 1986. Engineers and managers apparently did not discuss constructively their opposing views on the safety of flying the shuttle in cold weather.[21] The explosion seconds after takeoff cost lives and crippled the American space effort. Failure to discuss opposing views is also a major contributor to commercial airplane crashes. Flight crew members often have the information that could avert crashes, but hesitate to challenge the pilot in command.[22]

Corporate raiders have argued that boards of directors do not have the independence, courage, and information to challenge management, and, as a consequence, do not defend the rights of shareholders properly. Harold S. Geneen, former CEO of ITT, argued that boards are unable to protect stockholders and seldom act until the company is near ruin. Investors, raiders, and managers are making boards more assertive.

The costs of ineffective controversy are not limited to disasters or the boardroom. Every day employees avoid discussing their strongly held views and frustrations directly with their boss, and continue to work in unproductive ways. Managers find it prudent to pretend to agree, withhold information, and not to challenge inadequate decisions. Alternatively, they badger, fight, and build coalitions to get their position accepted to make themselves look good. The more powerful, cunning, and persistent win, but their decisions may be wrong.[23]

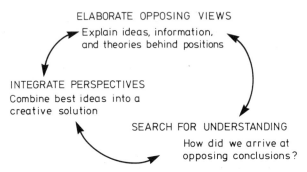

**Figure 11.1**   Dynamics of controversy

# DYNAMICS OF CONSTRUCTIVE CONTROVERSY

Controversy, the open discussion of opposing positions and views, comple-
ments unity. The most surprising findings from research on the interaction in
cooperative goals involve conflict. Cooperation does not avoid or suppress
conflict, but encourages open discussion and productive conflict management.[24] Employees who integrate their varied ideas are able to solve problems
and pursue their cooperative goals successfully.

*Controversy, when discussed in a cooperative context, promotes elaboration of
views, the search for new information and ideas, and the integration of apparently
opposing positions.* This controversy copes with the biases of closed-mindedness, inadequate evaluation of new information, simplifying the problem, and
unwarranted confidence in initial positions. These processes in turn result in
understanding opposing positions and the problem, development of alternatives, adoption of and commitment to high-quality solutions.[25] (See Figure
11.1.)

## ELABORATE

> To be persuasive we must be believable; to be believable we must be credible;
> to be credible, we must be truthful.
>
> > Edward R. Murrow, journalist

Employees with cooperative goals elaborate and explain their present
positions and ideas as they begin to disagree. They identify their positions and
the extent that they are confident or have reservations about them. They list
the facts, information, and theories that validate their theses, and provide a
logical structure that links the facts to the conclusion. Often people appreciate
their own positions, assume that their positions are superior, and want to
prove their ideas are 'right' and that their position should be accepted.

As the controversy is engaged, other employees elaborate their own views and these are often different and incompatible. The clash of opposing views interrupts any decision making and movement. Proponents may feel frustrated and argue their positions and develop their arguments more completely and forcefully. They repeat old and add new information, present more ideas, and elaborate on their positions.

## SEARCH

Difference of opinion leads to inquiry, and inquiry to truth.

Thomas Jefferson

The opposing ideas and positions challenge and provoke searching. People criticize each other's arguments, and point out weaknesses and possible strengths. They rebut counter-arguments and elaborate, but they also come to doubt the wisdom and correctness of their own position. The ideas and logic of others create internal, cognitive conflict that challenges whether their original position is as useful and sensible as they had assumed.

People become uncertain about the validity of their original thesis. With this conceptual conflict, they actively search for new information. They read more relevant material and ask others for information. They ask their protagonists to clarify their positions and rephrase their arguments so that they can understand the opposing position more thoroughly.

Because of their curiosity, they know and remember the arguments, reasoning, and facts that support alternative positions. They can take the perspective of their opponents, anticipate how they might think about future issues, and identify the kind of reasoning they like to employ.

## INTEGRATE

When a fixed idea makes its appearance, a great ass also makes its appearance.

Nietzsche

One completely overcomes only what one assimilates.

André Gide

The elaboration and search leave people much more open-minded and knowledgeable about the issue. They have approached the issue from several perspectives, and are not rigidly fixed to their own. They can synthesize and integrate different ideas and facts into a single position. They sense new patterns, incorporate other's information and reasoning into their own, and develop a position responsive to several points of view. Repeated exposure to conflictful discussion fosters more sophisticated and higher-level reasoning and cognitive development.[26]

# CONSEQUENCES

Constructive controversy has been shown *to result in high-quality, innovative solutions and agreements.* The mix and clash of the discussion creates new positions not previously considered. These positions combine the arguments and perspectives of several people in elegant ways.

People are satisfied and feel they have benefited from the discussion. They enjoy the excitement, feel aroused by the challenges of the conflict, and develop positive attitudes toward the experience. They are committed to the new agreements and positions because they understand how they are related to their own interests and positions, and why the adopted position is superior to their original one. Controversy then is critical for successful participation in which people 'own' and feel committed to decisions.[27]

The rewards of constructive controversy are rich indeed. They are much more than proving that one is right or one's position should dominate. Controversy stimulates intellectually and emotionally, and, when cooperative goals are emphasized, results in effective solutions, high morale, and strengthened work relationships.

# THE TEMPTATION TO AVOID CONTROVERSY

To do nothing at all is the most difficult thing to do in the world . . .
                                                                                    Oscar Wilde

The hottest places in Hell are reserved for those who, in a time of great moral crisis, maintained their neutrality.
                                                                                    Dante

Despite the value of controversy, employees in many teams and organizations go to great lengths to avoid discussing their opposing views and ideas openly. They try hard to be up-beat and optimistic, and look at the good side of things. They want to 'cooperate' and 'support' each other. They don't want to rock the boat, upset the team, or create waves. They fear looking dumb by asking the embarrassing questions or making a mistake by being 'wrong.' Head nodding and smiles are straightforward ways to avoid. Silence often gives the illusion of agreement.

Employees are imaginative in the ways they smooth over differences. They may gush warmth and carry on with small talk until there is just no time to talk about issues. They may debate a trivial issue strongly so that everyone is too distracted and exhausted to debate the real one. A manager may talk so long about how much he values openness and participation that no one dares embarrass the manager by implying that there has been little openness.

Team members pressure each other to conform and avoid controversy. They let each other know that it is dangerous to disagree openly and directly by the explicit or implicit messages such as: 'Our team is too fragile to withstand a clash of opinions'; 'We don't have much time so debate is counter-productive'; 'I'll hold it against you if you make me look bad by disagreeing with me'; 'We all know what we're doing so what is the point of questioning it.'

Pressure to avoid also comes from internalized values. Team members assume that an explicit disagreement will upset and frustrate. Everyone can remember when an apparently innocent discussion soon escalated into a hostile argument and created a rift not easily mended. Team members often believe that the risks of open controversy are too high, especially when the other person is a powerful boss who likes to be 'right.'

Avoiding controversy becomes for many teams a matter of habit. They fail to express their own opinions because they assume that everyone agrees with the team's decision.[28] That they should try to be smooth, mature, and rational by avoiding conflictful discussions is so obvious and ingrained that they never think of challenging the assumption. Their failure to deal with controversy becomes 'undiscussable.'[29]

Controversy requires a great deal. People have to be open about their positions and the ideas and logic that support them. They must also be open-minded and consider a different perspective. They must grapple with new information and change their thinking. Even if they believe they have the skills, they may doubt that others do.

Perhaps the overriding reason that so many groups spend so much effort avoiding controversy is the false assumption that conflict is inevitably disruptive and antagonistic. Relatedly, the risks of discussing differences openly seem immediate and tangible whereas the value of controversy for productivity and people is more distant. Lack of confidence and knowledge about how to make controversy productive also inhibits.

Avoiding does not solve the problem or dissolve the opposing perspectives. People may pay lip-service to the group's decision, but grumble and gossip in private and only appear to implement the group's decision. They may engage in a variety of political actions to pursue their positions indirectly. They may form coalitions of people of similar mind and situation for quiet warfare.[30] The coalitions help them resist the majority, spread rumors discrediting the current policy, and plot how to elevate one of their own as leader. It is unlikely that this political infighting will be organizationally useful.[31]

## STRUCTURING CONTROVERSY

Direction, unity, and empowerment prepare teams to engage in open, constructive controversy. Feeling united in cooperative goals creates a willingness to conflict openly and an ability to make it productive.[32] Feeling confident and respectful to each other, and having mutual influence, also contribute to productive controversy and decision making.

This section outlines how team leaders and members can develop the social support and procedures to express opposing views openly to explore problems and create solutions. Cohesion within a group can increase the pressures to conform, but it can also strengthen the resolve of people to disagree.[33] A minority can persuade the majority through information influence.[34]

## ELABORATE OPPOSING VIEWS

Teams can promote a healthy exchange by understanding the positive role of controversy, developing norms that support it, and gaining experience and training.[35] They have several ways to encourage the open expression of opposing views:

(1) *Include diverse people* People who differ in background, expertise, opinions, outlook, and organization position are likely to disagree. Independent thinkers and people from different departments and organizations are likely to make controversy more likely. Mixed-sex groups are at times more productive than one-gender groups.[36]

(2) *Establish openness norms* Everyone should be encouraged to express their opinions, doubts, uncertainties, and hunches. Ideas should not be dismissed because they first appear too unusual, impractical, or undeveloped.

(3) *Protect rights* The right to dissent and free speech reduces fears of retribution for speaking out.

(4) *Assign sub-groups* Coalitions are formed and given opposing positions to present and defend.

(5) *Identify a devil's advocate* One person is assigned to take a critical evaluation role by attacking the group's current preference.

(6) *Foster participation* Managers actively encourage various viewpoints and indicate that they are willing to change their own position.

## SEARCH FOR UNDERSTANDING

Team members actively search for new information in several ways:

(1) *Ask questions* Team members stop defending their own views long enough to ask each other for more information and arguments. They want others to clarify and to explain the support for their position. These are not rhetorical questions or statements in the form of questions, but are attempts to understand others thoroughly.

(2) *Put self in the other's shoes* Conflict is an opportunity to understand another's feelings, views, and thinking. Team members listen carefully and reflect back the other's position and arguments. They show they are trying to appreciate the problem fully, understand all sides, and be in a better position to develop solutions that work for all.

(3) *Use the golden rule of controversy* This simple, but often misunderstood and ignored rule is: discuss issues with others as you want them to discuss with you. If you want people to listen to you, then listen to them. If you want them to take your perspective, then take theirs. If you want others to compromise, then you compromise. The golden rule is one way to influence others, even those considered unyielding and closed-minded.

(4) *Consult relevant sources* Articles, books, consultants, and experts can provide experiences and ideas that can help the group decide which course of action is superior. Visits to organizations that have grappled with the same issue can be very enlightening. Typically, teams need to use various ideas to create their own solution rather than simply follow the advice of others.

(5) *Emphasize common ground* People in controversy can forget that they have common goals. Throughout the discussion, they remind each other that they are working for a solution that benefits all. Efforts to pursue individual objectives at others' expense are discouraged. They say 'We are all in this together' and 'Let's see a solution that is good for everyone,' not 'I am right, and you are wrong.' Decision makers avoid looking for winners and losers but focus on a productive solution to the common problem.

(6) *Show personal regard* Decision makers can quickly assume that because they are criticizing each other's ideas, they are challenging each other's face of competence.[37] They should listen to everyone's ideas respectfully, and criticize these ideas rather than attack an individual's motivation and personality. Insults or implications that challenge another's integrity, intelligence, and motives are avoided. Communication of acceptance of the person ('We are friends,' 'I am interested in what you have to say') is accompanied by disagreement with that person's current position ('I don't agree with you on that point,' 'I've come to a different conclusion').

(7) *Avoid premature evaluation* Teams should explore and try to understand various options thoroughly before they begin to evaluate them.[38] They may suspend evaluation for some time to encourage brainstorming.

## INTEGRATE PERSPECTIVES

Teams encourage integration by various means:

(1) *Work to resolve* Team members recognize that they want to resolve the controversy so they can make a decision and accomplish common goals.

Unending or escalating conflict can be very costly. Group members remind each other of the benefit for everyone if a high-quality decision is reached.

(2) *Define issues jointly* Team members know what the major issues are and stick to the problem. They avoid diversion to side issues by taking the discussion too personally, feeling indignant, or trying to save face.

(3) *Influence collaboratively* Controversy requires people to persuade, inform, and convince in order to make the discussion stimulating and involving. People have the conviction and willingness to argue their positions forcefully and to persuade, but they avoid dominating and coercion. They say 'I want you to consider this seriously' and 'You will probably find this convincing,' not 'You must accept this point' and 'You have no choice but to agree.' There is give and take, not dominance or passivity.

(4) *Strive for consensus* Requiring consensus decision making encourages full participation and people with doubts to speak out. Majority vote can degenerate into attempts to get a majority and force that decision on others.[39]

(5) *Combine ideas* Team members avoid 'either my way or your way' thinking and try to use as many ideas as possible to create new, useful solutions. They may be able to create a totally new solution. Sometimes they can find creative compromises where people agree to another's ideas in areas of primary importance to that person, or are able to cut the costs for the adopted position.[40]

## GUIDES FOR ACTION

- Elaborate positions and ideas.
- List facts, information, and theories.
- Ask for clarification.
- Clarify opposing ideas.
- Challenge opposing ideas and positions.
- Reaffirm your confidence in those who differ.
- Identify strengths in opposing arguments.
- Search for new information.
- Integrate various information and reasoning.
- Create a solution responsive to several points of view.

## PITFALLS TO AVOID

- Assume your position is superior.
- Prove your ideas are 'right' and must be accepted.

- Interpret opposition to your ideas as a personal attack.
- Refuse to admit weaknesses in your position.
- Pretend to listen.

## EXPLORING IN RESEARCH & DEVELOPMENT

Miles had briefed the TLC on progress that his area was making in dealing directly with the mistrust between whites, blacks, and Asians, and between males and females.

'Like Art said about his group two weeks ago, we too are moving slowly but quickly,' Miles summarized. 'Nothing dramatic has happened in terms that can be quickly measured—our productivity hasn't increased noticeably. But there's a change in attitude not only toward other groups, but also toward ourselves and our jobs. We feel more in charge and on top of our problems, and feel more united too. We have more of that "can do" feeling that is hard to quantify but really makes a difference.'

'My new product teams need some of that "can do" feeling,' Scott said. 'As my boss wanted, we have our teams made up of Marketing, R&D people, Engineering, and Production, and they talk, but it just seems to go around and around. There are no big conflicts or emotional displays to blame.'

'What do you think is going on?' Marian asked.

'I used to think that there was too much teamwork, too much unity, but after talking about our model it hit me that perhaps there isn't enough,' Scott said. 'Kyle and I got to talking about it and he offered to sit in on one of the team's meetings. We thought that they would be less inhibited with him than with me.'

'The group I sat in on was very polite,' Kyle offered. 'Everyone is proper, and no one raises their voice, but they really don't seem to dig very far. Scott and I decided that we perhaps needed to work more on the exploring side of these teams.'

'A little structured controversy can go a long way,' Marian said. 'It can break open the log jam and help them see that a united team needs to explore alternative points of view seriously.'

'Let them mix it up, I agree,' Scott said. 'But I have already in a sense told them to do that. I told them to speak up, and that the reason for having this team is to give the various groups a chance to work out problems together and early rather than have each department work on a new product sequentially.'

'I can see the heads nodding and the faces smiling, as they tell themselves you must be bucking for a promotion,' Art teased.

'Let's give Scott the benefit of the doubt,' Marian said, laughing with the group. 'Perhaps they did understand you and they may even have believed you.'

'You do have a wild imagination, especially for someone from Human Resources,' Art deadpanned.

'Even if they did accept what you were saying, that does not mean that they know how to disagree constructively,' Marian said. 'We've been told over and over again that competent managers take charge and don't get ruffled; mature people are cool and don't get emotional. It is hard to go from this mindset to a "let it all hang out" one.'

'You're saying they need some help,' Scott said.

'Right, and there are lots of ways to structure controversy and I can give you all some reading on that,' Marian said. 'But the one I think is particularly useful to get groups to appreciate the value of controversy and develop some confidence is advocacy sub-groups. Essentially, you select two or more positions and assign people to defend these positions. Give them some time to gather information and develop their reasoning. Then have them present and defend their positions to each other. That controversy should get a lot of facts and arguments out on the table, and then have the groups drop their assigned positions and the team as a whole integrates the best arguments into a new solution.'

'The team I observed seems to be stuck on whether they should refine the frozen potato line or go for the high-risk, high-return microwave option,' Kyle said.

'We have all heard that one before,' Art said. 'That's been an ongoing issue for some time.'

'Your group probably reflects the different positions of the areas in Savory', Marian said. 'Marketing wants microwave, Production is negative, and the technical people are ambivalent.'

'That's about it,' Scott said.

'Your group is a place where that issue can be directly grappled with rather than be hung up in this kind of political battle,' Marian said.

'Now, we haven't moved on it because there's been no consensus, and Allan has not forced the issue and said which position he favors,' Art said.

'He probably doesn't want to offend anyone,' Kyle speculated.

'And he may not know what to do,' Miles said.

'These advocacy sub-groups might just polarize the new product team,'

Scott said. 'Marketing becomes more committed to its position, and Production to its.'

'It's important that you mix the groups up,' Marian said. 'Put pro frozen and pro microwave in each sub-group. Let them defend the other side for a while.'

'I can see where it could be liberating,' Scott said.

'You'd be surprised at how committed these groups can get,' Marian said. 'One thing to watch out for is that people will still argue their assigned position after you ask them to integrate views. You have to remind them that the purpose is to arrive at a common position that helps the whole team. You are using controversy to promote unity.'

'Let me look over that material and see if I can come up with a plan for these advocacy sub-groups,' Scott said.

'I'd be glad to help,' Kyle said.

'That would be good,' agreed Scott.


## ADVOCACY SUB-GROUPS FOR DECISION MAKING

The best way ever devised for seeking the truth in any given situation is advocacy: presenting the pros and cons from different, informed points of view and digging down deep into the facts.

Harold S. Geneen, former CEO, ITT

Advocacy sub-groups is a systematic, thorough way to structure productive controversy.

*Phase 1: The team selects a problem important enough to warrant the time and resources needed to explore it comprehensively.* The leader identifies the major alternative positions.

*Phase 2: Advocacy sub-groups are formed and each one is assigned a major alternative.* Members are given the time and resources to find all the supporting facts, information, evidence, and reasons for their alternative. They plan how they can present their arguments so that everyone is well aware of the strengths of their position. Their goal is not to win the debate by getting their position accepted, but they still want to present their arguments forcefully and thoroughly so that their position is seriously considered.

*Phase 3: Each sub-group presents its arguments and position fully and persuasively; at the same time members open-mindedly listen to the other positions.* In this free discussion, they develop their own arguments, advocate their position, defend it against refutation, and counter opposing arguments. They take notes, and challenge inadequate facts and reasoning. They may paraphrase each other's position and arguments to demonstrate that they have listened and understood them. Throughout the discussion, they remember that their purpose is for the whole group to develop as strong a position as possible.

*Phase 4: Reach a consensus decision.* The subgroups drop their assigned position, and using all the facts and arguments identified, reach a general agreement on the best course of action. They change their minds because of the logic and evidence, not because others are more powerful or argue more loudly. The decision reflects their best joint reflected judgment.

*Phase 5: Approach management and others to make and implement the decision.* Making a decision in an organization is more than getting the right answer. Decisions are not puzzles to be solved; they are part of the stream of working and managing. The solution must be accepted and implemented, its impact assessed, and new problems identified.

After the decision, the team as a whole meets to reflect and talk about how the members used conflict to make decisions. Though the approach can be exciting, involving, and worthwhile, it is not easy. It can be tempting to fall back into the typical mode of trying to dominate and 'win' by getting one's position accepted. Team members can easily get caught up in proving they were right and the others wrong. They have to remind themselves that what counts is *not who was right at first but that the group is right at the end.*


## ADVOCACY SUB-GROUPS GUIDES


Phase 1: Select a problem that warrants a comprehensive evaluation.
       Identify the major alternative positions.
Phase 2: Assign sub-groups opposing positions.
       Provide resources for teams to gather argumentsand information for
       their position.
Phase 3: Each sub-group presents its arguments.
       Others listen open-mindedly.
       Constructively challenge positions.
Phase 4: Members drop assigned positions.
       Examine all the evidence and arguments.
       Reach a consensus decision.
Phase 5: Approach those who can make and implement the decision.

## CONCLUDING COMMENTS

Problems test teams. If they can explore them in depth and create workable solutions, teams stay on course, overcome obstacles, and further their vision. If they are stymied and unable to develop confidence in their decisions, then teams can sputter and splinter. Common goals and confidence are lost as people feel demoralized and begin to pin blame. Constructive controversy unlocks the power of team problem solving.

Controversy tests teams. Teams need the values, skills, and procedures to make conflict positive. Team members must express their ideas forcefully, but also be open to understanding other points of view. They dig into the issues to develop a complex understanding of the problem and incorporate various ideas into useful recommendations. They gain consensus and agreement through direct, open discussion of conflicting opinions.

There is a growing recognition of the value of team and conflict in organizational decision making. Researchers have proposed different ways to heighten conflict. Structuring businesses into family groups and exploiting the heterogeneous viewpoints and backgrounds within a corporation have been considered critical for companies to rejuvenate their products and services and cope with intense competition.[41] Empirical work has investigated devil's advocate, dialectic inquiry, and other procedures to stimulate conflict and improve strategic decision making.[42] During a crisis, decision makers may successfully cope by creating and then objecting to a series of positions.[43]

Although harmony has traditionally been much lauded, avoiding controversy undermines decision making. When team members suppress their differences, they can make poor decisions that threaten the credibility and vitality of the company. They remain ignorant of risks and opportunities, and make decisions without thoughtful analysis. They court disaster as well as stagnation.

People working together can explore issues and combine ideas, and feel the confidence and power necessary to take new developments as opportunities, not threats. To solve problems together, team members must express their opposing views openly. Then they doubt their original position, ask questions to explore alternatives, take opposing information seriously, develop a more accurate view of the situation, and incorporate opposing positions into their own thinking and decisions. Through productive controversy, team members create solutions and competitive advantages.

## REFERENCES

1. Jackson, S. E. and Dutton, J. E. (1988). Discerning threats and opportunities. *Administrative Science Quarterly*, **33**, 370–387.

2. Hill, G. W. (1982). Group versus individual performance: are N + 1 heads better than one? *Psychological Bulletin*, **91**, 517–539. Johnson, D. W., Maruyama, G., Johnson, R. T., Nelson, D. and Skon, S. (1981). Effects of cooperative, competitive, and individualistic goal structures on achievement: a meta-analysis. *Psychological Bulletin*, **89**, 47–62. Kelley, H. H. and Thibaut, J. W. (1968). Group problem solving. In G. Lindzey and E. Aronson, *Handbook of Social Psychology*. Reading, MA: Addison-Wesley, **3**, 1–105.

3. Johnson, D. W., Maruyama, G., Johnson, R. T., Nelson, D. and Skon, S. (1981). Effects of cooperative, competitive, and individualistic goal structures on achievement: a meta-analysis. *Psychological Bulletin*, **89**, 47–62. Johnson, D. W. and Johnson, R. T. (1989). *Cooperation and Competition: Theory and Research*. Edina, MN: Interaction Book Company.

4. Halverson, R. and Pallak, M. (1978). Commitment, ego-involvement, and resistance to attack. *Journal of Experimental Social Psychology*, **14**, 1–12. Hollenbeck, J. R., Williams, C. R. and Klein, H. J. (1989). An empirical examination of the antecedents of commitment to difficult goals. *Journal of Applied Psychology*, **74**, 18–23. Kiesler, C. (1971). *The Psychology of Commitment: Experiments Linking Behavior to Belief*. New York: Academic Press. Lewin, K. (1943). *Forces behind Food Habits and Methods of Change: The Problem of Changing Food Habits*. (NRC Bulletin No. 108). Washington, DC: National Research Council: Committee on Food Habits.

5. Walsh, J. P. (1988). Selectivity and selective perception: an investigation of managers' belief structure and information processing. *Academy of Management Journal*, **31**, 873–896.

6. Simon, H. A. (1976). *Administrative Behavior*. New York: Free Press.

7. Barnes, H. H., Jr (1984). Cognitive biases and their impact on strategic planning. *Strategic Management Journal*, **5**, 129–137. Cyert, R. M. and March, J. G. (1963). *A Behavioral Theory of the Firm*. Englewood Cliffs, NJ: Prentice-Hall. Schuster, M. (1984). The Scanlon Plan: a longitudinal analysis. *Journal of Applied Behavioral Science*, **20**, 23–38. Schwenk, C. R. (1984). Cognitive simplification processes in strategic decision-making. *Strategic Management Journal*, **5**, 111–128.

8. Hogarth, R. M. and Makridakis, S. (1981). Forecasting and planning; an evaluation. *Management Science*, **27**, 115–138. Slovic, P., Fischhoff, B. and Lichtenstein, S. (1977). Behavioral decision theory. *Annual Review of Psychology*, **28**, 1–39.

9. Levine, J. M. (1989). Reaction to opinion deviance in small groups. In P. B. Paulus (ed.), *Psychology of Group Influence*. Hillsdale, NJ: Erlbaum. 2nd edn, 187–231. Tversky, A. and Kahneman, D. (1974). Judgement under uncertainty; heuristics and biases. *Science*, **185**, 1124–1131.

10. Brockner, J., Houser, R., Birnbaum, G., Lloyd, K., Deitcher, J., Nathanson, S. and Rubin, J. Z. (1986). Escalation of commitment to an ineffective course of action: the effects of feedback having negative implications for self-identity. *Administrative Science Quarterly*, **31**, 109–126.

11. Tversky, A. and Kahneman, D. (1974). Judgement under uncertainty; heuristics and biases. *Science*, **185**, 1124–1131.

12. Schwenk, C. R. (1984). Cognitive simplification processes in strategic decision-making. *Strategic Management Journal*, **5**, 111–128.

13. Tversky, A. and Kahneman, D. (1974). Judgement under uncertainty; heuristics and biases. *Science*, **185**, 1124–1131.

14. Cohen, M. D. and March, J. B. (1974). *Leadership and Ambiguity*. New York: McGraw-Hill.

15. Hegedus, D. M. and Rasmussen, R. V. (1986). Task effectiveness and interaction

process of a modified Nominal Group Technique in solving an evaluation problem. *Journal of Management*, **12**, 545–560.

16. Johnson, D. W. and Johnson, R. T. (1989). *Cooperation and Competition: Theory and Research*. Edina, MN: Interaction Book Company.

17. Stasser, G. and Titus, W. (1987). Effects of information load and percentage of shared information on the dissemination of unshared information during group discussion. *Journal of Personality and Social Psychology*, **53**, 81–93.

18. Mulder, M. and Wilkie, H. (1970). Participation and power equalization. *Organizational Behavior and Human Performance*, **5**, 430–448.

19. Janis, I. L. (1972). *Victims of Groupthink*. Boston, MA: Houghton Mifflin. Mann, L. and Janis, I. (1983). Decisional conflict in organizations. In D. Tjosvold and D. W. Johnson (eds), *Productive Conflict Management: Perspectives for Organizations*. Minneapolis, MN: Team Media, 16–45.

20. Janis, I. L. (1972). *Victims of Groupthink*. Boston: Houghton Mifflin.

21. Kruglanski, A. W. (1986). Freeze-think and the Challenger. *Psychology Today*, August, 48–49.

22. Foushee, H. C. (1984). Dyads and triads at 35,500 feet: factors affecting group process and aircrew performance. *American Psychologist*, **39**, 886–893.

23. Eisenhardt, K. M. and Bourgeois, L. J., III (1988). Politics of strategic decision making in high-velocity environments: toward a midrange theory. *Academy of Management Journal*, **31**, 737–770.

24. Deutsch, M. (1973). *The Resolution of Conflict*. New Haven, CT: Yale University Press. Tjosvold, D. (1985). Implications of controversy research for management. *Journal of Management*, **11**, 21–37.

25. Tjosvold, D. (1987). Participation: a close look at its dynamics. *Journal of Management*, **13**, 739–750. Tjosvold, D. and McNeely, L. T. (1988). Innovation through communication in an educational bureaucracy. *Communication Research*, **15**, 568–581.

26. Rest, J. (1986). Studies in cognitive development. *Research in Educational Research*.

27. Tjosvold, D. (1987). Participation: a close look at its dynamics. *Journal of Management*, **13**, 739–750.

28. Harvey, J. B. (1988). *The Abilene Paradox and Other Mediations on Management*. Lexington, MA: Lexington Books.

29. Argyris, C. and Schon, D. (1978). *Organizational Learning*. Reading, MA: Addison-Wesley.

30. Eisenhardt, K. M. and Bourgeois, L. J., III (1988). Politics of strategic decision making in high-velocity environments: toward a midrange theory. *Academy of Management Journal*, **31**, 737–770. Pfeffer, J. (1981). *Power in Organizations*. Boston: Pitman.

31. Eisenhardt, K. M. and Bourgeois, L. J., III (1988). Politics of strategic decision making in high-velocity environments: toward a midrange theory. *Academy of Management Journal*, **31**, 737–770.

32. Tjosvold, D. (1985). Implications of controversy research for management. *Journal of Management*, **11**, 21–37. Van Berklom, M. and Tjosvold, D. (1981). The effects of social context on engaging in controversy. *Journal of Psychology*, **107**, 141–145.

33. Leana, C. R. (1985). A partial test of Janis' Groupthink Model: effects of group cohesiveness and leader behavior on defective decision making. *Journal of Management*, **11**, 5–17.

34. Kaplan, M. F. (1987). The influencing process in group decision making. In C. Hendrick (ed.), *Group Processes*. Newbury Park, CA: Sage, 189–212. Nemeth, C.

(1986). Differential contribution of majority and minority influence. *Psychological Review*, **93**, 23–32.

35. Basadur, M., Graen, G. B. and Scandura, T. A. (1986). Training effects on attitudes toward divergent thinking among manufacturing engineers. *Journal of Applied Psychology*, **71**, 612–617.

36. Wood, W. (1987). Meta-analytic review of sex differences in group performance. *Psychological Bulletin*, **102**, 53–71.

37. Tjosvold, D. (1983). Social face in conflict: a critique. *International Journal of Group Tensions*, **13**, 49–64.

38. Maier, N. R. F. (1970). *Problem-solving and Creativity in Individuals and Groups*. Belmont, CA: Brooks/Cole.

39. Thompson, L. L., Mannix, E. A. and Bazerman, M. H. (1988). Group negotiation: effects of decision rule, agenda, and aspiration. *Journal of Personality and Social Psychology*, **54**, 86–95.

40. Pruitt, D. G. and Syna, H. (1989). Successful problem solving. In D. Tjosvold and D. W. Johnson (eds), *Productive Conflict Management: Perspectives for Organizations*. Minneapolis, MN, Team Media, 69–90.

41. Charkravarthy, B. S. (1984). Strategic self-renewal: a planning framework for today. *Academy of Management Review*, **9**, 536–547. Porter, M. (1985). *Competitive Advantage*. New York: Free Press.

42. Cosier, R. A. (1978). The effects of three potential aids for making strategic decisions on prediction accuracy. *Organizational Behavior and Human Performance*, **22**, 295–306. Cosier, R. A. and Schwenk, C. R. (1990). Agreement and thinking alike: ingredients for poor decisions. *Academy of Management Executive*, **4**, 69–74. George, A. (1974). Adaptation to stress in political decision-making: the individual, small group, and organizational contexts. In G. V. Coelho, D. A. Hamburg and J. E. Adams (eds), *Coping and Adaptation*, New York: Basic Books. Mason, R. O. and Mitroff, I. I. (1981). *Challenging Strategic Planning Assumptions*. New York: Wiley. Schweiger, D. M., Sandberg, W. R. and Ragan, J. W. (1986). Group approaches for improving strategic decision making: a comparative analysis of dialectical inquiry, devil's advocacy, and consensus. *Academy of Management Journal*, **29**, 51–71. Schweiger, D. M., Sandberg, W. R. and Rechner, P. L. (1989). Experimental effects of dialectical inquiry, devil's advocacy, and consensus approaches to strategic decision making. *Academy of Management Journal*, **32**, 745–772.

43. Anderson, P. A. (1983). Decision making by objection and the Cuban Missile Crisis. *Administrative Science Quarterly*, **28**, 201–222.

# 12   Reflecting

Our advocacy sub-groups really got into whether we should invest in improvements in our frozen line or open up a microwave line of potato products,' Kyle reported to the TLC.

'Each group had banners and slogans, as well as demographic charts and expert testimony from technology types,' Scott said.

'I think we all got a better understanding of why there is no simple answer to this issue,' Kyle said. 'The data, the logic are not all on one side.'

'We did come to a general consensus that microwave was a great gamble, but the future probably was there too,' Scott said.

'So you decided to go that way?' Art asked.

'Yes, but not totally,' Scott said. 'We still think people will go for some frozen foods if we can keep improving quality. Who knows, the market may expand despite all the experts. We should also invest in some potato microwave products. Funny, but we came to see that not moving in this way was very risky, perhaps too risky. We might be shut out altogether in a real hot market and lose big.'

'Observing the fun this new product group had got me to thinking how boring our accounting group is,' Kyle said.

'Bean-counting—boring?' Miles teased.

'I think you let yourself in for all kinds of accounting jokes,' Marian said with a sympathetic laugh.

'Sometimes stereotypes are true,' Kyle said.

'Aren't you identifying with the enemy?' Art teased Kyle.

'Actually, we have a good group of people,' Kyle said. 'By and large, accountants are nice people who want to be helpful. But our accounting group seems to have more than its share of hang-ups. I've heard some stories, but it's hard to put my finger on what the issues are and decide what to do.'

'What have you been thinking?' Miles asked.

'We seem to have a cantankerous guy who has been with the company for decades who's gotten sour on lots of operations people who are also sour on him. I'm afraid it hurts the whole group.'

'Cut out the cancer,' Miles offered.

'But he is a loyal guy, and given his all for Savory. How could I just let him go?' Kyle asked.

'Perhaps you should get the whole team involved in diagnosis and let them come up with some ways to strengthen the team,' Marian suggested.

'I guess I don't have to have the answers,' Kyle said.

'It's better that they come up with the answers,' Marian said. 'The answers may be superior and better known and implemented.'

'I'll still be leading?' Kyle asked.

'You're leading by asking them to reflect on their experiences to improve their performance,' Marian said.

They brainstormed about how Kyle might proceed. Kyle decided that they would modify slightly Marian's sample questionnaire and interviews. The interviews and questionnaires would be held confidentially; a summary of the responses to the questionnaires and the issues uncovered would be distributed to the accounting group. The group would be asked to consider this information and generate more, diagnose how the group members work together, and plan how to strengthen it. Scott offered to interview some people who might feel more comfortable talking to someone other than their boss.

## THE PULL OF REFLECTION

Teams celebrate success with parties and toasts. Failures bring recriminations and vows to redouble efforts. How the team is working together, as well as its progress on its business task, stimulates reflection and evaluation. Sincere support leaves people feeling grateful. Angry conflicts get people to re-evaluate their strategies and attitudes, and, if productively discussed, improve their collaboration.

Team members want to reflect. They have weekend retreats, all-day sessions, and hire consultants to do team building. Much more reflection goes on informally. They confide in spouses, friends, and therapists. At lunch, over drinks after work, and in the hallway, they turn to talking about their team's progress and people. They describe and analyze, complain and criticize, praise and thank, appreciate and blame.

Teams are rich experiences. Working with others involves central human needs and aspirations. Team membership offers the possibility to achieve and be respected. Our innermost thoughts and feelings concerning who we are depend upon how others treat us.[1] People want to know how they come across to others as a way to know themselves.

It is intellectually challenging to try to understand the complex dynamics within teams. Why does Art find it easy to believe in the value of teams whereas Scott is skeptical? How did Miles develop his easy, warm ways of working with other people? What motivated Marian to study teamwork?

There are inevitably hitches and hiccups. Even in the best of relationships, people have frustrations, annoyances, and conflicts. Conflict is especially prevalent and important in close relationships because many needs and values are involved. People dismiss slights from strangers, but are deeply worried when colleagues are inattentive. The strong emotions and troubling questions of conflict propel people to talk. *The issue is not whether teams will conflict and reflect, but how open and useful discussions will be.*

Teams want to evaluate 'bottom-line' progress on their task and examine their internal workings. Team members collect and consider data about their success in getting the job done and establishing productive relationships. The need to evaluate task progress is well understood and how it is done depends very much on the nature of the task. This chapter focuses on reflecting on how people are working together.

## ONGOING EVALUATION AND DEVELOPMENT

> For things we have to learn before we do them, we learn by doing them.
>
> Aristotle

Reflection may seem out of place in the breakneck speed of contemporary business. But coasting, going through the motions, and rigidly following outworn procedures are no longer acceptable. Reflection helps teams and organizations respond by recognizing how their present ways of operating are obsolete. *Experience itself does not teach; people learn from reflecting on their experience.* By evaluating its strengths and weaknesses, a team prepares itself to act more effectively.

Reflection is the vital link between action and ideas. Ideas in this book can help you understand teamwork and make plans about how to establish and work within a team. However, you must experiment with these ideas and procedures, reflect and learn, and try again. Then you will deepen your

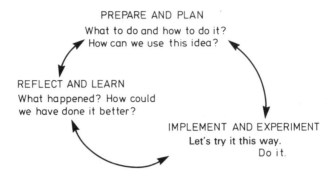

**Figure 12.1**  Ongoing evaluation and development

understanding of teamwork and strengthen your capacity to develop teams. Without experimenting, the ideas in this book will remain abstract. Without reflection, you will not use your experience to improve your abilities. (See Figure 12.1.)

Reflection contributes critically to team productivity.[2] Conflicts cannot be allowed to simmer and rip relationships apart. Teams must adjust to the changing organization's vision and requirements and the changing needs and aspirations of individuals. Feeling competitive and wanting to work alone threaten unity. Doubts and setbacks can demoralize. Norms that pressure conformity must be corrected. A team has to be able to take stock of itself and the situation, develop a useful analysis, and adjust and make plans. A team is not a machine to wind up, set on course, and let go: it needs adjusting, nurturing, and strengthening.

## REFLECTING AT EATON CORPORATION

Eaton Corporation has been experimenting with participative management since the 1960s. According to Jon Wendenhof,[3] corporate director of industrial relations, the company had a general feeling that it could develop much better links with unionized employees, and tried several experiments. By learning from its experiences, the company gradually extended participative management.

In 1968, a team of operations and human resource people, charged with designing a productive work environment for a new engine valve manufacturing plant, was struck how differently the salaried and the unionized employees behaved at established plants. Team members concluded that the company showed much more trust of salaried employees; they had no time clock to punch or laundry list of rules. As a consequence, salaried employees were much more committed and motivated. Hourly workers reciprocated mistrust with their own;

they would, for example, work just to the minimum of acceptable standards.

At the new 'greenfield' site, Eaton adopted the same management style for workers as for salaried. There were no preferred parking areas or separate dining rooms; no list of rules, probationary periods, or time clocks; no obsession about precedent-setting implications of individual decisions; and far fewer secrets about key business issues. Their first experiences were positive, so they continued to use this approach in new plants.

Eaton wanted to measure the impact of this management style on productivity. They saw striking differences between the 'new philosophy' plants and the old style ones. Operators at the new style plants, manufacturing identical parts with equal processes and equipment, were consistently 30–40% more productive, and had absentee rates of 1% rather than 5%. Employees in the new style plants often came back to work in their own time, whereas in the old plants workers would line up to punch out.

In 1983, Chairman Del de Windt, concerned how the new philosophy survived the years of recession, charged a team of managers to interview people at the plants. The team found that the new philosophy, especially in plants where local management emphasized communication and working together, was very instrumental in the success of the company through the recession. Plants that reverted to old ways of working were less successful. The managers also learned the limitations of the program. Even at plants that stayed with the new style, they found there was not much experimenting with new ways to implement it. Turnover of top managers and the growth of plants above 400 workers also made it more difficult to maintain trust and teamwork. Non-union office people often felt neglected.

The audit encouraged Eaton to implement the new philosophy in old plants. It highlighted that the company should experiment with longer tenure for top managers, smaller sizes for factories, and programs to involve office personnel. Working as a team in participative management is a powerful idea, but as Eaton demonstrated, it must be experimented with, examined, and re-acted upon.

## BARRIERS TO OPEN REFLECTION

But why is it, by most accounts, that shared, open reflection is so uncommon in organizations? Why are its benefits ignored and the costs of gossiping and private reflection incurred? It is not simply that people don't want to. As we have seen, the powerful needs to achieve, be respected, know oneself, and be part of a productive team are tied to open reflection. What is behind the failure to appreciate clearly the value of shared reflection and make use of it?

## SHORT-TERM TASK ORIENTATION

Many managers and employees are highly oriented to getting the task done without a firm recognition of the need to build and maintain relationships among people. Sharing technical information and solving task problems are seen as highly legitimate and useful. Sharing feelings about how people are treated is considered difficult and obstructive. But why do so many managers and employees fail to see the need to invest and work on the relationships through which things get done?

The crushing emphasis on the short run reinforces the neglect of relationships. Managers and employees often feel under the gun to get the letter out by 5 o'clock, the project done by Friday, and the profits in by the end of the quarter. Competitive pressures in the marketplace and investor pressure on stocks can make this short-term orientation seem even more important today. From this perspective, spending time having people talk about their feelings toward each other and complaining about their conflicts may seem superfluous, perhaps a bit crazy. From a long-term view, discussing how people can strengthen their communication and teamwork to be increasingly effective seems very sensible.

## EDUCATION

Secondary, vocational, professional, and managerial education emphasizes task skills and procedures, and ignores the complexity of working with other people. There is an assumption that because people have obtained degrees they have also learned to collaborate. Of course, everyone has some skills because they have had to live and work with others. However, many people fail to appreciate the sensitivity and skills needed to work with others in contemporary organizations. Here they must work with people they do not know, with much different training, perspectives, and orientations, and they must quickly perform efficiently. Yet they and their managers have little appreciation that relationships must be built and nurtured.

Chris Argyris[4] argued that professional education reinforces managers with values and beliefs that result in defining interpersonal issues as 'undiscussable.' Though managers espouse openness and cooperation, they act to exert unilateral control, to win, and to hide feelings. The discrepancy between action and ideals is a double-bind message that immobilizes managers and employees. Employees conspire to let managers maintain the illusion of participation and collaboration. To reflect openly and talk about feelings would reveal the manager's competitiveness and control orientation, expose employees' duplicity, and embarrass everyone. Managers and employees experience a deep sense of hypocrisy between the ideal and the reality, but the very discrepancy prevents them from reflecting on their behaviour.

## MISATTRIBUTIONS

Inaccuracies also inhibit reflection. Studies document fundamental errors in attributing responsibility. People are willing to accept responsibility for success, but attribute poor performance to others. Similarly, people are much more aware of their own positive contributions than of the contributions of others.[5] These conclusions can make people feel they are being blamed unjustly and are unappreciated. These feelings cause disgruntlement and a desire to leave the group.[6]

However, attributions are not invariably biased and inaccurate. Taking the long term, for example, has been found to reduce attribution errors. People who understand that they need to work together in the future on important tasks are more forthcoming in accepting responsibilities.[7] Team members with cooperative goals have been found to make enabling attributions. Rather than become demoralized by attributing failure to factors outside their control, they understand that there are situations they can change to improve their future performance.[8] Attribution research underlines the need for shared reflection. Team members will make attributions but, without an open discussion about them, they may well blame each other and expect others, not themselves, to improve performance.

The short-term, get things done orientation coupled with concerns about blaming and being blamed and fears that open discussions may get out of hand result in a 'if it ain't broke, don't fix it' approach to interpersonal issues: Let's hope that people will work together and that any problems will naturally sort themselves out. If relationships explode and it becomes obvious that the job is not getting done, then we'll try to pick up the pieces, hire a consultant, and have a weekend for team building. But by then suspicions and anger can be so intense that finding and dealing with underlying issues is very emotionally trying and time consuming. The team may be stalled in a quagmire with no practical means to extradite itself.

## PROGRAM FOR EVALUATION AND DEVELOPMENT

The team should strive for an *ongoing, developing approach to relationships*, rather than try to put the pieces back together after an escalating conflict or embarrassing failure. Here team members recognize the complexity and difficulties of working together effectively, and appreciate there will be inevitable frustrations, misunderstandings, and conflict. These are not in themselves great obstacles; indeed, *conflicts, when properly discussed, help them know each other better, develop more effective ways of working, and leave them feeling united and directed toward their vision.*

Reflection needs to be a mutual process. It is risky for an employee to talk about feelings and relationships alone. They may look aggressive or be suspected of 'playing games' and putting other people on the spot. One person cannot manage a conflict alone; it takes two to get entangled in a conflict and it takes two to get untangled. Teams need to encourage joint discussion so that people talk openly and directly to develop a shared understanding of the team and a joint commitment to future improvements, and avoid gossiping and forming divisive coalitions behind closed-door offices.

## USING THE TEAM ORGANIZATION MODEL

Feeling directed, unified, empowered, and able to explore issues helps teams reflect openly and productively. Then team members understand that reflection will be used to keep them on course, promote mutual benefit, strengthen their abilities, and use problem solving to examine their teamwork. Teams also need norms, procedures, and skills to identify and overcome interpersonal conflicts, deal with failures, and celebrate successes as they work together to get things done.

Teams have a great number of ways to reflect. They may complete questionnaires, be interviewed, and use observations. They may discuss the data and identify an action plan after a team meeting, at a weekend retreat, or as a conflict arises. The structure may be formalized and the time set, or spontaneous. They may do it with their own resources, or invite a consultant from the firm's human resource group or the outside to assist them. The concrete way to proceed will depend upon a great number of practical considerations as well as the particular styles and wishes of the team members. *What is critical is that the team members create valid, useful data and together recognize their accomplishments and obstacles. Then they can celebrate their successes, and deal with limitations and conflicts to strengthen their team.*

## STRENGTHS

It is often assumed that a team should concentrate on its weaknesses, as if it can only learn from mistakes and limitations. But teams improve by recognizing their accomplishments and abilities. They are aware of what they are capable of doing, and the persistence that it takes to succeed. Their greater confidence gives them more energy to pursue, and makes them less defensive and more able to recognize the weaknesses they need to work on to be more effective. They believe they are on course and believe in each other. Success breeds success.

Teams should celebrate their accomplishments together. As Renn Zaphiro-poulos, president and CEO at Versatec put it, 'If you are going to give someone a check, don't just mail it. Have a celebration.' The sense of common success and mutual congratulation makes the achievement more meaningful, and reinforces the sense of team confidence and competence. It is much more fun to share a victory than to have to blow one's horn alone.

## WEAKNESSES

Team members need to face their weaknesses head on. Problems that the team do not know about will do it in; those that it does not work on will paralyze it. The team avoids blaming individuals and shares the responsibility and digs into doing something about it.

Although blaming is avoided, *individual team members are held accountable.* In the division of labor and assignment of roles, they have been assigned particular responsibilities. Those who have not fulfilled them should be confronted and the reasons for their inadequate performance explored.[9] But even here the team has a shared responsibility to work with the individual, help remove obstacles, and provide the resources for individual and group success. Often individuals failed to perform because they felt unsupported and inadequately informed. Of course, individuals who continue to refuse to do their jobs risk punishment and expulsion.

## TEAM SKILLS AND EXECUTIVE SUCCESS

Although management education does not emphasize interpersonal skills, the real world of work does. The failure to reflect on and use experience to develop skills in working with peers, superiors, and subordinates can be disastrous. McCall and Lambardo[10] found the reasons why top executives were derailed and did not fulfill their potential were:

(1) Insensitivity to others.
(2) Coldness, aloofness, and arrogance.

(3) Untrustworthiness.
(4) Playing politics and pushing too hard to promote themselves.
(5) Failure to admit a problem.
(6) Failure to delegate and build a team.
(7) Inability to select and develop a staff.
(8) Inability to think strategically and broadly.
(9) Unable to adapt to a superior with a different style.
(10) Overdependence on a superior or mentor.

# REFLECTING

Team members should work to understand their situation and problems rather than jump quickly to a solution. They want to investigate the past, not to find fault but to analyze it and understand the reasons why problems arose. They use available information and reasoning to dig into issues, understand their relationships, and identify barriers and obstacles. They compare their present skill and work relationships with the ideals of the team organization model. They develop a common understanding of their strengths and weaknesses. Then they are prepared to develop and implement plans.

## COLLECTING DATA

There are various ways to collect information. What is critical is that team members are able to discuss their views, reach a general understanding of the team's working, and be mutually motivated to strengthen it.

(1) *Use questionnaires for general information and comparisons* Questionnaires are relatively inexpensive ways for team members to indicate how they view the group's vision, unity, empowerment, exploring, and reflection. (See Sample Questionnaire in the appendix at the end of this chapter.) However, questionnaires ask people to make generalizations, and team members may use much different paths to draw conclusions. They may also differ in their use of the rating scale; a rating of 'very much' is unlikely to mean the same for everyone. Questionnaires provide general conclusions, but do not themselves give specific behaviors and incidents behind them.

(2) *Interview for rich information* Team members can explain the specific behaviors and incidents that lie behind their perceptions and generalizations about the group. (See Sample Interview Schedule in the appendix.) When team members interview each other, it allows for a mutual, two-way communication and shared understanding. However, interviews require training,

skill, and time, and the results are often difficult to summarize and feed back to the group.

(3) *Observe to describe the actual behaviors of team members* A team member, an employee from another group, or an outside consultant reports what they have seen going on in the group. (See Sample Observation Sheet in the appendix.) The group gets a much better picture of its actual workings. Observations, like interviews, require training and time. Unlike interviewing, observation focuses on overt behavior, and does not directly tell us how people think and feel about each other.

(4) *Have the team draw its portrait* People, either together or separately, draw a picture of the group, a collage that represents the group, or decide what kind of animal the group resembles. This method can be a fun way to get an overview of the group, but does not provide direct evidence of behavior or feelings.

(5) *Provide confidentiality if appropriate* People complete questionnaires or are interviewed with the understanding that only group scores will be made public, and their own responses will not be attributable to them. This confidentiality can help people reveal their true feelings and beliefs when they fear that openly doing so is too risky. If confidentiality is extended, then it needs to be protected. However, the team should work toward direct exchange of feelings and feedback. Team members will then get to know each other much better, and deal more effectively with issues. Confidentiality can still be maintained within the group: team members do not disclose events that might embarrass each other.

The strengths and uses of these methods complement each other, and teams will often want to use them together. For example, after team members have discussed questionnaire results, they can interview each other to understand each person's thinking. Then in a general discussion, people can relate their observations about how they see the group working.

## OPEN DISCUSSION

All employees, regardless of their power and prestige in the team, express their opinions and feelings and the information and reasoning that lie behind them. They don't just speak out and assert themselves, but communicate their responses in ways that help others talk about theirs. They listen carefully and paraphrase each other's comments to make sure they understand. They avoid pressures to conform and coalitions to protect sub-groups. The team as a whole analyzes itself and reaches a consensus on its strengths and issues.

(1) *Structure a suitable time and place* Ten minutes at the end of the meeting, a semi-annual retreat, or other regularly scheduled session facilitates reflec-

tion. Team members do not catch each other off guard, but select a situation when all have the energy, time, and openness to discuss the problem.

(2) *Put self in other shoes* Team members ask about and try to know each other's perspective so they appreciate the problem fully, understand all sides, and develop solutions that work for all. They stop defending their own views long enough to listen carefully to others, and demonstrate their understanding of the others' positions and arguments. People who believe others are trying and do understand them are open to listening to others and resolving issues.

(3) *Define issues specifically* Teams resolve concrete conflicts more easily than general principles and grand ideas. People fight over issues, not personalities. They identify specific behaviors (how they develop the budget) rather than personalities (the accountants are bossy and arrogant). They stick to the issue and main problem without bringing up tangential issues that diffuse and confuse. They avoid diversion to side issues by taking the discussion too personally, feeling indignant, or trying to save face.

(4) *Describe perceptions and feelings about each other's behavior* The emphasis is on sharing information and understanding, not evaluating. People talk about their feelings and reactions to the team and its members and describe what led them to draw their conclusions. They use 'I' and 'my' to emphasize that they are talking about their perspective.

(5) *Minimize labeling and judgment* Abstract labels tend to be confusing, evaluative, and difficult for the person to do something about. People who feel that they are being evaluated often become defensive and closed-minded. Labels and abstract terms do not clearly communicate observations and reactions. Specific behaviors coupled with clear ownership are less threatening and more useful. For example, instead of the analysis 'You're compulsive' use 'I'm annoyed and feeling untrusted because you asked me three times within an hour to get that report to you later today.'

(6) *Convey feelings* Our feelings are windows through which others know us and our experiences. Feelings do not just happen; nor do others' actions cause feelings. People interpret the actions of the team and these interpretations result in feelings.[11] If a team member challenges our position and we interpret it as an attack to make us look bad, we are apt to be angry, and plot how to get back. However, if we believe that the challenge was an honest difference of opinion and an attempt to explore with us the underlying issues, we feel invigorated and search to understand opposing views and work toward a mutually acceptable solution. *By knowing others' feelings and interpretations, we understand them as individuals and are more able to work with them.*

## TEAM FEEDBACK

Groups have a variety of ways to give each other feedback:[12]

(1) Each team member has a sheet of newsprint on the wall. All team

members write on these sheets the things they want the person to (a) begin doing, (b) stop doing, and (c) keep doing.

(2) Team members make the same requests as above, but instead send notes to the person in an envelope.

(3) Each member reviews how they view their performance in the team, and others confirm or disconfirm these views.

(4) Team members complete a questionnaire, results are analyzed and distributed, and the team confirms or contradicts the diagnosis.

(5) Each person asks for feedback to identify areas of effectiveness and weaknesses.

(6) Each team member suggests what others should do to improve team performance.

## PLAN AND IMPLEMENT

A thorough, joint diagnosis is the basis for developing action plans and carrying through. Team members are not rigidly committed to their original position, but encourage opposing views and use them to create workable, effective solutions. The best ideas, information, and reasoning are combined to formulate ways to improve work relationships. They focus on the issues and select a solution based on the facts of the situation that promotes everyone's interests. The responsibility to implement the solution is shared so that all employees know how they should act to strengthen the team.

(1) *Recognize the gains for resolving conflicts, and the costs for not* It takes a team to get itself into a pickle, and it takes the team to get out of it. When everyone realizes the costs and the benefits, discussion is apt to be fruitful and team members motivated to implement solutions.

(2) *Use exploring and controversy skills detailed in Chapter 11* Team members invite various possibilities, avoid assuming that it has to be one person's way or another's, and combine ideas. They elaborate their opposing views and ideas. They search to try to understand each other and the benefits and costs of different courses of action. They integrate their views to create mutually acceptable and beneficial solutions.

(3) *Be firm, yet flexible* Team members should be firm in their resolution to develop useful solutions, but flexible about what those might be.[13] They may use *cost cutting* in which one person gets what they want while cutting another person's costs in conceding. Or they may try *logrolling* in which each person agrees to the other person's demands in areas of primary importance to that person—no one gets all that they want but all get what they most want. *Bridging* is often possible. Here a totally new option is developed that satisfies

the interests of all, and may even leave all of them better off than any original proposal.

(4) *Negotiate feelings* Feelings are often thought to be givens and unnegotiable. People will say that they have a 'gut' suspicion of another as if the feeling is undiscussable and unchangeable. The power of feelings can be misused. Some people use their anger to overpower. When confronted, they argue that they are just angry and no explanation is necessary or possible. They demand that others change or face continued hostility. But *talking about feelings, clarifying others' intentions, reinterpreting events, and planning how to work in the future change feelings.*

(5) *Strive for ongoing improvement* Teams need time to develop, and some interpersonal problems are not easily solved. The goal should be to make progress through repeated discussions rather than to solve all issues quickly and become a completely successful team instantly. Open reflection and discussion should be a regular, accepted part of working as a team. Open discussions are convincing evidence that the team is making progress. They celebrate small as well as major gains. While recognizing their weaknesses, they feel confident that they can cope with them and can get better with experience.

## OVERVIEW OF REFLECTION PROGRAM

(1) *Build in reflection* Team members recognize that they will have opportunities to discuss their feelings and deal with issues to strengthen their relationships and prevent deterioration.

(2) *Use the team model* The team should improve its abilities to envision, unite, empower, and explore.

(3) *Collect data through questionnaires, interviews, and observations* A combination of methods provides a rich, broad understanding of the team's dynamics.

(4) *Dialogue* All employees dig into the data and present their views of the team and their personal experiences.

(5) *Deal with conflicts* Making interpersonal frustrations public is often the most difficult part. Once identified, the team can develop new ways of working that reduce frustrations and improve productivity.

(6) *Use good feedback skills* Team members describe their perceptions and feelings, and avoid labeling, and judging.

(7) *Search for a diagnosis* The team objectively assesses its strengths and weaknesses.

(8) *Use constructive controversy* The team openly discusses alternative positions about how it should proceed and combines ideas into

creative, workable solutions that are mutually acceptable. It avoids win–lose arguing.

(9) *Celebrate strengths* The team appreciates and values its accomplishments and abilities. It understands that admitting and dealing with problems and weaknesses are valuable assets and signs of team competence.

## CONCLUDING COMMENTS

There is either growth or decay; teams are either getting more effective or less effective; team members are either strengthening their relationships or letting them slide. Developing a team is not a one-time effort, but an ongoing process. Repeated reflection is the route to a team doing things right and doing the right thing.

The team organization model provides a framework for reflection. It explains that reflection is part of the ongoing process to develop a team and to further its vision. It directs reflection toward examining how the team envisions, unites, empowers, and explores. It indicates what are strengths that should be celebrated and built upon; it suggests what might be barriers and how they can be overcome.

## APPENDIX: SAMPLE DATA COLLECTION INSTRUMENTS FOR TEAM ORGANIZATION

The sample questionnaire, interview schedule, and observation form in this appendix have not been subject to rigorous empirical development, though they have been field tested. No claims are made for their reliability or validity.

### QUESTIONNAIRE TEAM ORGANIZATION

The following questions ask you to indicate your opinions on how much your company has now developed a strong team organization and feeling. Your individual response will be held confidential. We will summarize the responses of the group as a whole. Completing the questionnaire can help you understand teamwork in your company and make realistic plans for improving it. Thank you.

Please use the following scale for each question:

| 1 | 2 | 3 | 4 | 5 |
|---|---|---|---|---|
| Very little amount | A limited amount | A moderate amount | A considerable amount | A great amount |

## I. Envision

(1) To what extent are you committed to the direction top
management wants the company to move toward in the future? ——————

2) To what extent do you believe that the company offers
the challenges and opportunities that you want in a job? ——————

## II. Unite

(1) To what extent do people at this company have a 'we
are in this together' attitude? ——————

(2) To what extent do people at this company work against
each other in their efforts to look better than others? ——————

(3) To what extent do people at this company do their own
thing in that they work for their own individual and
independent objectives and advantage? ——————

## III. Empower

(1) To what extent do you have opportunities to discuss
issues with your co-workers at this company? ——————

(2) To what extent do you feel confident that you have
the people skills to work effectively with others at
this company? ——————

(3) To what extent do you have the technical skills to
do your job well? ——————

## IV. Explore

(1) When issues and problems occur, to what extent do
people here express their own views fully? ——————

(2) When problems occur, to what extent do people try to
blame each other? ——————

(3) When problems and conflicts occur, to what extent do
people explore all sides to seek a solution good and
acceptable to all? ——————

## V. Reflect

(1) To what extent do you and co-workers take time to

consider how you are working to identify strengths and
areas that need improvement?                                    ———
(2) To what extent is the company committed to ongoing
improvement and development?                                     ———
(3) To what extent is management open to new ideas and
improved ways of working?                                       ———

## SAMPLE OBSERVATION

Put a check for each time the person performs one of the behaviors. Be
prepared to discuss your results with the team.

Person                                    1     2     3     4     5

### I. Vision and Goal

Reaffirms value
   of goal
Clarifies task
Other

### II. Unity

Emphasizes mutual goals
'We' statements
Emphasizes win–lose
   competition
Other

### III. Empower

Describes own strengths
Recognizes others' abilities
Specifies group's resources
Other

## IV. Explore

States own position
Asks for others' ideas
Asks for proofs and facts
Disagrees with others'
    ideas
Integrates positions
Smooths over differences
Criticizes others as
    persons
Other

## V. Reflect

Asks for feedback
Gives feedback
Deals with conflicts
Celebrates achievements
Avoids discussing
    conflicts
Other

## SAMPLE INTERVIEWING

Interviewing requires creating the conditions under which people will be able to recall information accurately and willingly disclose it. The team organization model has implications here. Interviewees who believe they understand the purpose of the interview believe their goals are cooperative with the interviewee, feel confident they have the skills to provide information, and explore issues that are likely to be forthcoming.

There is no magic formula or set phrase that establishes a cooperative trust link between interviewer and interviewee. Interviewing is a challenging, complex skill that is learned through experience. However, the following guides are useful.

## I. Climate of respect, openness, and confidentiality

(1) Indicate purpose of interview.

(2) Set ground rules re: uses of information and confidentiality.
(3) Show warmth and interest in the other person.
(4) Invite interviewee to express any concerns about the interview.

## II. Explore

(5) Identify teamwork as the subject of the interview.
(6) If appropriate, explain and clarify the issues of vision, unity, empower, explore, and reflect.
(7) Ask open-ended questions about how the interviewee sees and evaluates the group re: vision, unity, empower, explore, reflect, and other relevant areas.
(8) Have interviewee describe specific examples to illustrate major ways the group works together effectively and ineffectively.
(9) Demonstrate listening to the interviewee.
(10) Respond to interviewee's feelings.

## III. Thank and Close

(11) Show appreciation for the interviewee's openness and effort.
(12) Reaffirm purpose and ground rules of the interview.

# REFERENCES

1. Brockner, J. (1988). *Self-esteem: Theory, Research, and Practice.* Lexington, MA: Lexington Books.
2. Matsui, T., Kakuyama, T. and Onglatco, M. L. U. (1987). Effects of goals and feedback on performance in groups. *Journal of Applied Psychology,* **72,** 407–415.
3. Wendenhof, J. (1987). People innovation at Eaton. In Y. K. Shetty and V. M. Buehler (eds), *Quality, Productivity and Innovation: Strategies for Gaining Competitive Advantage.* New York: Elsevier, 93–101.
4. Argyris, C. (1970). *Intervention Theory and Method: A Behavioral Science View.* Reading, MA: Addison-Wesley. Argyris, C. and Schon, D. (1978). *Organizational Learning.* Reading, MA: Addison-Wesley.
5. Brawley, L. R. (1984). Unintentional egocentric biases in attributions. *Journal of Sport Psychology,* **6,** 264–278. Ross, M. and Sicoly, F. (1979). Egocentric biases in availability and attribution. *Journal of Personality and Social Psychology,* **37,** 322–336.
6. Shaw, M. E. and Breed, G. R. (1970). Effects of attribution of responsibility for negative events on behavior in small groups. *Sociometry,* **33,** 382–393.
7. Wortman, C., Costanzo, P. R. and Witt, T. R. (1973). Effects of anticipated

performance on the attribution of causality to self and others. *Journal of Personality and Social Psychology*, **27**, 372–381.

8. Johnson, D. W. and Johnson, R. T. (1985). Motivational processes in cooperative, competitive, and individualistic learning situations. In C. Ames and R. Ames (eds), *Research on Motivation in Education 2*, New York: Academic Press.

9. Matsui, T., Kakuyama, T. and Onglatco, M. L. U. (1987). Effects of goals and feedback on performance in groups. *Journal of Applied Psychology*, **72**, 407–415.

10. McCall, M. W. and Lombardo, M. M. (1983). *Off the Track: Why and How Successful Executives Get Derailed*. Greensboro, NC: Center for Creative Leadership.

11. Ellis, A. (1987). The impossibility of maintaining consistently good mental health. *American Psychologist*, **42**, 364–375.

12. Dyer, W. G. (1987). *Team Building: Issues and Alternatives*. Reading, MA: Addison-Wesley.

13. Pruitt, D. G. and Syna, H. (1989). Successful problem solving. In D. Tjosvold and D. W. Johnson (eds), *Productive Conflict Management: Perspectives for Organizations*. Minneapolis, MN: Team Media, 69–90.

# Part IV: Toward an Integrated Company

Two are better than one, because they have a good reward for their toil. For if they fall, one will lift up his fellow; but woe to him who is alone when he falls and has not another to lift him up . . . And though a man might prevail against one who is alone, two will withstand him. A threefold cord is not quickly broken.

Ecclesiastes 4: 9–12

The five separate fingers are five independent units. Close them and a fist multiplies strength. This is organization.

J. C. Penney

No one team, not even top management, makes a company successful. Marshalling its full resources is critical for a company's competitive advantage. Chapter 13 discusses vertical integration to unite management and workers. Chapter 14 focuses on horizontal integration of synergy between departments and divisions. The final chapter describes the principles and steps to become a team organization, argues the need for teamwork across organizational boundaries, and poses challenges for managers, employees, and researchers.

# 13 Labor–Management Relations

It took employee involvement to bring us together tonight. It took employee involvement to foster a new spirit and attitude that flourished at the bargaining table only seven months ago. And it took employee involvement to chart a new standard for labor and management relations . . . I believe that we are just beginning to grasp the potential that lies ahead . . . I want Ford to be recognized by our human enterprise as well as our economic enterprise . . . We are here because we believe in employee involvement and in mutual commitment to common goals.

> Donald E. Petersen, Ford Motor Company

We are a team. We must treat each other with trust and respect.

> Mission, Values, and Guiding Principles, Ford Motor Company

'Are you still having fun with your TLC?' Jerry asked Marian as he walked into her office.

'We keep digging away, trying this and trying that . . . we all keep working at it, though progress is not always a straight line upward.'

'Well, our friendly VP wants me to take the lead and approach union people about getting them involved in a large-scale employee involvement program.'

'Did you laugh?'

'No, I told him sure thing.'

'Isn't that kind of soft for a hard-headed person like you?' Marian teased.

'Sometimes I surprise myself. But you know I wasn't against your teamwork idea, just skeptical.'

'Interesting distinction,' Marian deadpanned.

'I wasn't anti-teams; I just doubted whether the company was sincere.'

'Didn't you say that all this talk about cooperation was just a plan to get everyone to shut up and forget their interests?'

'I did have my suspicions—OK, perhaps I was too skeptical.' Jerry enjoyed Marian's teasing; they both knew, though never discussed, that behind his gruff appearance Jerry was a soft, compassionate person. 'Wouldn't it be a dull world if we all thought alike?'

'True, but what would the world be like if everyone thought like you. Have you thought of that?'

'Maybe that would be too much of a good thing! Give me credit though. At least I was not closed-minded. When I saw what Miles is doing with that valuing differences program, I got interested. It's not just a program good for the company, but good for employees too.'

'That program got diversity out of the closet, and people seem to be appreciating their differences,' Marian agreed.

'Miles's work also had an impact on the attitudes of the union leaders.'

'They've been skeptical,' Marian said.

'They want to believe, but they have their reasons for not. We've played a few games with them over the years. It's a great myth that union leaders want strife and strike. Strikes are hard on them. They get pressured to be tough and to compromise. There're lots of ways they lose. Workers go back to work; the media portrays them as villains; the management gets mad and locks them out.'

'So you think the union leaders may be receptive to new cooperative efforts?'

'I think they're convinced that management is sincere and is not trying to do the union in or smooth over problems and conflicts.'

'I thought you said union leaders don't like strife and strikes.'

'They don't, but they're quite comfortable dealing with conflict, banging the table, and negotiating. They like to mix it up, and believe that it is necessary for meaningful cooperation.'

'I agree with them. I have an idea. Why don't you join us at TLC? I could send you some readings and we can discuss our approach to developing teams.'

Jerry agreed. 'There are lots of different ways that companies can develop labor–management cooperation—quality circles, quality of work life, autonomous work teams, socio-technical. But they all seem to use teams.'

'I think you'll see the need not only for shop-floor teams, but teams to connect work groups, departments, and union and management people. I can see a team of you and union leaders, with stewards and supervisors.'

'This could be a real undertaking,' Jerry said somberly.

'If it was easy, it would have already been done. But we'll have fun too.'

# INDUSTRIAL RELATIONS AS A COMPETITIVE ADVANTAGE

Many companies are overhauling their industrial relations system. Inflexibility, feather bedding, unearned pay increases, rigid bargaining, and strikes jointly caused by management and labor are no longer acceptable. In the past, managers could avoid these issues and argue that because other companies had the same troubles they were not disadvantaged. Today many managers realize that industrial relations is a critical competitive advantage.

## CHALLENGES TO TRADITIONAL PRACTICES

Mounting pressures challenge the complacency based on the argument that labor costs and the ineffective management of labor were taken out of competition. North American and European companies must compete directly with firms operating with a much different industrial relations system with lower, sometimes much lower, wage structures. In addition, some of these systems work better in terms of productivity improvements, strikes, and lost workdays.

Traditional labor–management relations are anti-team. Both management and union see themselves as separate and distinct, with independent agendas, rights, responsibilities, and constituents. They often have different backgrounds and training, and socialize with different people. Sometimes they even think of each other as the enemy, not at all as partners.

They do not feel empowered, rather they worry about who might have the upper hand. They hide information, and use it to further their own interests at the expense of the other. When they do meet face to face, it tends to be in adversarial settings of dealing with a poorly handled grievance or collective bargaining. Issues are not explored, but each side uses power and cunning to see if they can assert their rights. Rather than reflect and develop the relationship, managers and employees complain about each other. Leaders on both sides want to be strong and tough, and avoid any appearance of weakness through compromise and quick agreement.

These practices and attitudes are costly. Strikes not only disrupt a firm's operations, but depress stock prices and cost shareholders.[1] Any day managers, supervisors, employees, and union officials may be embroiled in petty squabbles and bitter fights; they are distracted from doing their jobs and planning for the future. Plans to involve employees in improving product quality sound unrealistic to these managers and exploitative to workers.

## POSSIBILITY OF AUTHENTIC COOPERATION

Industrial relations has been viewed from unitarian, Marxist, and mixed-motive perspectives. The unitarian view that the interests of management and workers are one is widely considered too unrealistic a basis upon which to build a viable industrial relations system.[2] Marxist industrial relations theorists argue that competitive goals result from the opposed interests caused by class conflict over ownership of the means of production. Management wants to reduce the costs of labor, and workers want to increase its costs. The third, and dominant perspective among industrial relations researchers, is that management and employees have a mixed-motive relationship. They have opposing interests over issues such as wages but overlapping interests on such issues as safety and financial solvency of the firm. They must negotiate their differences so that they can continue to work toward their common goals.

The team organization model poses a fourth alternative. It recognizes that management and labor have opposing and common interests, but holds that *what is critical is how managers and workers consider and frame their interests.* They can decide they have largely competitive interests: management seeks profits and power at the expense of workers. Or they can decide their goals are basically cooperative: they have the common goals to promote the success of the company and the competence and job security of employees. They also have the common goal to create a quality relationship that helps them work together to pursue their joint interests.

As previously reviewed research suggests, *the conclusion by union and management that their goals are primarily cooperative rather than competitive dramatically affects the dynamics and outcomes of labor relations.* Concession bargaining, union representation on boards, profit sharing, quality of worklife and employee involvement programs have been considered signs of a transformation of the US industrial relations system.

## CHANGES IN INDUSTRIAL RELATIONS

Beginning in the 1960s and taking hold in the 1970s, many companies in the US and elsewhere have deployed an aggressive, successful employee relations strategy, often to prevent unionization.[3] They developed personnel policies that undercut incentives to unionize: they paid employees well; invested in technology and training of employees; stabilized employment and minimized layoffs; involved employees in making decisions; developed a rational wage and salary administration and performance appraisal that rewarded both merit and seniority; and selected sites and people who would not be pro-union. IBM, Eastman Kodak, Digital Equipment Corporation, Motorola, Du Pont, Michelin Tires, Marriott Hotels, and Sears Roebuck have found these strategies promoted the company's goals and avoided unions.

Current research supports these companies' conclusion that cooperative relationships with the workforce contribute to organizational success. Savvy Japanese firms have used information sharing as a strategic industrial relations policy to improve firm performance. Motohiro Morishima[4] has found that Japanese firms that used joint consultation committees were more profitable and productive than those that did not. Information sharing appears to moderate union demands and make them more open to accepting lower wage settlements.[5]

In the US, effective industrial relations programs have contributed to productivity. Organizations with low grievance rates and disciplinary action were found to have low absenteeism and high participation in suggestions programs; these dynamics in turn appear to contribute to labor efficiency and product quality.[6] Concession bargaining can contribute substantially to the firm's value and shareholder equity, and potentially to future worker gains.[7]

Cooperative relations with workers, whether unionized or not, is a powerful strategy for firms to adjust to market pressures and gain competitive advantages. Quality labor–management relationships and joint consultation are likely to result in wage concessions when needed and acceptance of employee involvement programs to improve quality and reduce costs.

## UNIONS' POTENTIAL CONTRIBUTION

Many managers assume that unions make more difficult, even preclude, constructive employee relations. Yet Ford and many companies are finding union leaders to be partners and allies in developing more constructive labor relations.[8] Union leaders, if convinced that management is sincere, help persuade workers to trust management and experiment with employee involvement. Union leaders can help set up forums and avenues for workers and managers to work together. They remind managers of the need to discuss conflicts and differences openly and constructively.

Workers do not see an inevitable tradeoff between company and union. *With a cooperative management–union relationship, workers can be highly committed to their company as well as to their union.*[9] The quality of the relationship between management and workers is critical for employee relations, not whether workers are unionized.

## A TEAM APPROACH

Pronouncements about cooperation are insufficient; a team organization is needed to make an industrial relations system authentic. Managers and workers, management and union must together commit themselves to an ongoing effort to develop a cooperative relationship and industrial relations system. The team organization model specifies the nature of a productive relationship and suggests the procedures to make the system work.

Management and employee leaders, whether union or non-union, agree together to develop honest, cooperative relations. Without joint sponsorship, both managers and workers may think that participation makes them appear as if they are weak and giving in. In many programs, a central team of industrial relations and other managers and union leaders and workers provide the thrust and oversee developments.[10] Middle management and union or employee representatives work together to encourage and overcome barriers. On the shop floor, workers and their supervisors together identify and solve frustrations and bottlenecks so that they can work productively. *Teamwork is needed between management and union up and down the hierarchy to forge a new relationship.*

Joint management–labor committees can use guides discussed in earlier chapters to create a vision that serves stockholders and executives, but also improves the quality of life and job pride for workers. Gainsharing, where workers receive a percentage of costs they saved the company or the income they generated, gives them a vested interest in the program. Similarly, bonuses based on company performance, profit sharing, and stock ownership underline their cooperative goals with the company.

Personal communication and open dialogue build trust between worker and manager. Employees have their questions answered and their suspicions dealt with. Through participation in shop-floor problem solving and company management committees, workers have an opportunity to understand problems and create solutions.

## TEAM LABOR RELATIONS AT FORD MOTOR COMPANY

Jolted by recession, fuel price increases, record imports of Japanese cars, and huge losses, Ford executives and United Automobile Workers union officials realized they needed to involve employees more fully to make Ford a viable company.[11] In the 1979 negotiations, they agreed to form a team, the National Joint Committee on Employee Involvement, to oversee and encourage participative management.

To begin, employees and supervisors formed *problem-solving groups* to deal with shop-floor problems. With experience and confidence, Ford managers and salaried and hourly employees found all kinds of teams useful. *Interface groups* worked on problems that cut across work groups. *Opportunity teams* were *ad hoc* groups to oversee implementation of new technology, product changes, and facilities improvements. *Special project teams* managed specific events such as an auto show or open house. *Linking teams* dealt with issues that required input from several shifts and departments. *Launch teams* coordinated across process and design needed to launch a successful new project. *Vendor quality teams* dealt with specific issues and developing ongoing communication with suppliers both inside and outside the company. *Resource committees* certified consultants' competence, trained hourly employee facilitators and union national representatives, and provided consulting and training upon request.

Ford managers and union officials attribute much of Ford's great success in the 1980s to the ongoing process of forming teams to involve employees. Communication and learning between management and workers, departments, plants, and suppliers increased. In addition to high-quality products (50% improvement by company indices), and moving from losses in 1980 that were greater than any company had ever incurred to handsome profits in the late 1980s, the program brought for the first time, according to UAW official, Al Hendricks, real and meaningful 'Dignity and Respect in the Workplace.'

Platitudes and quick changes did not produce such success, but a transformation was required in culture and structure. Executives had to work with the union to *envision* an inspiring, common aspiration: managers and workers were a team that created high-quality products they all could be proud of. Throughout the company, people had to feel *united* and trusting so that they worked together: they would share fairly in the fruits of their joint success. They had to feel *empowered*: they developed and 'owned' forms of involvement and were trained in group skills. Employees and managers *explored* issues: they had many opportunities to exchange ideas, solve frustrating problems, and create valued processes and products. They *reflected* on their progress and countered pressures to 'revert to the familiar': they established the Mutual Growth Forum for ongoing discussion and systematic fact finding. Some 500 Ford managers, employees, and union officials met at the First National UAW–Ford Employee Involvement Conference to encourage each other, share experiences, attend workshops, and discuss future plans. They saw employee involvement as an ongoing process to be made into a way of life; they realized they have to build on their momentum to succeed in the future.

Well-managed teams promoted the *innovation* Ford needed to respond to changes in the marketplace. The status quo was no longer acceptable. Ford had to build high-quality products that would win back savvy, demanding customers with a great range of automobile needs. These teams also evoked the *commitment* of employees and managers to provide the energy, determination, and creativity necessary for the company to adapt.

Teamwork between management and labor is very valuable, but it does not insure continuous prosperity. Ford will undoubtedly experience ups and downs in the competitive automobile market. It also needs teamwork throughout the organization. As the 1990s begin, Ford's Centers of Responsibilities that tie design centers in England, West Germany, and Dearborn, Michigan together to produce cars for world-wide marketing do not appear to be very effective.[12] As CEO Petersen admitted, 'It has been slogging hard work.' Without smartly designed cars targeted for the right markets, Ford will suffer despite its team labor–management relations and manufacturing capabilities.

## PRINCIPLES OF EMPLOYEE INVOLVEMENT AT FORD MOTOR COMPANY

Unions do not prevent developing a team organization with employees. At Ford and many other companies, employee involvement becomes a joint management–union endeavor.[13]

(1) Employee involvement projects are separate from and not substitutes for collective bargaining, grievance procedures, and other contract provisions.
(2) Participation is voluntary.
(3) Projects are based on local circumstances and needs.
(4) Elected union leaders are fully involved.
(5) Programs should proceed in a reasonable and prudent manner over time.
(6) No single program works for all locations.
(7) Local management and union leaders can terminate a project at any time.

## CONCLUDING COMMENTS

Employee leaders or union officials need to join forces with management to create effective team industrial relations. Executives from the company and top union leaders jointly announce the effort to change their relationship. Appropriate employee representatives on the national, division, plant, and shop-floor committees can be responsible for employee involvement. A team approach is used to develop a team industrial relations system.

There is no single fix that makes the labor–management relationship work. Sharing rewards, whether it be through bonuses for developing specific cost-effective solutions in gainsharing, or distributing money in profit sharing, or compensating with stock ownership, does not itself guarantee employee cooperation. Effective involvement of employees in participation programs is also required to develop a productive labor–management relationship.[14]

Cooperative labor relations are possible, but not inevitable. Neither is competition. Management and labor have a choice. But they must jointly decide and have the skills and procedures to make their cooperative teamwork rich and rewarding.

# REFERENCES

1. Davidson, W. N., III, Worrell, D. L. and Garrison, S. H. (1988). Effect of strike activity on firm value. *Academy of Management Journal*, **31**, 387–394.
2. Kochan, T. A. and Katz, H. C. (1988). *Collective Bargaining and Industrial Relations. From Theory to Policy and Practice*. Homewood, IL: Irwin. Kochan, T. A. (1980). *Collective Bargaining and Industrial Relations*. Homewood, IL: Irwin.
3. Katz, H. C., Kochan, T. A. and Weber, M. R. (1985). Assessing the effects of industrial relations systems and efforts to improve the quality of working life on organizational effectiveness. *Academy of Management Journal*, **28**, 509–526.
4. Morishima, M. (in press). Information sharing and collective bargaining in Japan: effects of wage negotiation. *Industrial Relations Review*. Morishima, M. (in press). Information sharing and firm performance in Japan: do joint consultation committees help? *Industrial Relations Review*.
5. Morishima, M. (in press). Information sharing and collective bargaining in Japan: effects of wage negotiation. *Industrial Relations Review*.
6. Katz, H. C., Kochan, T. A. and Gobeille, K. R. (1983). Industrial relations performance, economic performance, and QWL programs: an interplant analysis. *Industrial and Labor Relations Review*, **37**, 3–17. Katz, H. C., Kochan, T. A. and Weber, M. R. (1985). Assessing the effects of industrial relations systems and efforts to improve the quality of working life on organizational effectiveness. *Academy of Management Journal*, **28**, 509–526.
7. Becker, B. E. (1988). Concession bargaining: the meaning of union gains. *Academy of Management Journal*, **31**, 377–387.
8. Banas, P. A. (1988). Employee involvement: a sustained labor/management initiative at the Ford Motor Company. In J. P. Campbell and R. J. Campbell (eds), *Productivity in Organizations: New Perspectives from Industrial and Organizational Psychology*. San Francisco: Jossey-Bass, 388–416.
9. Angle, H. L. and Perry, J. L. (1986). Dual commitment and labor–management relationship climates. *Academy of Management Journal*, **29**, 31–50. Magennau, J. M., Martin, J. E. and Peterson, M. M. (1988). Dual and unilateral commitment among stewards and rank-and-file union members. *Academy of Management Journal*, **31**, 359–376.
10. Bushe, G. and Shani, A. (1990). *Parallel Learning Structures*. Reading, MA: Addison-Wesley. Pasmore, W. W. and Friedlander, F. (1982). An action-research program for increasing employee involvement in problem-solving. *Administrative Science Quarterly*, **27**, 343–362.
11. Banas, P. A. (1988). Employee involvement: a sustained labor/management initia-

tive at the Ford Motor Company. In J. P. Campbell and R. J. Campbell (eds), *Productivity in Organizations: New Perspectives from Industrial and Organizational Psychology*. San Francisco: Jossey-Bass, 388–416. Jusela, G. E., Chairman, P., Ball, R. A., Tyson, C. E. and Dannermiller, K. D. Work innovations at Ford Motor. In Y. K. Shetty and V. M. Buehler (eds), *Quality Productivity and Innovation: Strategies for Gaining Competitive Advantage*. New York: Elsevier, 123–145.

12. Taylor, A., III (1989). Caution: bumps ahead at Ford. *Fortune*, December 18, 93–96.

13. Banas, P. A. (1988). Employee involvement: a sustained labor/management initiative at the Ford Motor Company. In J. P. Campbell and R. J. Campbell (eds), *Productivity in Organizations: New Perspectives from Industrial and Organizational Psychology*. San Francisco: Jossey-Bass, 388–416.

14. Klein, K. J. (1987). Employee stock ownership and employee attitudes: a test of three models. *Journal of Applied Psychology*, **72**, 319–332.

# 14  Forging Synergy

The failure of synergy stemmed from the inability of companies to understand and implement it, not because of some basic flaw in the concept . . . Compelling forces . . . are increasing the competitive advantage to be gained by those firms that can identify and exploit interrelationships among distinct but related businesses. These interrelationships are not the fuzzy notions of 'fit' which underlie most discussions of synergy, but tangible opportunities to reduce costs or enhance differentiation in virtually any activity in the value chain . . . *Horizontal strategy* . . . perhaps the most critical item on the strategic agenda facing a diversified firm . . . is the mechanism by which a diversified firm enhances the competitive advantage of its business units.

Michael Porter, *Competitive Advantage*

'I want to thank you personally for your efforts to develop teamwork at Savory,' Allan said to Marian. Her VP had mentioned Marian's work with TLC as an example of positive change, and Allan thought it was a good opportunity for him to catch someone in the act of doing something right.

'Thank you very much . . . I'm very grateful,' Marian said. 'But the whole group should be given credit. The managers are the ones learning and experimenting with the ideas. They are the ones getting up at bat and hitting the ball.'

'That's a good team attitude,' Allan said with a smile. 'Give the credit to the whole group, I like that. That's the kind of leader we need here at Savory.'

'That's one thing we've been talking about in our group. Leadership and teamwork go together.'

'We need both. There're too many people who think they need to put themselves into the limelight and make themselves appear important. We don't have much room for such super-stars. For it is group effort that counts in business. Even myself, I can preach and preach about teamwork, but unless people like you take up the challenge and use your special abilities, not much is going to happen.'

'We've been saying in our group that leadership is a team thing, something that leaders and people do together. For our managers' group on teamwork, you set the climate and we used the opportunity.'

In addition to wanting to recognize Marian, Allan had a problem on his mind, and he hoped talking to Marian might help. Though he had learned to ask questions over the years, he still felt a little awkward asking someone in the company for help on how to manage. 'Something is bothering me and I was wondering if you could give me your thoughts.'

'Sure, I'd be glad to.' Marian had hoped the meeting would give her an opportunity to discuss something substantive, and wondered what it might be.

'I'm serious about this teamwork idea. We are decentralizing and giving more autonomy to the areas. The divisions in turn are instituting various kinds of employee involvement and participation programs. We've got a lot to learn, but I can feel the excitement.'

'People are talking—they're optimistic.'

'So far so good, and we'll have to learn as we go. But what's bothering me is that the company will not only be decentralized, but also out of control. Each area will be doing its thing. Some companies are a lot worse than we are about infighting and politics, but we could go that way.'

'But haven't the VPs been off to weekend retreats developing the corporate vision and mission?' Marian asked.

'I told them I want them to be a team. I want to lead through teamwork, just like you said. They like it, but they also seem to be pulled into their own separate directions.'

'Our areas are not at each other's throats, but they don't have a history of working together. Divisions have sort of done their own thing, with you and the other executives trying to coordinate. The new decentralization can, like you suggest, just exacerbate that problem.'

'Perhaps I shouldn't worry too much about it. It just may be the price we have to pay for teamwork.'

'The logic of teamwork applies for the whole company as well as for departments. We need to know what each area is about, how we can coordinate our efforts, how we can help each other out . . .'

'Your logic is compelling, especially from where I sit. But won't that require a lot of red tape and interference on the corporate level? Then we're back where we began.'

'What's critical is that the divisions themselves coordinate, rather than have you act as referee and police. The way I see it is that you want them to understand why it's important for them to work together and have them negotiate, coordinate, solve mutual problems, and all those good team things.'

'But the reason I end up policing is because the divisions don't do that sort of thing, and they don't appear to want to either.'

'Just like in a project team or in a department, "teamness" among areas has to be built up and worked on. You as leader, I think, want to create the situation in which divisions are able to work together.'

'So leaders develop teams.'

'Yes, and leaders work with people to create teams. The method is consistent with the goal.'

'Interesting, but, don't get me wrong, annoying too. How am I, or my team, supposed to do all of this?'

Marian explained the team organization model of envision, unite, empower, explore, and reflect and promised to send Allan related readings.

In response to Allan's question, Marian gave an overview of the major implications of the model. Marian argued that envisioning had already begun. Allan and the VPs were talking about the need for the company to build on its regional base and develop a global strategy to sell value added, high-tech products world-wide. Everyone should have an opportunity to talk about this vision and to see how their areas, departments, and groups fit into this vision and unite them.

'I certainly want everyone behind this vision,' Allan said.

'We want people to talk about it to see why it is important and to understand that other people are committed to it as well.'

Marian and Allan also discussed how shared compensation, perhaps a bonus based on company performance, would give everyone a vested interest in corporate success. Keeping everyone informed about the company adds to the feeling of united purpose. Training develops communication, group facilitation, and other collaboration skills. Project teams, task forces, and new product teams are forums for people with different viewpoints to create new solutions. Regular sessions can be established to discuss progress toward achieving business objectives and becoming a more effective organization.

'I'm going to have to think about this,' Allan said thoughtfully. 'But can we do all this even though we are unionized?'

'There are many companies using a team approach who are unionized. Some union leaders are staunch advocates of teamwork.'

'I have to fly off to Europe this week; perhaps I could read your materials then and get back to you.'

## THE CHALLENGE: SYNERGY IN THE DECENTRALIZED COMPANY

Savory and other companies are experimenting with ways to involve employees more fully in the company. Employee participation in teams, we have seen, is critical to upgrade the quality of products and cut costs. Quality products and services cannot be mandated from on high: loan officers themselves have to be warm, helpful, and efficient; production people have to work hard to 'do it right the first time.' Costs are not controlled by edict, but by many people finding ways to conserve and use company resources wisely. Quality improvements and cost reduction require the full participation and motivation of all employees.

Decentralization follows. Companies are pushing the decision-making responsibility low into the organization, to the people who have the knowledge to create workable solutions and who must implement those solutions. Divisions, plants, and departments become profit, revenue, and cost centers with their own budgets and targets and are given ongoing information about their progress. Their managers are asked to be entrepreneurial and act as if they are running their own independent business. Often they are rewarded with bonuses and recognition to the extent that their unit contributes to the corporate bottom line. This decentralization is expected to unleash managers and employees. The divisions can keep abreast of changes in markets and suppliers, adjust quickly, and exploit emerging opportunities.[1]

However, decentralization and participation are often carried out in ways that make synergy among the divisions less likely. The divisions need not only to be free of the layers of approvals and heavy handedness of the corporate office, but also from interference by other divisions. Each division becomes a separate strategic business unit that has the authority to manage its business. Transfer prices that reflect the market are to allow exchanges that both units find satisfactory.

Yet there are good reasons for a company to be synergistic. An integrated company uses its total resources to win market share, employs emerging technologies, makes progress in research and development, and adapts to political and business changes. Diversified firms related enough so that their business units can contribute to each other's success are valued more highly in the marketplace than unrelated diversified companies.[2] Business units within these firms are increasingly asked to share their resources.[3] One manufacturing capability, for example, is being employed to make several related products.

Unity is needed for a strategy that directs the total corporation to exploit opportunities and avoid pitfalls.[4] But there is no formula or simple tool: effective strategies must be hammered out by the top management team in conjunction with the company's strategic business units, divisions, and departments.[5] Nor can the top management alone put the plan into effect. All the areas at Savory must collaborate to develop, produce, and sell quality products for which consumers will pay premium prices. A team organization is needed to put the company in the right businesses and to do things right.

As Allan was finding, decentralization of authority and employee participation programs can splinter a company. Many companies are loosely coupled with weak central authority and few links between groups. Pushing down the decision making adds to these centrifugal forces. How can a company be loosely organized, yet tightly focused? *The challenge is to decentralize in order to involve people and groups fully, yet to integrate these groups into a coherent, synergistic company.*

## REALITY OF INTERDEPENDENCE

Treating divisions as if they were independent ignores reality. Executives will compare divisions on return on equity and sales volume and growth. To estimate more subjective issues like morale and potential for innovation, executives are even more apt to compare business units.

Investment decisions and budgets make divisions and departments interdependent. In providing the capital for investments and major expenses, the corporation makes inevitable comparisons and tradeoffs. Divisions must demonstrate that capital outlays are prudent, and, to some extent, will perform better than investments in other business units.

To consumers, bankers, and investors, business units are related. Consumers will generalize their experiences with one division's product to others'. Investors and bankers examine the balance sheet and potential of all divisions as they consider providing capital for one division.

Crises highlight that public recognition and private pride depend upon the company as a whole. The gas leak and subsequent tragedy at Bhopal embarrassed everyone at Dow Chemical. The disastrous Alaskan oil spill was a blow to the public esteem of all groups at Exxon. Praise of the company boosts employees' self and social esteem that they are part of a good company that serves its customers and the public well.

## SYNERGY AND POLITICS AT THE TOP

Synergy begins at the top. If the business units' heads, vice presidents, or department managers are not working together as a team, it is unlikely that those below them will have the mandate and incentives to share resources and collaborate.

Yet posturing, fights over budgets and scarce resources, and political infighting and intrigue sabotage synergy. Executives form coalitions behind the scenes, lobby powerful members, withhold information, and alter agendas to get their way to promote their special interests. Open, forthright discussions and pursuit of the common goals are mere shells and pretenses.

In their study of politics in top management teams, Kathleen Eisenhardt and Jay Bourgeois[6] interviewed the CEO and his immediate subordinates in eight microcomputer firms in the San Francisco area. Four firms were politically active, but in the four others consensus and direct controversy were the norm.

The CEOs in the four political firms tried to centralize power in themselves. As one vice president put it, 'When he makes a decision, it's like God.' Another said, 'Geoff is the decision-maker. He runs the show by edit, not by vote.' In the management meetings of one firm, it was 'as if a gun would go off' as the CEO would 'beat up on' people who did not reach their goals.

The executives in these firms lobbied each other before meeting as a group. They used 'outlaw' meetings to try to influence decisions before discussions with the president. Rather than form *ad hoc* coalitions on specific issues, they relied on personal friendships based on office location, previous association, and age to protect themselves and further their interests. Consequently, meetings were more like bargaining and trading sessions than direct exploration of issues. Executives played their cards close to the chest and competed against each other.

The politically inactive firms decentralized power. They adopted a team-oriented, consensus style of managing targeted for company benefit, not just for one function; super-egos were not tolerated. Executives felt that lobbying before meetings was not a good use of time. Top management meetings focused on important issues, and people changed their minds once confronted with useful ideas and data. Issues were not glossed over: they had many disagreements and some heated conflicts.

Executives in the four politically active firms were frustrated; one wished his CEO 'would go away for 6 months.' The political dynamics also appear to have greatly impacted the bottom line. One of the firms had declining sales, another was a moderate performer with low growth and modest profits, and the two others later went into bankruptcy. In contrast, executives in the team companies were energetic, committed, and successful. One company had sales growing 25% to 100% per quarter, another tripled its sales in the year of the study, and one had a 50% sales growth. The fourth company was still in a start-up mode, but the future looked promising.

Eisenhardt and Bourgeois concluded that centralized power and resulting political activity consume time, distort perceptions, divert attention, result in inferior solutions, and frustrate resource sharing among groups. A united top management team is empowered and able to explore issues so that it creates and implements a strategy that combines the company's full capabilities.

## COMPANY TEAMS

Task forces, management teams, budget meetings, liaison and project teams, and special events committees link departments and groups together. Through these company teams, representatives of different units bring various perspectives together to achieve common goals. It is impractical to have large divisions meet to make decisions, but interdepartmental teams are practical ways to make company-wide decisions.

A critical advantage of company teams is that they *give people from different parts of the organization a specific, common task.* Company goals tend to be general and over time can lose their meaning. Cross-divisional teams are given a specific assignment—to recommend how to make the company more customer-oriented, or to suggest a useful gainsharing program. Members realize that top management believes these tasks are priorities with high visibility within the organization. With this clear direction, employees understand that they have a common, important objective and that, if their group is successful, they will be recognized and rewarded.

Though they have great potential, company teams are not automatic solutions. They can alienate, disrupt, and undermine. People can sabotage them and use them to wage war and gain dominance. Company teams must, like other groups, be well managed. Team members discuss their common assignment so that they understand how they are united, feel empowered, and are able to make their controversies constructive. Teams must coordinate and manage conflict with people in the organization as they propose and gain support for their recommendations.

## THE BANK'S NEW PRODUCT TASK FORCE

This is a big deal, this new account. Huge deal! And very significant in the banking industry, and—it's kind of fun to be right in the middle of it!

VP, Compliance Officer

> It was . . . the first time in a long, long time where you could become
> creative . . . innovative. In the past we were so regulated—everyone
> offered exactly the same instrument. Just a whole lot of sameness.
>
> VP, Operations

A large East Coast bank saw the US Congress approval of new
product for banks, the first since the early 1930s, as a critical opportunity for them to get back deposits lost to money market funds.[7] The
president agreed with a vice president's argument that the bank
needed to strike a task force to develop the bank's new product.

The four key team members were the VP for compliance, the
treasurer who as a senior VP sat in on the company's top policy
group, the marketing VP, and the VP for operations. They were
enthusiastic and recognized that their task was vital to the company.
They had the diverse expert knowledge needed to put together a
product that would capture market share, protect the profitability of
the firm, fit in with its computers and operational system, and make
sense to the top management group.

The group first met immediately after the law was signed and even
before the Depository Institution Deregulation Committee had
detailed the regulations. At that meeting, and the other three
meetings over 34 days, one or two of them prepared a skeletal
document that focused the group's discussion. The group explored
issues and checked off items as they covered them, with each question
leading to another one. They used their specialized expertise as
bankers, but also their personal experiences as consumers. They
searched for a product that would help them break out of the pack of
sameness, yet keep risks at an acceptable level. Bells rang and lights
went on when the team made a significant decision.

They had to maintain some secrecy for competitive reasons and
resisted pressure from outsiders to shape the product to fit special
interests, but they also realized that various groups in the bank must
work together if the product was going to be marketed successfully.
They checked out the feasibility of certain features of the product
with specialists, and two people from operations joined them at a
meeting. The senior VP kept the president informed and relayed his
strong interest in the group's success.

The group decided that the new product would be an investment
account linked to personal checking at the second meeting,
hammered out operations at the third, and nailed down the final
product at the fourth meeting. As they represented the bank as a
whole, they were able to get operations, marketing, and retail people
on their side. The president went, for the first time, to branch offices

talking about how important the new product was for the bank. Branch managers trained their tellers to understand and explain it to customers. The information group integrated the product with the computer systems. Later, the task force chair sent a memo praising the team effort of all groups for the success of the new product.

The task force had a vision, felt united and empowered, explored issues and created solutions, and checked progress against its aspirations and deadline. The group also served to unite and empower the whole bank.

# COOPERATIVE LINKS BETWEEN GROUPS

Integration cannot just be mandated from the top, or achieved through company teams. Executives are not in a position to know the specific ways that divisions can use each other's technological, marketing, and management know-how. Even if they know, they may not be able to require collaboration. Groups and divisions that are in competition demand that their executives and representatives on company teams assert their positions, and feel betrayed by those 'weak' leaders who compromise. Synergy depends upon a team organization where the divisions and units seek each other out, share needs and capabilities, and negotiate agreements for exchange.

## RESEARCH ON COOPERATIVE SYNERGY

Contrary to common assumptions, competition between groups is neither inevitable nor generally useful for group solidarity and productivity. People within a business unit or division have common goals and tasks, the need to share resources, complementary roles, and other reasons to believe their goals are cooperative. Research studies, when taken together, indicate that while competition among groups can, in a few circumstances, increase productivity, generally it undermines motivation and success.[8] Groups in competition are sometimes quite unmotivated: those highly confident of victory do not see any pressing need to apply themselves; groups which doubt they can win do not see why they should try.

Cooperative goals, on the other hand, help divisions be productive. Cooperating divisions provide resources, serve as role models for learning, and inspire each other to be successful. Divisions give each other the technical assistance, managerial know-how, different perspectives, and emotional support needed to innovate.[9]

Cooperative goals between departments and divisions, for example, have been found critical for a company's ability to serve customers. Engineering consultants were much more successful in winning and fulfilling contracts and utility employees in responding to customer complaints with cooperative than with competitive or independent goals.[10] Cooperative goals may be more vital between groups than within them. Team members may be prepared to assist each other out of a general sense of belonging to the same group even if they do not have strong cooperative goals. However, people from different divisions, roles, and units may have no compelling reason to help unless they have cooperative goals.[11]

## THE POWER OF COMPETITION

However, divisions, departments, and groups in a company often compete. They try to outdo and disparage each other, even come to see each other as the enemy. As one manager said, 'Our divisions fight against each other so much, we don't have the time or inclination to go after the competition.'

Competition between groups can easily be established.[12] Just being aware of belonging to one group and not others can result in favoring one's own group at the expense of others. Asking groups to work on similar tasks without any attempt to see which one is better can lead people to assume that they are in competition. Groups that executives set up to be independent often believe they are in competition.

Competitive dynamics between business units and divisions in a company are often extremely potent because they have developed over time and involve important issues. Divisions have a definite identity and draw a border around themselves. Their common training, values, and experiences reinforce their distinct identity. They are physically set apart in the building, or even in another city. Tuned in to their own experiences, business units and divisions have skimpy, misleading information about others. Sensing a rivalry, they compete for vital, limited resources.[13]

## NEED FOR EXECUTIVE ACTION

Despite the value of company synergy, many executives are pessimistic about getting divisions to collaborate effectively. Every day they confront indifference and competition. Although they talk about the importance of synergy and pressure divisions to work together, they end up fire fighting and imposing exchange. Divisions hire outside experts rather than consult with specialists in other divisions. They want to do everything themselves, and are uninterested in innovations 'not developed here.'

Feeling powerless, top management avoids rather than deals direc conflicts between groups. Executives have a great variety of ways to rationalize their avoidance. They talk about such infighting as 'human nature.' They reconcile themselves to wanting hard-hitting, aggressive business leaders, and ·it is only to be expected that they will try to outdo and undo others. They may even come to see their role and contribution to the firm as moderating and keeping a lid on the fighting, and supporting and cajoling the 'losing' divisions. Executives get help avoiding these issues from the divisions themselves who recognize their competition is too much at odds with espoused theories of synergy and too 'hot' to discuss.

But perhaps the most significant reason for executive inaction is a lack of knowledge of how to create strong cooperative links among groups. The next section highlights how the team organization model can be used to achieve synergy.

## CREATING SYNERGY

In the team organization, groups, departments, and business units see themselves as united in a common vision and direction, empowered to collaborate, exploring their common issues and problems, and celebrating their achievements. In this way it becomes a synergistic, nimble company able to navigate among landmines and exploit opportunities.

### ENVISION

The company wants a meaningful vision that directs its efforts and reaffirms the value of the company to employees, shareholders, customers, and society. Top management sketches its vision, and then the business units, divisions, and groups complete it by developing their complementary visions. Not all units have to be in the same business, but it is important to show how the visions are related. A division unable to state its vision in ways consistent with corporate values runs the risk of being seen as expendable. Through discussions with top management and their own group meetings, employees are able to revise and fill out the vision of top management so that they believe it is significant and binds them together.

### UNITE

Many executives talk about the need to work together while rewarding and encouraging competition and independence. They compare divisions and give their managers bonuses based only on the performance of their own division. Division leaders should understand how their visions, rewards, and resources give them cooperative goals and why it is important for their own interest as well as the company's to make synergy happen.

Groups and divisions are given costs, budgets, profit reports, and stock prices of the company. This information reinforces that they have a common direction and vision, and depend upon each other to be successful. Each division recognizes that it is responsible for its contribution and for helping others improve theirs.

Departments typically do not have specific, immediate shared rewards to reinforce cooperative goals. Although their salaries, jobs, and prestige all depend eventually upon their common effort, this connection often seems distant. Compensation based on joint rewards such as stock ownership, gain-sharing programs, and profit-sharing plans unify. Leaders and employees recognize their tangible as well as intangible rewards depend upon the performance of the whole organization. Divisions have a vested interest in the effective performance of others.

Development and promotion values and practices reinforce unity. In formal and informal cross-divisional groups, managers discuss issues and refine their leadership skills and styles. They go through workshops together, discuss their learning, and help each other deal with specific problems they confront. They recognize that their leadership abilities to develop a team and work collaboratively with others are important criteria for promotion. Self-promotion and showing up others are not valued.

The company develops a compassionate, socially responsible culture that helps employees identify with the company and create a sense of community. Stories retold at lunch tables and at speeches and written up in the company newsletter illustrate the common history and values of the company. The company gets people together by such means as having them work in close proximity and attending common functions. Through job rotation, membership on task forces, and social gatherings, people establish personal links across divisions that make it easier to ask for and offer assistance.

## EMPOWER

People in different departments usually do not feel empowered to work together and manage their conflicts. Making a team organization work requires ongoing communication and coordination. The organization must support, provide opportunities, and develop skills for people from different divisions to work together productively.

To reinforce top management's commitment to synergy, it provides opportunities for communication. Regular meetings, weekend retreats, conferences, physical proximity of offices and work stations, electronic mail, and information systems help employees from different areas keep in touch and work together. Top management strikes a task force to explore company-wide issues, and pledges to consider their recommendations seriously.

Instead of top management making budget decisions unilaterally, division managers together examine budget requests and develop a budget good for the company as a whole. Internal and external consultants back up readings, workshops, and reflection to develop skills to communicate, discuss controversy, and manage conflict.

## EXPLORE

Top management involves divisions in decisions that affect them and the company. The emphasis is on debate and dialogue before action is taken to insure commitment and avoid charges of favoritism. Forward-looking, reflective decision making is used rather than crisis management.

In addition to task forces and other company teams, executives structure advocacy teams. Executives assign teams opposing views on an important issue, give them time to prepare their arguments, and then use the information and ideas from the debate to make decisions. Alternatively, two groups are asked to present their best solution and, based on their presentation, top management decides what to do. Companies like Honeywell and 3M have instituted ideas fairs for employees to discuss projects and ideas and hook up with others who can use and develop them.

## REFLECT

The company commits itself to ongoing development. It updates its vision, improves compensation and promotion practices to strengthen unity, provides opportunities and skills for divisions to collaborate, and structures decision making so that various ideas are expressed and used. Becoming a quality organization is a continuous climb, not a push just to get over the next ridge.

Newsletters, regular updates, and annual reports keep people abreast of the company and its performance. At regular meetings, employees examine the balance sheet and ask questions about the company's performance. An executive, for example, meets with the division quarterly; the division discusses its and the company's fortunes at monthly meetings. Managers and employees examine the results of a regular survey on how people believe the company is furthering its vision, feeling united and empowered, and exploring issues. Actions are taken to strengthen relationships within the company.

## CONCLUDING COMMENTS

Synergy is needed to create and implement strategy and gain competitive advantages. A strategy must be hammered out and created broadly within the organization to make sure that divisions and groups have the capabilities and motivation to realize it. A vision to which only top management or one division is committed divides a company.

Executives can overcome significant roadblocks to synergy. They lead by establishing a team organization in which divisions are motivated and able to find ways to help each other become more effective. A compelling vision, compensation based on company performance, and promotion based on teamwork emphasize cooperative interdependence. Training programs in interpersonal skills and membership on joint task forces empower people to work together. Representatives from the divisions openly debate alternative approaches and recommend company procedures. In this way, a company lives its vision and earns credibility.

## REFERENCES

1. Lawrence, P. and Lorsch, J. (1967). *Organizations and Environments.* Boston, MA: Harvard Business School. Porter, M. (1981). *Competitive Edge.* New York: Free Press.
2. Rumelt, R. P. (1982). Diversification strategy and profitability. *Strategic Management Journal*, **3**, 359–369.
3. Govindarajan, V. (1988). A contingency approach to strategy implementation at the business-level: integrating administrative mechanisms with strategy. *Academy of Management Journal*, **31**, 828–853. Gupta, A. K. and Govindarajan, V. (1986). Resource sharing among SBUs: strategic antecedents and administrative implications. *Academy of Management Journal*, **29**, 695–714.
4. Porter, M. (1985). *Competitive Advantage.* New York: Free Press.
5. Hambrick, D. C. (1987). The top management team: key to strategy success. *California Management Review*, Fall, 89–108.
6. Eisenhardt, K. M. and Bourgeois, L. J., III (1988). Politics of strategic decision making in high-velocity environments: toward a midrange theory. *Academy of Management Journal*, **31**, 737–770.
7. Gersick, C. J. G. (1990). The bankers. In J. R. Hackman (ed.), *Groups that Work (and Those that Don't).* San Francisco, Jossey-Bass, 126–145.
8. Johnson, D. W. and Johnson, R. T. (1989). *Cooperation and Competition: Theory and Research.* Edina, MN: Interaction Book Company. Johnson, D. W., Maruyama, G., Johnson, R. T., Nelson, D. and Skon, S. (1981). Effects of cooperative, competitive, and individualistic goal structures on achievement: a meta-analysis. *Psychological Bulletin*, **89**, 47–62.
9. Tjosvold, D. and McNeely, L. T. (1988). Innovation through communication in an educational bureaucracy. *Communication Research*, **15**, 568–581.
10. Tjosvold, D. (1988). Cooperative and competitive interdependence: collaboration

between departments to serve customers. *Group and Organization Studies,* **13,** 274–289.
11. Tjosvold, D. (1988). Cooperation and competitive dynamics within and between organizational units. *Human Relations,* **41,** 425–436. Tjosvold, D. (1988). Interdependence and power between managers and employees: a study of the leader relationship. *Journal of Management,* **15,** 49–64. Tjosvold, D. (1988). Cooperative and competitive interdependence: collaboration between departments to serve customers. *Group and Organization Studies,* **13,** 274–289. Tjosvold, D. and Weicker, D. (1990). *The entrepreneurial network: a study of goal interdependence.* Paper, Academy of Management Meetings, San Francisco.
12. Ferguson, E. K. and Kelley, H. H. (1964). Significant factors in overevaluation of own-group's product. *Journal of Abnormal and Social Psychology,* **69,** 223–231.
13. Friedkin, N. E. and Simpson, M. J. (1985). Effects of competition on members' identification with their subunits. *Administrative Science Quarterly,* **30,** 377–394.

# 15 Becoming a Team Organization

Knowing is not enough; we must apply. Willing is not enough; we must do.
Goethe

The hand is the cutting edge of the mind.
Jacob Bronowski

Success for Savory and other organizations requires an array of teamwork. Workers must identify and overcome barriers that threaten the production of consistently high-quality frozen and microwave foods. Supervisors must understand the frustrations of workers and take their ideas and suggestions seriously to keep standards high and reduce waste and costs. The accounting group needs to provide timely data to help managers make sensible business decisions. Marketing has to develop the channels to foreign markets and to expand markets in order to justify the costs of research and development of new products. Marketing, Engineering, and Production must collaborate to develop new products that Savory can make efficiently and sell broadly.

Allan, Marian, and others are learning *the need to invest in the relationships between people and groups*. Buildings, capital, patent, brand names, and machinery do not by themselves make a company work or profitable. People need to breathe life into these resources. But it is not independent effort, but joint, coordinated work that drives a company. Relationships are the life-blood of organizations, through which the energy, knowledge, and support needed to get things done flow.

## PRINCIPLES OF CHANGE

Teamwork is needed to create the team organization. A leader cannot simply decree or wish it so, nor can employees. Together they create their team.

The team organization model outlines ideals to be striven for, and suggests how they can be accomplished. *The model is both the end and the means* to develop the team organization. Employees work in teams to learn and apply the model to their organization. These teams have a vision and cooperativ. unity to strengthen their organization. They dig into issues, explore alternative points of view, and solve problems. They recognize that creating a team organization is an ongoing process, not a one-shot affair. The methods to create the team organization reinforce the message.

People gain a deeper understanding of what it takes to be an effective team as they apply the model to themselves. Team members collect valid, useful data through questionnaire surveys, interviews, and observations to identify their strengths and weaknesses. They put this understanding to work by developing plans to improve their team. *They are strengthening their team as they learn to analyze and lead teams.*

*Employees work simultaneously on developing themselves as a unified force as well as dealing with business issues.* They use their team understanding and skills to explore important problems and make specific operational business decisions.

## STEPS FOR CHANGE

Leaders and employees learn and apply the team organization model to make their organization into a flexible, united force. They are convinced of the value of teamwork, have a common understanding of the nature of effective teamwork, work together to find the values and procedures suitable for them, and extend and strengthen cooperative teamwork throughout the organization.

### SHARED CONVICTION

Managers and employees first get exposure to the model and gain a sense of its power and usefulness. Reading this and other books and articles, getting involved in discussions about teamwork, attending seminars and presentations, and talking to people already using teamwork and the team model can get people to explore the issues further. Perhaps the most convincing evidence is the experience of using the model.

### COMMON KNOWLEDGE BASE

Team members learn the model and begin to decide its applications together. They are on the same wavelength in their commitment to strengthening the team and have a shared set of aspirations for it, though they may have opposing ideas of how specifically to create that kind of team.

Workshops and discussions are essential; the specific format of the workshop depends upon the circumstances and needs of the team. For example, the leader may describe her vision for the team. Working in groups, others discuss this vision and give their input. They ask questions, emphasize certain points, and fill out the meaning the vision has for them and their areas. The workshop facilitator then discusses how teams can further the vision, and indeed how the team organization model is an essential part of the vision. The facilitator involves the participants in learning and teaching each other the components of the team organization model and how the components reinforce each other.

## MUTUAL WORK

At workshops and meetings, the team takes joint action to strengthen itself and the company. After learning the model, workshop participants form task forces that report recommendations for how their team can strengthen its vision, feel more united, be more empowered, explore issues thoroughly, and reflect for continuous improvement.

They work to achieve a living, workable consensus on the company's direction. They structure job assignments, rewards, and norms to strengthen unity. They refine communication and productive conflict skills to feel empowered. They use conflict to identify and solve problems. They reflect on their experiences, celebrate successes, and use their learning to strive for ongoing improvement. Task forces and other groups use their team skills to explore specific business issues, make decisions, and implement solutions.

## CONTINUOUS DEVELOPMENT

Recognizing the need to continue to invest in their groups and organizations or risk creating suspicions and unresolved hostilities, team members commit themselves to dealing with conflicts directly and openly. They schedule regular sessions to reflect on how they are working together.

They extend teamwork by applying the team organization model to the people that report to them. Executives might use workshops to become a productive team, then use their learning to develop teamwork in their divisions. Each division develops a shared conviction, a common knowledge base and takes joint action. The executives form a leader development group in which they discuss their plans, get help to overcome barriers, and celebrate successes as they create cooperative teams.

# NETWORKING ACROSS ORGANIZATIONS

Teamwork spills out across organizations. Companies are finding, as individuals have, that they cannot do it all by themselves. They work with suppliers to improve quality, use community resources to develop a business, and form joint ventures to take advantage of opportunities. Their associations promote a business climate and lobby government for favorable legislation and rulings. They assist community services, environmental groups, and schools to promote the quality of life of their employees and the development of future employees. Organizations depend on their environment, and need teamwork to respond and influence it.

## SUPPLIERS

Manufacturers are working with suppliers to improve the quality of their products and the reliability of their deliveries. Components purchased from suppliers, for example, are usually over half the cost of a car. Automobile companies recognize that their success depends upon having successful suppliers, and have instituted programs to get them involved in quality programs.

One morning in August, 1985, a General Motors' sales manager informed Velcro that it was dropped from its highest supplier quality rating to its fourth.[1] It had 90 days to begin a program of total quality control or face the prospect of losing an important customer. GM was dissatisfied that Velcro was not building quality into the product, was throwing away from 5% to 8% of the tape, and passing the costs on to it. Velcro, GM made it clear, had to be organized around ongoing improvement.

Velcro used those 90 days to orient employees, establish improvement teams, and set up a steering committee to monitor progress of these teams. Having the president and the heads of Sales, Finance, Personnel, Marketing, Manufacturing, R&D, Quality, and Management Information System (MIS) on the steering committee clearly signaled that quality was a priority. GM agreed that Velcro was on the right track and would check up again in six months.

The first 90 days were just the beginning. Velcro had to involve everybody from the top down to show them how quality was vital to the survival of the company; the message from GM made that credible. The steering committee met regularly every two weeks to hear progress reports from continuous improvement teams. The president also modeled the way by being a member of one of the quality improvement teams. The company's newsletter usually had a lead article featuring quality, written by an improvement team. Employee teams trained operators, repaired and redesigned machinery, and measured and reported quality results. Teams also focused on the organization to improve up-and-down communication and accuracy of payroll, and to reduce paperwork. Indeed, about half of the 50 teams operating at any one time work on administrative issues.

The quality program paid off; Velcro reduced waste as a percentage of total manufacturing expense by 50% in 1987 from 1986, and another 45% in 1988 from 1987. GM recognized Velcro's success by improving its quality rating, but it and other auto makers keep raising standards and expectations in the drive for quality improvement.

## COOPERATIVE AGREEMENTS AND JOINT VENTURES

The global economy threatens companies like Savory as new competitors gain footholds in their traditional markets, but it also opens up opportunities. Savory is forming joint ventures and marketing arrangements with companies around the world. Other companies adapt its products to the tastes of different regions, promote its products effectively, and distribute them in stores for consumers to buy. Teamwork is necessary to take advantage of the opportunities as well as ward off the threats of the international marketplace.

Joint ventures and other cooperative agreements are the major vehicles for international expansion.[2] Whereas US companies own 10 000 foreign subsidiaries fully, they share ownership in another 15 000, and have 30 000 overseas agreements with little or no equity stake. Cooperative arrangements are even more popular for European and Japanese firms.

Cooperative ventures have many advantages. They allow for expansion yet reduce risks for any one firm. Combined resources and technology exchange make the venture stronger than independent action. A local company may have the marketing contacts and savvy necessary to succeed in that country; the foreign-based one has access to technology and favorably priced capital. Agreements limit costly competition as potential competitors agree to work together. Joint ventures meet government concerns and barriers against foreign ownership.

Cooperative arrangements are a vital, practical tool. General Electric, for example, has 10 000 products, and cannot invest in all of them. It has scores of foreign affiliates, several hundred licensing and production contracts, and minority joint ventures to manufacture and market its products world-wide.

Yet these arrangements have pitfalls. A company may use access to its partner's technology to become a competitor. Demands to communicate and negotiate agreements—exacerbated by cultural barriers, suspicion, and geographical separation—may require a great deal of top management's attention and distract from other opportunities. Credible teamwork is necessary to make these cooperative arrangements succeed.

## ENTREPRENEURS

But surely entrepreneurs are free of the need to work as a team? The entrepreneur, folklore has it, is a lone-wolf who single-handedly creates a business because of inner needs to take risks, assert independence, and break out of structured ways of working. We now recognize that entrepreneurs develop a network to support their activities.[3] Birley[4] found that entrepreneurs relied extensively on the informal network of family, friends, and business people and also on the formal network of banks, accountants, and lawyers.

This network can be very useful.[5] Entrepreneurs need to keep abreast of current trends if they are going to adapt and implement their business plans successfully. Knowledge of emerging technologies, changing consumer trends, and new ways to manage and solve problems have important implications for how they position their products and manage their companies. They also turn to others for support and encouragement to maintain long-term motivation and overcome obstacles. Indeed, entrepreneurs reported that they spend 59% of their time with people outside their own company; financially successful entrepreneurs were particularly active in networking with business people, regulators, and union representatives.[6]

Entrepreneurs are independent business people free from an immediate boss, but they are not independent. To the extent that they develop cooperative goals and discuss issues openly entrepreneurs have been found to use a network of business and community people to help them learn, find support, and gain resources necessary to develop their business.[7]

# WE ARE THE WORLD

> . . . without the assistance and co-operation of many thousands, the very meanest person in a civilized country could not be provided, even according to . . . the easy and simple manner in which he is commonly accommodated.
>
> In civilized society [man] stands at all times in need of the co-operation and assistance of great multitudes, while his whole life is scarce sufficient to gain the friendship of a few persons.
>
> Adam Smith, *Wealth of Nations*

## ECONOMIC INTERDEPENDENCE

The international marketplace makes countries highly interdependent. Countries have been trading for thousands of years. Egyptian ships imported gold from Africa in 2500 BC. Ship convoys were used in the thirteenth century BC. The Dutch East India Company began its world trading exploits in 1600. But the impact of international trade has never been greater. A strong market for grain in the Soviet Union means higher prices for Iowa corn producers. The speed of information, the flow of capital, and the exchange of goods make the interdependence among nations deeper.

The world economy offers great potential. Sales of corn to the Soviet Union help Iowa farmers escape bankruptcy. Japanese investments rescue a depressed English town. The efficient assembly of electronics in Singapore helps consumers in other countries enjoy affordable computers at work and at home. The efficient production of fruits in California helps consumers around the world enjoy sweet oranges. The world can produce more valued goods and services through such division of labor.

However, increased interdependence poses great risks and makes countries much more vulnerable. A stock crash in New York soon rebounds to the Pacific and Europe. Inflation spreads from one country to another. Bankruptcies in underdeveloped countries destabilize banking in developed countries. The interdependence among nations must be managed and conflicts dealt with.

Yet there are competitive interests that pit countries against each other. One country will suspect that another is trying to push its interests without regard for theirs. Some countries close their borders to trade because they believe they will be swamped with superior foreign goods and find it impossible to sell their own. They fear that they will be unable to discuss problems that arise.


PEACE


World peace as well as prosperity requires a cooperative effort. The United States and the Soviet Union have invested heavily in the attempt to protect themselves and their allies. The failure to manage the superpower relationship constructively has cost hundreds of billions of dollars and rubles, and drastically curtailed standards of living.

Because of mistrust, strategists on both sides have tried to pursue their security independently.[8] Without accurate communication, they assumed the other country would use their weapons offensively. To counter the other's offensive capability, strategists persuaded their country to develop a new system. However, these strategists failed to appreciate that the other country would see the new system as a dangerous offensive weapon and would develop their own system to offset it. This cycle has enormously escalated arms spending. Even more, the attempt to increase security independently of the other has only increased mutual terror and insecurity as each country has the capacity to destroy the other many times over.

The 1990s offer the opportunity of a more effective security based on trust, perspective taking, and mutual effort. Both countries and their allies should demonstrate their shared commitment to mutual security, have a common understanding of the nature of effective cooperation, and work together for this mutually beneficial relationship. With that vision and cooperative goal, they can develop mechanisms to communicate and explore concerns and issues. The cooperative vision and goal of mutual security would be strengthened by a mutual commitment to the prosperity and productivity of both countries.

One of the major costs of the cold war and the policy of threat and deterrence is that countries have not invested much in the values, strategies, and procedures to develop a cooperative relationship between the superpowers and East and West. Coordinating mechanisms and conflict management capabilities are needed to strengthen the relationships in the post-cold war era.

The implications of the team organization model for world interdependence require another book. Teams representing national interests must continually emphasize the need to work together to further the common vision of a prosperous, peaceful world and the communality of their long-term interests. The United Nations and tariff negotiations offer forums for communication. Task forces and frequent conferences explore issues and try to create workable solutions. Countries must recognize the need to reflect on their relationships and work to strengthen them. Managing global interdependence will continue to challenge politicians, diplomats, specialists, and business people.

## CHALLENGES

Teamwork is both an ancient practice and a contemporary challenge. *Homo sapiens* has hunted and gathered in groups for over 60 000 years. Jordan valley had large cities by the year 6000 BC. China had cities of over 2 million people by the year 2000 BC. Oxford University was founded in the fourteenth century and the Hudson's Bay Company in 1670.

But today people have to develop teamwork under much different circumstances. Project teams of diversely trained specialists belonging to different departments are asked to design a high-tech pulp mill, and then work with nationals to build and operate it in another country. The popularity of cooperative strategies in international business insures that people will increasingly be asked to work with unfamiliar others who do not share their culture, language, nationality, or organization. The pressures for higher quality products and reduced costs are likely to heighten.

For example, Bellingham Cold Storage and a Russian company, Sovrybflot, formed Marine Resources in Seattle after the Russians were excluded from fishing within 200 miles of the US coast.[9] The Americans, who could catch the fish, had no capacity to process special varieties of fish in sufficient quantity to make even a modest profit nor the expertise to market these products internationally. The joint venture contracted with Americans to catch fish and supply Soviet factory ships in the middle of the Pacific, which processed the fish and sold it directly to Japan and Korea. People in Seattle, Nakhodka, the Soviet Union, American fishing boats, and Soviet processing ships had to collaborate to make this business work.

## NEED FOR LEADERSHIP

Teamwork cannot be taken for granted. A collection of people does not automatically become a productive team, but must confront and overcome roadblocks. Putting people in a group, having a meeting, or forming a task force does not insure teamwork. Teamwork demands leadership. Working with employees, leaders create the understanding, skills, and procedures needed for vital teamwork.

People placed in a group will wonder whether they really do have common goals and interests. They may well be suspicious, not because they are hostile and nasty, but because competition and independence are real alternatives. We have all worked with people who were egocentric and cared little about the welfare of others. Some people compete and take great pleasure in showing others up and proving they themselves are the brightest.

Even cooperative goals are not sufficient. Team members will wonder whether the group has the wherewithal to be successful and whether their work will prove worthwhile. The team must also have the skills to make decisions and deal with interpersonal frustrations and conflicts that inevitably occur.

*The team organization model provides a framework for how to invest in relationships and create teamwork.* A meaningful vision, cooperative unity, empowering of resources and skills, exploring different points of view, and reflecting on their experience guide the effort of leaders and team members. The team model becomes part of the team's vision, and identifies major steps to reach that vision.

## NEED FOR EXPERIMENTING

> Do not repeat the tactics which have gained you one victory, but let your methods be regulated by the infinite variety of circumstances.
>
> Sun Tzu, *The Art of War*

There is no simple step, no quick fix for teamwork. Art learned that unity could not be imposed, but that people themselves had to believe their goals were cooperative. He worked with his assistants and a task force to develop proposals for bonuses and events that would create a feeling of united purpose. Marian led the TLC group to discuss their vision and goals, how everyone could benefit from learning about teams, and the nature of productive teams. Miles thought getting employees to appreciate and value each other in their diversity was a vital first step to teamwork. Based on his observations, Scott worked to have the new product teams explore issues and discuss opposing opinions openly. Kyle had his people reflect and take stock on how they have worked together and manage their conflicts to identify how they might strengthen themselves.

The team model guides but does not prescribe what leaders and employees should do. The model is psychological; it identifies the perceptions, skills, and behaviors that promote teamwork. The specific ways to develop teamwork depend upon the styles, needs, and values of people involved, the circumstances of their work, and their purposes.

Management researchers have argued that leaders must adapt their style and actions to the situation. Leaders do not want to employ teams for every purpose; the task has to be important and complex enough to warrant and require the effort of several persons. In addition, how leaders and employees develop their team depends upon the circumstances. Teamwork is needed on the shop floor, in the executive offices, and in the storefront, but managers and employees must experiment with different ways to create their teams.

## NEED FOR RESEARCH

The team organization is based on theories tested and developed by many social scientists over decades of empirical research. This book suggests the research base and identifies references that interested readers can pursue. Yet much more work is needed to extend our knowledge. What are the specific ways that lead people in organizations to believe their goals are cooperative, competitive, or independent? How does the mix of these interdependencies affect people's orientations and behaviors? How do people in non-Western countries communicate they have cooperative goals? How do they explore different points of view and manage their conflicts? How can the team organization be used with people from different cultural backgrounds? Studies are also needed to evaluate programs to develop cooperative teams in organizations. The considerable research progress opens up new avenues.

## FINAL COMMENTS

Relationships—'who you know,' 'connections'—are central to doing business. It is through people working together that deals are made and things get done.

Several people provide the proposal, capital, determination, and know-how to develop a new business. Several people working together identify and exploit opportunities, and create solutions to problems. The image of the business leader doing it all alone is no longer valid, if it ever was. Entrepreneurs continually work with other people inside and outside the firm to develop ideas, secure financial backing, market products, and gain the support needed for long-term commitment.

Developing links between individuals and groups is not just a thing that is nice to do if the company is fat and has time, but is essential for a business that wants to survive and compete in the long run. These links are the ultimate competitive advantage for they sustain a viable direction and mission, and provide the energy, passion, and muscle needed to achieve objectives. The team organization invents, implements, and revises competitive advantages.

The great experimenting with teamwork is well under way. Managers and employees are trying new ways to design their organizations, assign tasks and roles, and train and compensate. No one knows where this experimenting will take the organization of tomorrow, although teamwork will continue to be pervasive and central. You and I may well be surprised by the creative ways teams will enable people and enliven organizations.

# REFERENCES

1. Krantz, K. T. (1989). How Velcro got hooked on quality. *Harvard Business Review*, September–October, 34–39.
2. Contractor, F. J. and Lorange, P. (1988). Why should firms cooperate? The strategy and economics basis for cooperative ventures. In F. J. Contractor and P. Lorange (eds), *Cooperative Strategies in International Business*. Lexington, MA: Lexington Books, 3–30.
3. Dollinger, M. J. (1985). Environmental contacts and financial performance of the small firm. *Journal of Small Business Management*, **23**, 24–30. Low, M. B. and MacMillan, I. C. (1988). Entrepreneurship: past research and future challenges. *Journal of Management*, **14**, 139–161. Schein, E. H. (1983). The role of the founder in creating organizational culture. *Organizational Dynamics*, **12** (1), 13–28.
4. Birley, S. (1985). The role of networks in the entrepreneurial process. *Journal of Business Venturing*, **1**, 107–117.
5. Aldrich, H. and Zimmer, C. (1986). Entrepreneurship through social networks. In D. L. Sexton and R. W. Smilor (eds), *The Art and Science of Entrepreneurship*. Cambridge, MA: Ballinger, 2–23. Dollinger, M. J. (1985). Environmental contacts and financial performance of the small firm. *Journal of Small Business Management*, **23**, 24–30. Gillingham, D. W. and Loucks, K. E. Forming new entrepreneurial ventures through the use of venture group sessions. *Journal of Small Business Management*, **20**, 5–12.
6. Dollinger, M. J. (1985). Environmental contacts and financial performance of the small firm. *Journal of Small Business Management*, **23**, 24–30.

7. Tjosvold, D. and Weicker, D. (1990). *Networking by entrepreneurs: a study of goal interdependence*. Paper, Academy Management Meeting, San Francisco.
8. Deutsch, M. (1980). Fifty years of conflict. In L. Festinger (ed.), *Retrospections on Social Psychology*. New York: Oxford University Press, 46–77.
9. Pereyra, W. T. (1981). Some preliminary results of a U.S.–Soviet joint fishing venture. *Journal of Contemporary Business*, **10,** 7.

# Index

*Index compiled by Jenny Tjosvold*